FATE KNOCKS AT THE DOOR

A NOVEL

WILL LEVINGTON COMFORT

1st WORLD
LIBRARY
Literary Society

Fate Knocks at the Door

Will Levington Comfort

© 1st World Library, 2007
PO Box 2211
Fairfield, IA 52556
www.1stworldlibrary.com
First Edition

LCCN: 2007934213

Softcover ISBN: 978-1-4218-9686-1
Hardcover ISBN: 978-1-4218-9786-8
eBook ISBN: 978-1-4218-9586-4

Purchase *"Fate Knocks at the Door"*
as a traditional bound book at:
www.1stWorldLibrary.com/purchase.asp?ISBN=978-1-4218-9686-1

1st World Library is a literary, educational organization
dedicated to:

- Creating a free internet library of downloadable ebooks

- Hosting writing competitions and offering book publishing
scholarships.

Interested in more 1st World Library books? contact:
literacy@1stworldlibrary.com
Check us out at: www.1stworldlibrary.com

1st World Library Literary Society

Giving Back to the World

"If you want to work on the core problem, it's early school literacy."

- **James Barksdale, former CEO of Netscape**

"No skill is more crucial to the future of a child, or to a democratic and prosperous society, than literacy."

- **Los Angeles Times**

"Literacy... means far more than learning how to read and write... The aim is to transmit... knowledge and promote social participation."

- **UNESCO**

"Literacy is not a luxury, it is a right and a responsibility. If our world is to meet the challenges of the twenty-first century we must harness the energy and creativity of all our citizens."

- **President Bill Clinton**

"Parents should be encouraged to read to their children, and teachers should be equipped with all available techniques for teaching literacy, so the varying needs and capacities of individual kids can be taken into account."

- **Hugh Mackay**

In speaking of the first four notes of the opening movement, Beethoven said, some time after he had finished the Fifth Symphony: "So pocht das Shicksal an die Pforte" ("Thus Fate Knocks at the Door"); and between that opening knock, and the tremendous rush and sweep of the Finale, the emotions which come into play in the great conflicts of life are depicted.

—From Upton's *Standard Symphonies*

To

THE MOTHERS OF MEN

CONTENTS

I. ASIA. (*Allegro con brio.*)

First Chapter: The Great Wind Strikes 13

Second Chapter: The Pack-Train in Luzon 23

Third Chapter: Red Pigment of Service 31

Fourth Chapter: That Adelaide Passion 43

Fifth Chapter: A Flock of Flying Swans 57

Sixth Chapter: That Island Somewhere 69

Seventh Chapter: *Andante con Moto*—Fifth 82

Eighth Chapter: The Man from *The Pleiad* *94*

II. NEW YORK. (*Andante con moto.*)

Ninth Chapter: The Long-Awaited Woman 103

Tenth Chapter: The Jews and the Romans 116

Eleventh Chapter: Two Davids Come to Beth 130

Twelfth Chapter: Two Lesser Adventures 142

Thirteenth Chapter: About Shadowy Sisters 150

Fourteenth Chapter: This Clay-and-Paint Age 155

Fifteenth Chapter: The Story of the Mother 170

Sixteenth Chapter: "Through Desire for Her." 184

Seventeenth Chapter: The Plan of the Builder 189

Eighteenth Chapter: That Park Predicament 200

Nineteenth Chapter: In the House of Grey One 207

Twentieth Chapter: A Chemistry of Scandal 218

Twenty-first Chapter: The Singing Distances........233

Twenty-second Chapter: Beth Signs the Picture....244

Twenty-third Chapter: The Last Ride Together.....257

Twenty-fourth Chapter: A Parable
of Two Horses 272

III. EQUATORIA. (*Allegro. Scherzo.*)

Twenty-fifth Chapter: Bedient for *The Pleiad* 285

Twenty-sixth Chapter: How Startling is Truth 295

Twenty-seventh Chapter: The Art of
Miss Mallory 304

Twenty-eighth Chapter: A Further Note
from Rey..........................312

Twenty-ninth Chapter: At *Treasure Island Inn* 322

Thirtieth Chapter: Miss Mallory's Mastery............332

Thirty-first Chapter: The Glow-worm's
One Hour 342

Thirty-second Chapter: In the Little Room Next...354

Thirty-third Chapter: The Hills and the Skies........362

Thirty-fourth Chapter: The Supreme Adventure ...368

Thirty-fifth Chapter: Fate Knocks at the Door.......374

IV. NEW YORK. (*Allegro. Finale.*)

Thirty-sixth Chapter: The Great Prince House 381

Thirty-seventh Chapter: Beth and Adith Mallory..388

Thirty-eighth Chapter: A Self-Conscious
                                 Woman 399
Thirty-ninth Chapter: Another *Smilax* Affair.........406
Fortieth Chapter: Full Day Upon the Plain 417

I. ASIA

Allegro con brio

FIRST CHAPTER

THE GREAT WIND STRIKES

Andrew Bedient, at the age of seventeen, in a single afternoon,—indeed, in one moment of a single afternoon,—performed an action which brought him financial abundance for his mature years. Although this narrative less concerns the boy Bedient than the man as he approaches twice seventeen, the action is worthy of account, beyond the riches that it brought, because it seems to draw him into somewhat clearer vision from the shadows of a very strange boyhood.

April, 1895, the *Truxton*, of which Andrew was cook, found herself becalmed in the China Sea, midway between Manila and Hong Kong, her nose to the North. She was a smart clipper of sixty tons burden, with a slightly uptilted stern, and as clever a line forward as a pleasure yacht. She was English, comparatively new, and, properly used by the weather, was as swift and sprightly of service as an affectionate woman. Her master was Captain Carreras, a tubby little man of forty-five, bald, modest, and known among the shipping as "a perfect lady." He wore a skull-cap out of port; and as constantly, except during meals, carried one of a set of rarely-colored meerschaum-bowls, to which were attachable, bamboo-stems, amber-tipped and of various lengths.

The little Captain was fastidious in dress, wearing soft shirts of white silk, fine duck trousers and scented silk handkerchiefs, which he carried in his left hand with the meerschaum-bowl. The Carreras perfume, mingled with fresh tobacco, was never burdensome, and unlike any other. The silk handkerchief was as much a feature of the Captain's appearance as the skull-cap. To it was due the really remarkable polish of the perfect clays so regularly cushioned in his palm. Always for dinner, the Captain's toilet was fresh throughout. Invariably, too, he brought with him an unfolded handkerchief upon which he placed, at the farther end of the table when the weather was fair (and in the socket of the fruit-bowl when the weather-frames were on), a ready-filled pipe. This he took to hand when coffee was brought.

His voice was seldom raised. He found great difficulty in expressing himself, except upon affairs of the ship; yet, queerly enough, there were times when he seemed deeply eager to say the things which came of his endless silences. As unlikely a man as you would find in the Pacific, or any other merchant-service, was this Carreras; a gentleman, if a very bashful one; a deeply-read and kindly man, although it was quite as difficult for him to extend a generous action, directly to be found out,—and his mind was continually furnishing inclinations of this sort,—as it was to express his thoughts. Either brought on a nervous tension which left him shaken and drained. The right woman would have adored Captain Carreras, and doubtless would have called forth from his breast a love of heroic dimension; but she would have been forced to do the winning; to speak and take the initiative in all but the giving of happiness. Temperate for a bachelor, clean throughout, charmingly innocent of the world, and a splendid seaman. To one of fine sensibilities, there was something about the person of Captain Carreras of softly glowing warmth, and rarely tender.

Bedient had been with him as cook for over a year, during which the *Truxton* had swung down to Australia and New South Wales, and called at half the Asiatic and insular ports from Vladivostok to Bombay. Since he was a little chap (back of which were the New York memories, vague, but strange and persistent), there had always been some ship for Bedient, but the *Truxton* was by far the happiest.... It was from the *Truxton* just a few months before that he had gone ashore day after day for a fortnight at Adelaide; and a wee woman five years older, and a cycle wiser, had invariably been waiting with new mysteries in her house.... Moreover, on the *Truxton*, he had nothing to do with the forecastle galley—there was a Chinese for that—and Captain Carreras, fancying him from the beginning, had quartered him aft, where, except on days like this, when Mother Earth's pneumatic cushion seemed limp and flattened, there was a breeze to hammock in, and plenty of candles for night reading.

Then the Captain had a box of books, the marvel of which cannot begin to be described. Andrew's books were but five or six, chosen for great quantity and small bulk; tightly and toughly bound little books of which the Bible was first. This was his book of fairies, his Aesop; his book of wanderings and story, of character and mystery; his revelations, the source of his ideality, the great expander of limitations; his book of love and adventure and war; the book unjudgable and the bed-rock of all literary judgment. He knew the Bible as only one can who has played with it as a child; as only one can who has found it alone available, when an insatiable love of print has swept across the young mind. Nothing could change him now; this was his book of Fate.

Except for those vision-times in the big city, Andrew could not remember when he had not read the Bible, nor did he remember learning to read. He seemed to have forgotten how to read before he came to sea at seven, but when an old sailor pointed out on the stern of the jolly-boat, the letters that formed the name of his first ship—it had all come back to the child; and then he found his first Bible. Slowly conceiving its immensity, its fullness *for him*—he was almost lifted from his body with the upward winging of happiness. It was his first great exaltation, and there was a sacredness about it which kept him from telling anybody.... And now all the structures of the great Scripture were tenoned in his brain; so that he knew the frame of every part, but the inner meanings of more and more marvellous dimension seemed inexhaustible. Always excepting the great Messianic Figure—the white tower of his consciousness—he loved Saint Paul and the Forerunner best among the men....

There was also a big book in the Captain's chest—*Life and Death on the Ocean*—quarto-sized and printed in agate. It was filled with mutiny, murder, storm, open-boat cannibalism and agonies of thirst, handspike and cutlass inhumanities. No shark, pirate nor man-killing whale had been missed; no ghastly wreck, derelict nor horrifying phantom of the sea had escaped the nameless, furious compiler. For four days and nights, Andrew glared consumingly into this terrible book, and when he came to the writhing "Finis," involved in a sort of typhoon tailpiece—he was whipped, and never could bring himself to touch the book again. One reading had burned out his entire interest. It was not Life nor Death nor Ocean, as he had seen them in ten solid years at sea. He had given the book his every emotion, and discovered it gave nothing back; but had shaken, terrified, played furious *tarantellas* upon his feelings—and replenished naught. So he turned for unguent to his Book of Books. Here was the strong steady light in contrast to which the other was an "angled spar." True, here crawled hate, avarice, lust, flesh and its myriad forms of death—not in their own elemental darkness—but as scurrying vermin forms suddenly drenched with light.... There were other and really wonderful books in Captain Carreras' chest—

a bashful welcome to his cabin, and such eager lending from the Captain himself!

This had become a pleasant feature in the young man's life— the queer kindly heart of the Captain. There were few confidences between them, but a fine unspoken regard, pleasing and permanent like the Carreras perfume. Bedient's desire to show his gratitude and admiration was expressed in ways that could not possibly shock the Captain's delicacy—in the small excellences of his art, for instance. To say that the boy was consummate in the limited way of a ship's cook does not overstate his effectiveness. He did unheard-of things— even fruit and berry-pies, from preserves two years, at least, remote from vine and orchard. The two mates and boatswain, who also messed aft, bolted without speech, but marvelled between meals. To these three, the tension of the Captain's embarrassment became insupportable, beyond four or five minutes; so that Carreras, a discriminating, though not a valiant trencherman, was always the last to leave the table.

And once after a first supper at sea out of Singapore (there had been a green salad, a fish baked whole, a cut of ham with new potatoes, and a peach-preserve tart), the Captain put down his napkin and coffee-cup, drank a *liqueur*, reached for his pipe and handkerchief, and suddenly encountering the eyes of Andrew, who lit a flare for him, jerked up decisively, as one encountering a crisis. His face became hectic, and the desperate sentence he uttered was almost lost in the frantic clearing of his throat:

"You're a very prime and wonderful chap, sir!"

Moreover, Bedient's arm had been pressed for an instant by the softest, plumpest hand seaman ever carried. Coughing alarmingly in the first fragrant cloud from his Latakia and Virginia leaf, the Captain beat forth to recover himself on deck.

The *Truxton* was now six days out of Manila. For the past thirty-six hours, she might as well have been sunk in pitch, for any progress she made.... The ship's bell had just struck four. Bedient had finished clearing away tiffin things, and stepped on deck. The planking was like the galley-range he had left, and the fresh white paint of the three boats raised in blisters. The sea had an ugly look, yellow-green and dead, save where a shark's fin knifed the surface. The crew was lying forward under the awnings—a fiend-tempered outfit of Laskars and Chinese. Captain Carreras appeared on deck through the companion-way still farther aft and nodded to Bedient. Then both men looked at the sky, which was brassy above, but thickening in the North. It augmented darkly and streakily—like a tub of water into which bluing is added drop by drop.... A Chinese arose and tossed a handful of joss-tatters into the still air. And now the voice of the Captain brought the rest of the crew to its feet.

The China Sea can generate much deviltry to a square mile. The calm of death and the burn of perdition are in its bosom. Cholera, glutted with victims, steals to his couch in the China Sea; and since it is the pool of a thousand unclean rivers, the sins of Asia find a hiding-place there. It has ended for all time the voyages of brave mariners and mighty ships, and become a vault for the cargoes, and a tomb for the bones of men. The China Sea fostered the pirate, aided him in his bloody ways, and dragged him down, riches and all. Bed of disease, secret-place of the unclean, and graveyard of the seas; yet, this yellow-breasted fiend, ancient in devil-lore, can smile innocently as a child at the morning sun, and beguile the torrid stars to twinkling.

It was in this black heart that was first conceived the Tai Fung (typhoon), and there the great wind has its being

Will Levington Comfort

to-day, resting and rising.

The Captain's eyes were deep in the North. Bedient's soul seemed to sense the awful solemnity on the face of the waters. He was unable afterward to describe his varying states of consciousness, from that first moment. He remembered thinking what a fine little man the Captain was; that their sailing together was done.... A sympathetic disorder was brewing deep down on the ocean floor; the water now had a charged appearance, and was foul as the roadstead along the mouths of the Godivari—a thick, whipped, yeasty look. The changes were very rapid. Every few seconds, Bedient glanced at the Captain, and as often followed his gaze into the churning, blackening North.

A chill came into the deathly heat, but it was the cold of caverns, not of the vital open. The heat did not mix with it, but passed by in layers—a novel movement of the atmospheres. Had the coolness been clean and normal, the sailors would have sprung to the rigging to breathe it, and to bare their bodies to the rain—after two days of hell-pervading calm—but they only murmured now and fell to work.

An unearthly glitter, like the coloring of a dream, wavered in the East and West, while the North thickened and the South lay still in brilliant expectation.... In some hall-way when Bedient was a little boy, he recalled a light like this of the West and East. There had been a long narrow pane of yellow-green glass over the front door. The light used to come through that in the afternoon and fill the hall and frighten him. It was so on deck now.

The voices of the sailors had that same unearthly quality as the light—ineffectual, remote. Out of the hold of the *Truxton* came a ghostly sigh. Bedient couldn't explain, unless it was some new and mighty strain upon the keel and ribs.

A moment more and the Destroyer itself was visible in the changing North. It was sharp-lined—a great wedge of absolute night—and from it, the last vestiges of day dropped back affrighted. And Bedient heard the voice of It; all that the human ear could respond to of the awful dissonances of storm; yet he knew there were ranges of sound above and below the human register—for they awed and preyed upon his soul.... He thought of some papers dear to him, and dropped below for them. The ship smelled old—as if the life were gone from her timbers.

Above once more, he saw a hideous turmoil in the black fabric—just wind—an avalanche of wind that gouged the sea, that could have shaken mountains.... The poor little *Truxton* stared into the End—a puppy cowering on the track of a train.

And then It struck. Bedient was sprawled upon the deck. Blood broke from his nostrils and ears; from the little veins in his eyes and forehead. Parts of his body turned black afterward from the mysterious pressure at this moment. He felt he was being *born again into another world*.... The core of that Thing made of wind smashed the *Truxton*—a smash of air. It was like a thick sodden cushion, large as a battle-ship—hurled out of the North. The men had to breathe it—that seething havoc which tried to twist their souls free. When passages to the lungs were opened, the dreadful compression of the air crushed through, tearing the membrane of throat and nostril.

Water now came over the ship in huge tumbling walls. Bedient slid over the deck, like a bar of soap from an overturned pail—clutching, torn loose, clutching again.... Then the Thing eased to a common hurricane such as men know. Gray flicked into the blackness, a corpse-gray sky, and the ocean seemed shaken in a bottle.

Will Levington Comfort

Laskars and Chinese, their faces and hands dripping red, were trying to get a boat overside when Bedient regained a sort of consciousness. The *Truxton* was wallowing underfoot —as one in the saddle feels the tendons of his mount give way after a race. The Captain helped a huge Chinese to hold the wheel. The sea was insane.... They got the boat over and tumbled in—a dozen men. A big sea broke them and the little boat like a basket of eggs against the side of the ship.

Another boat was put over and filled with men. Another sea flattened them out and carried the stains away on the surge. There were only nine men left and a small boat that would hold but seven. Bedient helped to make a rigging to launch this over the stern. He saw that the thing might be done if the small craft were not broken in two against the rudder.

The Captain made no movement, had no thought to join these stragglers. He was alone at the wheel, which played with his strength. His face was calm, but a little dazed. It did not occur to him other than to go down with his ship—the old tradition. The fatuousness of this appealed suddenly to Bedient. Carreras was his friend—the only other white man left. The two mates and boatswain had tried out the first two boats—eagerly.

Bedient ran to the wheel, tore the Captain from it and carried him in his arms toward the stern. A Chinese tried to knife him, but the man died, *as if* struck by a flying bit of tackle. Bedient recaptured the Captain, who during the brief struggle had dumbly turned back to the wheel. It was all done in thirty seconds; Carreras was chucked into the stern-seat of the little boat, where he belonged. The body of a Laskar cushioned the craft from being broken against the rudder. And now they were seven.

The *Truxton* had been broken above and below. She

strangled—and was sucked down. Bedient saw her stern fling high like an arm; saw the big "X" in the centre of the name in the whitish light.

He remembered hearing that typhoons always double on their tracks; and that a ship is not done that manages to live through the first charge. This one never came back. They had five days of thirst and equatorial sun. Two men died; two fell into madness; Captain Carreras, Andrew Bedient and a Chinese made Hong Kong without fatal hurt.

Captain and cook took passage for London. The former declared he was through with the sea, except as a passenger. In twenty-five years he had never encountered serious accident before; he had believed himself accident-proof; and learning differently, did not propose to lose a second ship. He could bring himself to say very little about Bedient's action of the last moment on deck, but he asked the young man to share his fortunes. Captain Carreras intended to stay for a while at his mother's house in Surrey, but realized he could not stand that long.... Bedient told him he was not finished with Asia yet. On the day they parted, the Captain said there would be a letter for Bedient, on or before July first of every year, sent care the *"Marigold, New York."*... The old embarrassment intervened at the last moment—but the younger man did not miss the Captain's heart-break.

SECOND CHAPTER

THE PACK-TRAIN IN LUZON

The first letter from Captain Carreras was a real experience for Bedient. Hours were needed to adjust the memories of his timid old friend to this flowing and affectionate expression. Captain Carreras, shut in a room with pen and white paper, loosed his pent soul in utterance. A fine fragrant soul it was, and all its best poured out to his memorable boy.

The letter had been written in England, of which the Captain was already weary. He must have more space about, he confessed; and although he did not intend to break his pledge on the matter of navigating, he was soon to book a passage for the Americas. He imagined there was the proper sort of island for him somewhere in those waters. He had always had a weakness for "natives and hot weather." Bedient was asked to make his need known in any case of misfortune or extremity. This was the point of the first letter, and of all the letters....

At length Captain Carreras settled in Equatoria, a big island well out of travel-lines in the Caribbean. The second and third letters made it even plainer that the old heart valves ached for the young man's coming. A mysterious binding of the two seems to have taken place in the months preceding the day of the great wind; and in that instant of stress and fury the Captain realized his supreme human relationship. It grew strong as only can a bachelor's love for a man. Indeed, Carreras was probably the first to discover in Andrew Bedient a something different, which Bedient himself was yet far from realizing.... The latter wished that the letters from the West Indies would not always revert to the strength of his hands. It brought up a memory of the despoiled face of the Chinese with the knife, and of the inert figure afterward on the planking.... Bedient knew that sometime he would go to find his friend.

Three years after the great wind, the excitement in Manila called Bedient across the China Sea. There had been a *coup* of the American fleet, and soldiers from the States were on the way to the Islands.... In the following weeks, there was much to do and observe around that low large city of Luzon, the lights of which Andrew had seen many times at night from the harbor and the passage—lights which seemed to lie upon still waters. When Pack-train Thirteen finally took the field from the big corral, to carry grub and ammunition to the moving forces and the few outstanding garrisons, Bedient had already been tried out and found excellent as cook of the outfit.

It is to be doubted if history furnishes a more picturesque service than that which fell to Luzon pack-trains throughout the following two years. It was like Indian fighting, but more compact, rapid and surprising. The actions were small enough to be seen entire; they fell clean-cut into pictures and were instantly comprehensive. As the typhoon confirmed Carreras, this Luzon service brought to Bedient an important relation—his first real friendship with a boy of his own age.

In the fall of 1899, David Cairns, the youngest of the American war-correspondents, stood hungry and desolate in the plaza of the little town of Alphonso, two days' cavalry march below Manila—when Pack-train Thirteen arrived with provisions. The mules swung in with drooping heads and lolling tongues, under three-hundred-pound packs. The roars of Healy, the boss-packer, filled the dome of sky where a young moon was rising in a twilight of heavenly blue—dusk of the gods, indeed. A battalion of infantry in Alphonso had been hungry for three days—so the Train had come swiftly, ten hours on the trail, and forced going. It was a volunteer infantry outfit, and apt to be a bit lawless in the sight of food. Some of the men began pulling at the packs. Healy and his iron-handed, vitriol-tongued crew beat them back with the ferocity of devils—and had the battalion cowed and whimpering, before the officers withdrew the men and arranged an orderly issue of rations.

Meanwhile, David Cairns watched the tall, young cook, lean, tanned, and with an ugly triangle of fresh sunburn under his left shoulder-blade, where his shirt had been torn with a thorn that day. He loosed the *aparejos* and *mantas*, containing the kitchen-kit; almost magically a fire was started. Water was heating a moment later and slabs of bacon began to writhe.... Savage as he was from hunger, it was marvellously colorful to the fresh-eyed Cairns—his first view of a pack-train. The mules, relieved of their burdens, were rolling on the dusty turf. Thirty mountain-mules, under packs one-third their own weight, and through the pressure of a Luzon day; dry, empty, caked with sweat-salt—yet there were not a few of those gritty beasts that went into the air squealing, and launched a hind-foot at the nearest rib or the nearest star, or pressed close to muzzle the bell-mare—after the restoring roll. Then, some of the packers drove them down to water, while others made ready the forage and grain-bags; infantry fires were lit; the provisions turned over; detachments came meekly forward for rations, and the lifting aroma of coffee enchanted the warm winds. Cairns remembered all this when the sharp profile of battle-fronts grew dull in memory.

And now Bedient had three great pans of bacon sizzling, a young mountain of brown sugar piled upon a *Poncho*, a big can of hard-tack broken open, and the coffee had come to boil under his hands—three gallons at least. The watered mules had to do just so much kicking, so much braying at the young moon; had to be assured just so often, through their queer communications, that the bell-mare was still in the land of picket-line—before nose-bags were fastened. Then, with all the pack rigging in neat piles before the picket-line, and the untouched stores covered and piled, the packers came in with their mess-tins and coffee-cups.

Bedient had seen the hunger in the eyes of David Cairns, the empty haversack, and noted that he was neither officer nor enlisted man. Bedient had plenty of water, but with a smile he offered the other a pail and pointed to the stream. This was a pleasantry for the eyes of Boss Healy. Cairns appeared presently through the infantry, and around the end of the picket-line—a correspondent serving mule-riders with all the enthusiasm of a pitifully-tightened belt.... The packers were at their pipes and cigarettes and were spreading blanket-rolls, and groups of "chucked" infantry had warmed into singing— when the two boys sat down to supper. The cook said:

"I'm Andrew Bedient—and are you a correspondent?"

"A cub—and pretty nearly a starved cub.... There's been nothing to buy, you know, and this outfit was hung up here grubless. The trails aren't open enough to travel alone. Some of the officers might have taken me in—"

"We have plenty. The packers hadn't had their coffee when I gave you the pail," Bedient whispered. "They hate the doughboys. I wanted them to see you weren't enlisted.... I should say the trails *weren't* open for travelling alone. The niggers peppered at us all day. Healy rides through anything—says we make better time when the natives are shooting—"

"I saw how he went through the bunch that started to help you unpack," Cairns said laughing.

... Theirs was a quick love for each other. They had not known how lonely their hearts were, until they encountered this fine mutual attraction. Together they cleaned up the supper things, and spread their blankets side by side.... Later, when only the infantry sentries were awake, and the packers' running guard (and a little apart, the interminable glow from Healy's cigarettes), the two were still whispering, though the day had been terrific in physical expenditure. So aroused and gladdened by each other were they, that intimate matters poured forth in the fine way youths have, before the control and concealment is put on. Grown men imprison each other.... Their low tones trembled with emotion while the night whitened with stars. Cairns wished that something of terror or intensity might happen. He hated a knife to the very pith of his life, but now he would have welcomed a passage of steel in the dark—for a chance to defend the other.

And the cook had that absolute, laughing sort of courage. Cairns divined this—a courage so sure of itself that no boastful explanations were needed. They talked about men, books, their yearnings, the recent fights. Cairns was enthralled and mystified. Bedient did not seem to hope for great things in a worldly way, while the correspondent was driven daily by ambition and its self-dreams. Life apparently had shown this cook day by day what was wisest and easiest to do—the ways of little resistance. He appeared content to go on so; and this challenged Cairns to explain what he meant to do with the next few years. Bedient heard this with fine interest, but no quickening. Cairns was insatiable for details of a life that had been spent in Asia and upon ships of the Eastern seas. Everything that Bedient said had a shining exterior of mystery to the American. His vague memories of New York; the water-fronts that had since called his steps; different ships and captains; the men about him, Healy and the packers; his entire detachment from relatives, and his easy familiarity with the great unhasting years—all these formed into a luminous envelope, containing the new friend.

"I was always fed somehow," Bedient whispered, as he told about the dim little lad that was himself. "There was always some one good to me. I 'member one old sailor with rings in his ears—"

The David Cairns of twenty likewise gave all gladly. Queerly enough, he found the other especially fascinated in anything he told of his mother and sisters, and the life at home in New York, made easy by the infinite little cushions of wealth and culture. A youth eight months away on his first campaign can talk with power on these matters. Here Cairns was wonderful and authoritative and elect to Bedient— particularly in the possession of a living, breathing Mother. This filled the cup of dreams in a way that the dominant exterior matters of the young correspondent's mind— newspaper beats, New York honors, great war stories, and a writer's name—could never have done. Bedient was clearly an inveterate idealist. His dreams were strangely lustrous, but distant, not to be touched nor handled—an impersonal kind of dreaming. Cairns was not so astonished that the other had been of uncommon quality in the beginning, but that his life had not *made* him common was a miracle, no less.

Elements of glory were in this life he had lived, but those who belonged to it, whom Cairns had observed heretofore,

Will Levington Comfort

were thick-skinned; men of unlit consciousness and hardened hearts, gruelling companions to whom there was no deadly sin but physical cowardice, and only muscular virtues. Bedient was not of these, neither in body, mind nor memory, aspiration, language nor manner. And yet *they* believed in him, accepted him in a queer, tentative, subdued fashion; and he spoke to them warmly, and of them with affection. All this needed a deeper and more mellowed mind than Cairns' to comprehend; though it challenged him from the first moment in that swiftly-darkening night. "It's too good to be true," was his oft-recurring sentence.... Though apart, Bedient was not scoffed. Could it be that he was so finished as a cook, as a friend, as an indefatigable—so rhythmically superior, that the packers took no offense at his aloofness? Certainly, Bedient felt no necessity of impressing his values upon his companions, as do those who have come but a little way in culture.

Somehow, Alphonso smelled of roses that night, as the two lay together in that little plaza, where the mules were picketed and the satisfied infantry slept. In the jungle (which seemed very close in the moonlight), bamboo stalks creaked soothingly and stroked each other in the soft night winds, and the zenith sky boiled with millions of white-hot worlds.... Are not the best dreams of this earth to be heard from two rare boys whispering in the night? They have not been frightened by their first real failure, and the latest, most delicate bloom of the race has not yet been brushed from their thoughts. Curled within their minds, like an endless scroll, are the marvellous scriptures of millenniums, and yet their brain-surfaces are fresh for earth's newest concept.... What are they whispering? Their voices falter with emotion over vague bits of dreaming. They ask no greater stimulus to fly to the uttermost bounds of their limitations—than each other and the night. Reason dawns upon their stammered expressions, and farther they fly—thrilling like young birds, when their wings for the first time catch the sustaining cushions of air.... These are the vessels of the future—seals yet unbroken.

THIRD CHAPTER

RED PIGMENT OF SERVICE

Bedient explained that he had come to the Philippines pleased with the thought of seeing his own people, the Americans. He realized that he was not seeing them at their best under martial law. The pair exchanged narratives of action. Cairns pictured his first time under fire, ending:

"... First you see the smoke; then you hear the bullets—then the *sound* of the guns last—"

"Yes, that's the order," said Bedient, who laughed softly, and presently was telling of a recent and terrible baptism of fire. The Pack-train had spurred to the rescue of a small party of sick and footsore, making their way to garrison.

"Why that was the Pony Pack Massacre!" Cairns exclaimed. "I heard about it—one of the worst affairs we've had over here—and you saw it?"

"I wish I hadn't," Bedient answered. "The little party of Americans were down when I first saw them. Six or seven of the sixteen were dead; nearly all the rest wounded. The natives had fired from three sides—and would have finished their work with knives, except for Thirteen. The American lieutenant in charge was clear-grained. He had been trying to withdraw toward the town and carry his wounded—think of that. There were not two others besides himself unscathed. I'll never forget him—striding up and down praying and cursing—his first fight, you know—and his boy's voice—'Be cock sure they're dead, fellows, before you leave 'em behind for the bolos!... For the love of God don't leave your bunkies behind for the butchers!'

"In a half minute, I saw it all—what a thing for white men to be gathered for slaughter on a trail over here. The boys knew it—and fought horribly against it...."

Cairns started to say something about this, but the words didn't come quickly enough, and Bedient went on:

"There is a picture of that day which always means *war* to me. The soldier was hit mortally just as I got to him, but didn't fall at once, as one does when the spine or brain is touched. As my hands went out to him, he got it again and lost his legs, as if they were shot from under. His body, you see, fell the length of his legs. This second bullet was a Remington slug that shattered his hip. He had a full canteen strung over his shoulder, infantry fashion. The bullet that dropped him sitting on the trail, had gone through this to his hip. The canteen was spurting water. Mind you, it was the other wound that was killing him. There he sat dying on the road. I felt like dying for him—felt that I couldn't bear it if it took long. He was in my arms—and the canteen was emptying itself through the bullet-holes. Then he seemed to hear the water flopping out on the sand, and wriggled around to look at his hip, and I heard him mutter thickly: 'Look—look at the b-bl-blood run!'"

Cairns felt that his companion suffered in this telling—that behind the dark, the face close to his was deadly pale. He couldn't quite understand the depths of Bedient's horror. It was war. All America was behind it. One boy can't stand up against his nation. It was all very queer. He felt that Bedient had a crystal gameness, but here was the sensitiveness of a girl. Cairns thought of the heroes he had read of who were brave as a lion and gentle as a woman, and these memories helped him now to grasp his companion's point of view.... Hesitating, Bedient finished:

"You know, to me all else was hushed when I felt that boy in my arms. It was like a shouting and laughing suddenly ceased—as when a company of boys discover that one of their playmates is terribly hurt.... I imagine it would be like that—the sudden silence and sickness. It was all so unnecessary. And that boy's mother—he should have been in her arms, not mine. Poor little chap, he was all pimpled from beans, which are poison to some people. He shouldn't have been hurt like that.... There was another who had needed but one shot. The Remington had gone into his throat in front the size of a lead-pencil—and come out behind like a tea-cup. The natives had filed the tip of the lead, so that it accumulated destruction in the ugly way. It was like some one putting a stone in a snow-ball—so vicious. You can't blame the natives—but the war-game—"

Boss Healy growled at them to go to sleep.

*   *   *   *   *

Cairns remained with the Pack-train after that until the Rains. Never did a boy have more to write about in three months. Every phase and angle of that service, now half-forgotten, unfolded for his eyes. And the impossible theme running through it all, was the carabao—the great horned sponge that pulls vastly like an elephant and dies easily like a rabbit—when the water is out.... They make no noise about their dying, these mountains of flesh, merely droop farther and farther forward against the yoke, when their skins crack from dryness; the whites of their eyes become wider and wider—until they lay their tongues upon the sand. The Chinese call them "cow-cows" and understand them better than the Tagals, as they understand better the rice and the paddies.

Once Thirteen was yanked out of Healy's hand—as no volley of native shots had ever disordered. The mules were in a gorge trotting into the town of Indang. Natives in the high places about, were waiting for the Train to debouch upon the river-bank—so as to take a few shots at the outfit. Every one expected this, but just as the Train broke out of the gorge into the open, at the edge of the river-bed—there was a great sucking transfiguration from the shallows, a hideous sort of giving birth from the mud.

It was just a soaked carabao rising from his deep wallow in the stream, but that she-devil, the gray bell-mare, tried to climb the cliffs about it. The mules felt her panic, as if an electrode ran from her to the quick of every hide of them. When the fragments of the Train were finally gathered together in Indang, they formed an undone, hysterical mess. The packers were too tired to eat, but sat around dazed, softly cursing, and smoking cigarettes; as they did one day after a big fight, in which one of their number, Jimmy the Tough, was shot through the brain. For days the mules were nervous over the delicate condition of the bell.

Study of Andrew Bedient and weeks in which he learned, past the waver of a doubt, that his friend was knit with a glistening and imperishable fabric of courage, brought David Cairns to that high astonishing point, where he could say impatiently, "Rot!"—as his former ideals of manhood rose to mind. It was good for him to get this so young.... One

Will Levington Comfort

morning something went wrong with Benton, the farrier. He had been silent for days. Bedient had sensed some trouble in the little man's heart, and had often left Cairns to ride with him. Then came the evening when the farrier was missed. It was in the mountains near Naig. At length, just as the sun went down, the Train saw him gain a high cliff—and stand there for a moment against the red sky. Bedient reached over and gripped Cairns' arm. Turning, the latter saw that his friend's eyes were closed. The remarkable thing was that not one of the packers called to Benton—but all observed the lean tough little figure of one of the neatest men that ever lived afield—regarded in silence the hard handsome profile. Finally Benton drew out his pistol and looked at it, as if to see that the oil had kept out the dust from the hard day on the trail. Then he looked into the muzzle and fired—going over the cliff, as he had intended, and burying himself.

"Some awful inner hunger," Bedient whispered hours afterward. "You see, he couldn't talk—as you and I do.... I've noticed it so long—that these men can't talk to one another—only swear and joke."

Early the next morning Cairns awoke, doubtless missing Bedient subconsciously. It was in the first gray, an hour before Healy kicked his outfit awake. Bedient was back in camp in time to start breakfast, having made a big detour to reach the base of the gorge. It wasn't a thing to speak about, but he had made a pilgrimage to the pit where the farrier had fallen.... Another time, Cairns awoke in the same way. It was the absence of Bedient, not the actual leaving, that aroused him. The Train had camped in a little nameless town. Cairns, this time, found his companion playing with a child, at the doorway of one of the shacks of the village. Inside, was an old man sick with *beri-beri*—swollen, features erased, unconscious; and an old woman who also had been too weak to flee before the American party. These two, the child, and a few pariah dogs were all that remained. You could have put the tiny one in a haversack comfortably. A poor little mongrel head that shone bare and scabby in places, but big black eyes, full of puzzles and wonderings; and upon his arms and legs, those deep humors which come from scratching in the night. The infant sat upon a banana leaf—brown and naked and wonderful as possible—and Bedient knelt before him smiling happily, and feeding hard-tack that had been softened in bacon-gravy.

Cairns saw the old woman's face. It was sullen, haggard. The eyes were no strangers to hunger nor hatred. She watched the two Americans, as might a crippled tigress, that had learned at last how weak was her fury against chains. He saw that same look many times afterward in the eyes of these women of the riverbanks—as the white troops moved past. There was not even a sex-interest to complicate their hatred.

One day Thirteen overtook a big infantry column making a wide ford in the river before Bamban. It was high noon, but they found during the hold-up, a bit of shade and breeze on a commanding hill. Cairns and Bedient kicked off their shoes into the tall, moist grass, and luxuriously poked their feet into the coolness; and presently they were watching unfold a really pretty bit of action.

A thin glittering cloud of smoke across the river showed where the trenches of the natives were. The Americans in the river, held their rifles and ammunition-belts high, and wriggled their hips against the butting force of the stream. It all became very business-like. The battalion first across, set out to flank the native works; a rapid-fire gun started to boom from an opposite eminence, and the infantry took to firing at the emptying trenches. The Tagals were poked out of their positions, and in a sure leisurely way that held the essence of attraction.

After all, it was less the actual bits of fighting that cleared into memories of permanence, than certain subtleties of the campaign: a particular instant of one swift twilight, as in the plaza at Alphonso; a certain moment of a furious mid-day, when the sun was a python pressure, so that the scalp prickled with the congested blood in the brain, and men lifted their hats an inch or two as they rode, preserving the shade, but permitting the air to circulate; some guttural curse from a packer who could not lift his voice in the heat, nor think, but only curse, and grin in sickly fashion....

There were moments, reminders of which awoke Cairns in a sweat for many nights afterward: One day when he was badly in need of a fresh mount, he saw just ahead of the Train—a perfect little sorrel stallion fastened to the edge of the trail. He dismounted to change saddles. The Train was straggling along under an occasional fire. Cairns found that the pony was held by a tough wire, that led into the jungle. Such was the braiding at the throat, that only a sapper could have handled it. The correspondent started to follow the wire into the thicket—when Bedient caught him by the shoulder and half-lifted him from the ground. There was strength in that slim tanned hand that had nothing to do with the ordinary force of men. The cook smiled, but disdained explanation. It all dawned upon Cairns a second later. He would have followed the wire to the end in the jungle—where the trap of knives would spring.... The bolo-men need but a moment.... It was only two or three days later that one of the packers dropped behind the Train to tighten a cinch. No one had noticed, and Thirteen filed on.

"For Christ's sake—don't!" they heard from behind.

Wheeling, they found that the man had seen the end—as he had called out in that horrible echoing voice. He was not more than fifty yards behind the rear packer—and pinned to the trail. A bolo had been hammered with a stone—through the upper lip and the base of the brain, two or three inches into the earth.... He had been butchered besides.

At the end of a terrific ten days, Thirteen was crawling at nightfall into the large garrison at Lipa. Men and mules had been lost in the recent gruelling service. The trails and the miles had been long and hard; much hunger and thirst, and there was hell in the hearts of men this night. Even Bedient was shaking with fatigue; and Cairns beside him, felt that there wasn't the brain of a babe in his skull. His saddle seemed filled with spikes. His spur was gone, and for hours he had kept his half-dead, lolling-tongued pony on the way, by frequent jabbing from a broken lead-pencil.... And here was Lipa at last, the second Luzon town, and a corral for the mules. As they passed a nipa-shack, at the outer edge, a sound of music came softly forth. Some native was playing one of the queer Filipino mandolins. The Train pushed on, without Cairns and Bedient. All the famine and foulness and fever lifted from these two. They forgot blood and pain and glaring suns. The early stars changed to lily-gardens, vast and white and beautiful, and their eyes dulled with dreams.

They did not guess, at least Cairns did not, that the low music brought tears that night—because they were in dreadful need of it, because they were filled with inner agony for something beautiful, because they had been spiritually starved. And all the riding hard, shooting true and dying game—those poor ethics of the open—had not brought a crumb, not a crumb, of the real bread of life. Nor could mountains of mere energy nor icebergs of sheer nerve! In needing the bread of life—they were different from the others, and so they lingered, unable to speak, while a poor little Tagal—"one of the niggers"—all unconsciously played. "Surely," they thought, "his soul is no dead, dark thing when he can play like that."

Will Levington Comfort

... So often, Bedient watched admiringly while Cairns wrote. The correspondent didn't know it, but he was bringing a good temporal fame to Thirteen and himself in these nights. He had a boy's energy and sentiment; also a story to tell for every ride and wound and shot in the dark. The States were attuned to boyish things, as a country always is in war, and a boy was better than a man for the work.... Often Bedient would bring him a cup of coffee and arrange a blanket to keep the wind from the sputtering candles. The two bunks were invariably spread together; and Bedient was ever ready for a talk in the dark, when Cairns' brain dulled and refused to be driven to further work, even under the whip of bitter-black coffee.... They were never to forget these passionate nights—the mules, the mountains, nor the changing moon. Cairns was tampering with a drug that is hard to give up, in absorbing the odor and color of the oriental tropics. It filled his blood, and though, at the time, its magic was lost somewhat in the great loneliness for the States, and his mother and sisters—still, he was destined to know the craving when back on consecrated ground once more, and the carnal spirit of it all, died from his veins.

The most important lesson for Cairns to grasp was one that Andrew Bedient seemed to know from the beginning. It was this: To make what men call a good soldier means the breaking down for all time of that which is thrillingly brave and tender in man.

Healy is a type—a gamester, a fiend, a catapult. With a yell of "Hellsfire!" like a bursting shell, he would rowel his saddle-mule and lead the Train through flood or flame. His was a curse and a blow. He seemed a devil, condemned ever to pound miles behind him—bloody miles. Sometimes, there was a sullen baleful gleam in the black eye, shaded by a campaign hat, but more often it was wide-open and reckless like a man half-drunk. Rousingly picturesque in action, a boy would exclaim, "Oh, to be a man like that!" but a *man* would look at him pityingly and murmur, "God forbid!"... No other had the racy oaths of this boss-packer. Here was his art. Out of all his memories of Healy and the Train, one line stands out in the mind of Cairns, bringing the picture of pictures:

Again, it was a swift twilight among the gorges between Silang and Indang. It was after the suicide of the farrier, and there were sores and galls under the packs. If one cannot quickly start the healing by first intention, a sore back, in this climate, will ruin a mule. In a day or two, one is all but felled by the stench and corruption of the worm-filled wound— when the *aparejo* is lifted.... Just before the halt this night, an old gray mule, one of the tortured, had strayed from the bell; sick, indeed, when that jangle failed to hold her to the work. Something very strange and sorrowful about these mighty creatures. If they can but muzzle the flanks of the bell-mare once in twenty-four hours, often stopping a jolt from the heels of this temperamental monster—the mules appear morally refreshed for any fate.

Miraculous toilers, sexless hybrids—successful ventures into Nature's arcanum of cross-fertilization—steady, humorous, wise, enduring, and homely unto pain! The bond of their whole organization is the bell. It is the source inseparable in their intelligence from all that is lovely and of good report— not the sound, but what the sound represents. And this is the mystery: mare or gelding doesn't seem to matter, nor age, color, temper; just something set up and smelling like a horse. Thirteen's crest-jewel was an old roan Jezebel that smothered with hatred at the approach of the least or greatest of her slaves. She had a knock-out in four feet—but Beatrice, she was, to those mules.

When Healy found the old gray missing, he remembered she was badly off under the packs. It was an ordeal to halt and search, for Silang meant supper and pickets. But the boss led the way back—and his eye was first to find her.... There she was, silhouetted against the sunset as poor Benton had been—seventy or eighty feet above the trail. Her head was down, her tongue fallen. The old burden-bearer seemed to have clambered up the rocks—through some desperate impulse for a breeze—or to die! She lifted her head as the hoofs rang below—but still looked away toward some Mecca for good mules. You must needs have been there to get it all—the old gray against the red sky—and know first-hand the torture of the trails, the valor of labor, the awfulness of Luzon. To Cairns and Bedient there was something deep and heady to the picture, as they followed the eyes of Healy—and then his yell that filled the gorges for miles:

"Come down here—you scenery-lovin' son of—"

That was just the *vorspiel*. Mother Nature must have fed color to Healy. He did not paint, play nor write, but the rest of that curse dropped with raw pigment, like a painting of Sorolla. Prisms of English flashed with terrible attraction. It was a Homeric curse of all nations. Parts of it were dainty, too, as a butterfly dip. Cairns was hot and courageous under the spell. The whole train of mules huddled and fell to trembling. A three-legged pariah-dog sniffed, took on a sudden obsession, and went howling heinously dawn the gorge. Healy rolled a cigarette with his free hand, and the old gray let herself down, half-falling....

And then—the end of campaigning. The rains began gradually that season, so that the last days were steamy and sickening with the heavy sweet of tropical fragrance. Between clouds at night, the stars broke out more than ever brilliant and near, in the washed air. There were moments when the sky appeared ceiled with phosphor, which a misty cloud had just brushed and set to dazzling. Something in the soil made them talk of girls—and Bedient drew forth for Cairns (to see the hem of her garment)—a certain hushed vision named Adelaide.... At last, the Train made Manila, wreck that it was, after majestic service; and the great gray mantle, a sort of moveless twilight, settled down upon Luzon and the archipelago. Within its folds was a mammoth condenser, contracting to drench the land impartially, incessantly, for sixty days or more. And now the fruition of the rice-swamps waxed imperiously; the carabao soaked himself in endless ecstasy; the rock-ribbed gorges of Southern Luzon filled with booming and treachery. Fords were obliterated. Hundreds of little rivers, that had not even left their beds marked upon the land, burst into being like a new kind of swarm; and many like these poured into the Pasig, which swelled, became thick and angry with the drain of the hills, the overflow of the rice-lands, and the filth and fever-stuff of the cities. At last, the constant din of the rain became a part of the silence.

FOURTH CHAPTER

THAT ADELAIDE PASSION

Andrew Bedient did not call at all these Asiatic and insular ports and continue to meet only men. Indeed, he did not fail to encounter those white women who follow men to disrupted places, where blood is upon the ground,—nor those native women inevitably present. A man fallen to the dregs usually finds a woman to keep him company, but it is equally true that man never climbs so high that, looking upward, he may not see a woman there.

A little before the *Truxton's* last voyage, the clipper had remained in port for a fortnight at Adelaide, New South Wales. A woman in that city was destined to mean a great deal to the boy of seventeen.... It would be very easy to say that here was a creature whose way is the way of darkness. The striking thing is that Adelaide (in the thoughts of Bedient afterward, she gradually appropriated the name of her city) did not know she was evil.... Such a woman, it is curious to note, has appeared in the boyhood of many men of power and eminent equipment.

Adelaide was small and fragrant. Though formerly married, she was true to her kind in being childless. All her interests were in senses of her own; or in the senses of men and women who fell beneath her eye; pale, narrow temples were hers, but crowded with what sensational memories! A hundred and a few odd pounds, every ounce vivid with health and rhythmic with desire; every thought a kiss loved, missed, or hoped for; a frail little flame that needed only time to destroy an arena of gladiators. Curving, pearly nails with flecks of white in them, a light low laugh, a sweet low voice! Perhaps this was her charm, a sort of *samosen* tone— low lilting minors that have to do with dusk and gardens and starlight....

There is not even a laughing pretense here that Adelaide was a real woman; but real women, even in this era of woman, often fail to remember what pure attractions to man, are their silences and their minor tones.

Just a fortnight—but what a tearing it was to leave her! Old Mother Nature must have writhed at this parting—groaned at the sight of the boy staring back from the high stern of the *Truxton*, at the stars lowering over the city and the woman, Adelaide. Possibly she retained something from the depth of his individuality.... Bedient would not have said so; but there is no doubt that her importance in his life was that of a *mannequin* upon which to drape his ideals. Had he seen her, in the later years, he would have met the dull misery of disillusionment. Adelaide was a boy's sensational trophy. Her distant beauty and color was the art and pigment of his own mind.

A soul rudiment, a mental bud, and a beautiful prophylactic body—such was her equipment. He dreamed of her as a love flower of inextinguishable sweetness. The mere abstraction of her sex,—colorless enough to most grown men,—was a sort of miracle to the boy. He made it shining with his idealism.... Frail arms held out to him; cool arms that turned electric with fervor. Unashamed, she took him as her own....

Exquisite devourer, yet she had much to do in bringing forth from the latent, one of the rarest gifts a boy can have—lovelier than royalty and fine as genius—the blue flower of fastidiousness. Adelaide, all unconcerned, identified herself with this, and it lived in the foreground of his mind. She became his Southland, his isle of the sea. Winds from the South were her kisses—almost all the kisses he knew for years afterward. Living women were less to him than her memory. Facing the South, through many a hot-breathed night, he saw her—and the little house.... And what a drowsy-head she was! Nothing to do with the morning light, had she, save when it awakened, to shut it out impatiently, and turn over to the dimmest of walls until afternoon. She had never been truly alive until afternoon. How he had laughed at her for that!... A creature of languors; a mere system of inert dejected cells when alone, pure destructive principle, if you like,—yet she held this boy's heart to her, without a letter, possibly with little or no thought of him, across a thousand leagues of sea—and this, through those frequently ungovernable years in which so many men become thick and despicable with excess.

Bedient often questioned himself—why he had not given up his berth on the *Truxton* and remained longer in Adelaide. There were a dozen ships in the harbor to take him forth when he cared. This thought had not come to him at the time. Quite as remarkable was the formidable *something* which arose in his brain at the thought of going back. This was not to be fathomed then—nor willed away. The roots of his integrity were shaken at the thought of return. Andrew Bedient at thirty-four understood. His was a soul that could thrive on dreams and denials. Even half-formed, this soul was the source of a strange antagonism, against which the fleshly desire to return was powerless. Poise, indeed, for a cook among sailors and packers.

The time came when he heard other women—blessed women—speak of the Adelaide type of sister as the crowning abomination; he watched their eyes harden and glitter as only a mother-bird's can, in the circling shadow of a hawk; he lived to read in the havoc of men's faces that the ways of such women were ways of death; he believed all this—yet preserved something exquisite. Ten years afterward, winds from the South brought him the spirit of fragrance from her shoulders and hair. From his own ideals, he had focussed upon that Emptiness, the beauty and dimension of a Helen.

Other experiences, up to the real romance—and these were surprisingly few—were episodes, brief quickenings of the old flame...When the first American soldiers were being lightered ashore in Manila harbor, in fact, shortly after the cannonading in the harbor, a certain woman came over from the States and took a house in Manila. It was known as the Block-House. Some months afterward, and just before the long trip of the Train in which Cairns featured, Bedient met this woman on the *Escolta*. It was at dusk, and she was crossing the narrow pavement from the post-office entrance to her carriage-door. Their eyes met frankly. She was wise, under thirty, very slender, perfectly dressed; pretty, of course, but more than that; her little perfections were carried far beyond the appreciation of any but women physically faultless as herself.

Bedient was impressed with something passionate and courageous, possibly dangerous. He could not have told the source of this impression. It was not in the contour, in the white softness of skin, in the full brown eyes, fair brow, nor in the reddened arch of her lips. It was something from the whole, denoted possibly in the quick dilation of her delicate nostrils or in the startling discovery of such a woman in Manila.... She lowered her eyes, started for her carriage—

then turned again to the tall figure of Bedient in fresh white clothing. Or it may have been that her deep nature found delight in the excellent boyishness of the tanned face.

"Wouldn't you like to drive with me on the *Luneta*?" she asked pleasantly, and there was a low tone in her voice which made her instantly different.

"Why, yes, I should like to."

Her carriage was a *victoriette*, small to match the ponies—black stallions, noteworthy for style and spirit even in Manila, where one's equipage is the measure of fortune.... Bedient found that he could be silent without causing an abatement of her pleasure. And, indeed, she seemed a little embarrassed, too, although he did not accept this. Vaguely he was ruffled by the thought that he had merely been chosen as the principal of a nightly adventure.... This was untrue.

It was before the time of native concerts on the sea-drive, but in the night itself, and in the soft undertone from the sea, there was ardent atmosphere—with this woman beside him. The deeper current of his thoughts rushed with memories, but upon the surface played the adorable present, swift with adjustments as her swiftly-moving arms. The wonder of Womanhood was ever-new to him. Mighty gusts of animation surged through his body. He spoke from queer angles of consciousness, and did not remember. She could laugh charmingly.... To her, the Hour uprose. Here was clear manhood of twenty (and such an unhurt boy he had proved to be)—to make her very own!... She had taught herself to live by the hour; had forfeited the right to be loved long. She knew the time would soon come, when she could not hold nor attract men. It comes always to women who dissipate themselves among the many. Yet she loved the love of an hour; was a connoisseur of the love-tokens of men to her; no material loss was counted in the balance against a winning such as this promised to be. Here was a big intact passion which she called unto herself with every art; her developed senses felt it pouring upon her; this was a drug to die for. It made her brave and filled her mind with dreams—as wine does to some men. Already he was giving her love—of a sort that older men withhold from her kind. She put her hand upon his wrist—and told the native to drive them home.

... They sat in a hammock together on the rear balcony of the Block-House. It had been a dangerous moment passing through the house. There had been embarrassments, the telltale artifices of the establishment, but she would not suffer the work of the ride to be torn down. She held him in enchantment by sheer force of will; and now they were alone, and she was building again. There was wine. Over the balcony rail, they watched the Pasig running wickedly below; and across, stretching away to where the stars lay low in the rim of the horizon, the wet teeming rice-lands brooded in the night-mist.... The piano, which had seemed unstrung from the voyage, as he passed through the house, sounded but faintly now through several shut doors. The fragments were mellifluous....

She knew he was a civilian from his dress, and asked his work in Luzon. He told her he was cook of Pack-train Thirteen, just now quartered in the main corral. She laughed, but didn't believe. He was not the first to conceal his office from her. It was unpleasant; apt to be dangerous. She did not ask a second time.... There was just one other perilous moment. They had been together on the balcony but a half-hour, when she turned her face to him, her eyes shut, and said:

"You're a dear boy!... I haven't kissed anyone like that—oh, in long, long!... It makes me feel like a woman—how silly of me!"

Her face and throat looked ghastly white for a moment in the sheltered candles. "Isn't it silly of me—isn't it—*isn't it?*" she kept repeating, picking at his fingers, and touching his cheeks in frightened fashion.... She was reaching amazing deeps of him. The best of her was his, for she could give greatly. It was wonderful, if momentary. He felt the terrific strength of his hands, as if his fingers must strike sparks when he touched her flesh. The need of her flamed high within him. She was delight in every movement and expression; and so slender and fervent and sweet-voiced.... She had banished the one encroachment of sordidness. The high passion of this moment was builded upon basic attractions, as with children. Some strong intuition had prevailed upon her so to build. They had come to an end of words....

A knock at the door broke the *notturno appassionato*. She had left word not to be called for any reason. Furiously now she rushed across the room.... Bedient did not see the female servant at the door, but heard the frightened voice uttering the word, "Brigadier—." The answer from the woman who had left his arms was mercifully vague, but the voice at the door whimpered, "Only it was *the General*—!"...

It was all hideously clear. Bedient was left sterile, polar. The door slammed shut; the woman faced him—and understood. There was no restoring *this* ruin.... She now damned military rank and her establishment in a slow, dreadful voice. Her knuckles seemed driven into her temples. She wanted to weep, to be soothed and petted—to have her Hour brought back, but she saw that her beauty was gone from him—and all the mystery which had been in their relation a minute before.... Her rebellion, so far hard-held, now became fiendish. It was not against him, but herself. So vivid and terrible was her concentration of hatred upon the cause, that Bedient caught the picture of the Brigadier in her mind. He *saw* the man afterward—a fat and famous soldier.... She spat upon the floor. Her lower lip was drawn in and the small white teeth snapped upon it.

There was nothing in the Block-House ever to bring him back. Her last vestige of attraction for him had disintegrated. Bedient had nothing to say; he caught up her clenched hand and kissed it.... And in the street he heard feminine voices rising to the pitch of hysteria. A servant rushed forth for a surgeon. The woman had fallen into "one of her seizures."...

Pack-train Thirteen took the field a day or two afterward. Bedient was not at all himself.... In all the months that followed meeting David Cairns in Alphonso, the Block-House incident was too close and horrible for words— though Bedient spoke of Adelaide and the great wind and a hundred other matters.

There was another slight Manila experience, which took place after the first parting with David Cairns, the latter being called to China by rumors of uprising. Pack-train Thirteen had rubbed itself out in service—was just a name. Bedient was delighting in the thought of hunting up Cairns in China.... It was dusk again, that redolent hour. Bedient had just dined. So sensitive were his veins—that coffee roused him as brandy might another. His health was brought to such perfection, that its very processes were a subtle joy, which sharpened the mind and senses. Bedient had been so long in the field, that the sight of even a Filipino woman was novel. Strange, forbidding woman of the river-banks—yet in the twilight, and with the inspired eyes of young manhood, that dusk-softened line from the lobe of the ear to the point of the shoulder—a passing maid with a tray of fruit upon her head—was enough to startle him with the richness of romance. It was not desire—but the great rousing abstraction, Woman, which descends upon full-powered young men at certain times with the power of a psychic

Will Levington Comfort

visitation. His heart poured out in a greeting that girdled the world, to find the Woman—somewhere.

Bedient did not know at this time of the heart emptiness of the world's women—a longing so vast, so general, that interstellar space is needed to hold it all. Still, he had so much to give, it seemed that in the creative scheme of things there must be a woman to receive and ignite all these potentials of love.... In this mood his mind reverted to that isle of the sea—the woman, and the room that was her house.... He was sitting in the plaza before the *Hotel d'Oriente*. A little bamboo-table was before him and a long glass of claret and fruit-juice. The night was still; hanging-lanterns were lit, though the darkness was not yet complete. There was a mingling of mysterious lights and shadows among the palm-foliage that challenged the imagination— like an unfinished picture.... Only a few of the tables were occupied. The native servants were very quiet. Bedient heard a girlish voice out of the precious and perilous South.

... It was not Adelaide. He had only started to turn, when his consciousness told him that. But the voice was much like hers—the same low and lazy loveliness in the formation of certain words. The appeal was swift. Bedient did not turn, though he sat tingling and attentive.... At this time not a few of the American officers had been joined by their wives in Manila, and most of these were quartered at the *Oriente*.... He knew the man's voice, too, but in such a different way— the voice of a soldier heard afield.

What was said had little or no significance—a man's tolerant, sometimes laughing monosyllables; and silly, cuddling, unquotable nothings from his companion. It was the ardor in her tones—the sort of completion of sensuous happiness— and the strange kinship between her and the woman he had known—these, that brought to Bedient a sudden madness of hunger to hear such words for his own....

The man had but recently come in from field-work. The woman was fresh from a transport voyage from the States. He talked laughingly of the "niggers" his company had met—of small, close fighting and surprises. She wanted to hear more, more,—but alone. She was pressing him, less with words than manner, to come into the hotel and relate his adventures, where they could be quite alone.... She had been so passionately lonely without him—back in Washington ... and the long voyage.... Her voice enthralled Bedient.

They were married. The man laughed often. The tropics had enervated him, though he made no such confession. He wanted drink and lights. To him, the present was relishable. Their chairs scraped the tiles before Bedient turned.... They had not risen. She caught his eyes. Hers were not eyes of one who would be lonely in Washington nor during a long transport voyage. She was very young, but a vibrant feminine, her awakening already long-past. There was just a glimpse of light hair, a red-lipped profile and slow, shining dark eyes. She was not even like Adelaide, but a blood sister in temperament. Bedient saw this in her hands, wrists, lips and skin, in the pure elemental passion which came from her every tone and motion. One of the insatiate—yet frail and lovely and scented like a carnation; a white flower, red-tipped—sublimate of earthy perfume.

Bedient had seen the man in the field, a young West Point product, with a queer, rabbit face, lots of men friends, the love of his company, and a remarkable kind of physical courage—a splendid young chap, black from the heats, who was being talked about for his grisly humor under fire. This officer had seen his men down—and stayed with them.... His was a different and deeper love. He did not hurry. It seemed as if she would take his hand, after all, and lead him into the hotel. Just a little girl—little over twenty.

For the first time it struck Bedient that he must leave. He was startled that he had not left. His only palliation for such a venture into two lives—was the memories her voice roused. His lips tightened with scorn of self. And yet the thought became a fury as he walked rapidly through the dark toward the river—what it would mean to have a woman want him that way!.... His thoughts did not violate the soldier's domain. Quite clean, he was, from that; yet she had shown him afresh what was in the world. It was nearing midnight; sentries of the city, still under martial law, ordered him off the streets before he realized passing time.... And the hours did not bring to his mind the woman of the Block-House, nor anyone of those flaming desert-women who love so fiercely and so fruitlessly; whose relations with men do not weave, but only bind the selvage of the human fabric....

*　*　*　*　*

Bedient was glad to get away to sea.... David Cairns, overtaken in China, had changed a little. It appears that the very best of young men must change when they begin to wear their reputation. Riding with Thirteen had made easily the best newspaper fodder which the Luzon campaigns furnished, and the sparkling wine of recognition eventually found its own. It must be repeated that only a boy-mind can depict war in a way that fits into popular human interest.

The David Cairns whom Bedient met at the Taku forts, near the mouth of the Pei-ho, had a bit of iron tonic in his veins. His sentences were shorter, less faltering and more frequent. He *knew* things that he had formerly held tentatively. His conceptions (during night-talks) were called in quickly from the dream-borders, and given the garb and weight of matter. The stamina of decision had hardened. He was eager to call

Bedient his finest friend, but he had forgotten for the time the amazing subtleties which at first had deepened and broadened this wanderer's place in his inner life. A touch of success and the steady drive of ambition had gradually moved the abiding place of Cairns' consciousness from his heart to his brain. Few would have detected other than manliness and improvement. Bedient did not trust himself to think much about it, for fear he would do his friend an injustice. The fact that he could not see Cairns differently in the latter's first fame-flush, and observing past doubt, that he was lifted for the world's eyes, helped Bedient to realize that he was a bit weird in judgment. At all events, something was gone from the friendship. He was sore at heart, more than ever alone.... The two separated a second time in Peking after the relief of the Legations. Bedient went to Japan, where he made the acquaintance of an old Buddhist priest—a scabby, long-nailed Zarathustra who roamed the boxwood hills above Nikko, and meditated.

Bedient was farther from such things now, but he could not avoid noting that Japan is an old and easy shoe for the passions. The women of Japan are but finished children, preserving a sense of innocence in their bestowals. Many little Adelaides in fragrance, without will, without high hopes, only momentary and baby hopes—children happy in the little happinesses they give and take. This is the extraordinary feature of an empire of dangerous half-grown men. Moreover, above the delicate charm of sex, these little creatures are so remote and primitive in race and idea, so intrinsically foreign and undeveloped—that one leaves the fairest with a mitigated pang...

Bedient never repeated an action which once had brought home to him the sense of his own evil. The emotions here narrated are but moments in years. He accounted them quite as legitimate in the abstract as the strange visionings of his higher life, as yet untold. These latter have to do with his maturity, as wars and passions have to do with the approach to maturity in the life of men. To Bedient, evil concerned itself with the unclean. Wherever uncleanness (to him a pure destructive principle) revealed itself there was a balance of power in his nature which turned him from it, despite any concomitant attraction. The original Adelaide was a superb answer to the more earthy of his three natures; so utterly confined to her one plane as to be innocent of others. In the two Manila twilights which saw the dominance of his physical being, it was the Adelaide element which roused; and the scars they left behind marked the scorch of memories.

The fact that there were moments in which Bedient smoldered helplessly in a world of possible women is significant in the character of one destined to fare forth on the Supreme Adventure. It is true, he was preserved in comparative purity though he roamed unbridled around the world. Perhaps it was the same instinct which held him apart from men in their lower moments of indulgence. He could linger where there was wine until the dregs of the company were stirred by the stimulus. All delight left him then, and he found himself alone. His leaving was quite as natural as the departure from a stifling room of one who has learned to relish fresh air.... It was during his Japan stay that Bedient pleased himself often with the thought that somewhere in the world was a woman meant for him—a woman with a mind and soul, as well as flesh. If the waiting seemed long—why should he not be content, since she was waiting, too? He would know her instantly. The slightest errant fancy of doubt would be enough to assure him that she was *not* the One....

Send a boy out on a long journey (even to Circe and Calypso, and past the calling rocks of the sea), but if his mother has loved into his life, the rare flower of fastidious-ness, he will come back, with innocence aglow beneath the weathered countenance. It is the sons of strong women who have that fineness which makes them choice, even in their affairs of an hour. A beautiful spirit of race guardianship is behind this fastidiousness.... Miraculously, it seems to appear many times in the sons of women who have failed to find their own knight-errants. Missing happiness, they have taken disillusionment from common man; yet so truly have they held to their dreams, that *ever* their sons must go on searching for the true bread of life.

Will Levington Comfort

FIFTH CHAPTER

A FLOCK OF FLYING SWANS

One day (it was before he knew David Cairns) Bedient picked up the *Bhagavad Gita* from a book-stand in Shanghai. It was limp, little, strong, and looked meaty. As he raised his eyes wonderingly from a certain sentence, he encountered the glance of the fat old German dealer.

"Will this little book stand reading more than once, sir?" Bedient asked.

"Ja—but vat a little-boy question! Ven you haf read sefen times the year for sefen years—you a man vill haf become."

Bedient had been through the Song of the Divine One many times before he heard of it from anyone else. He had liked to think of it as a particular treasure which he shared with the queer old German, sick with fat. Now, it was the old Japanese sage who had turned the young man's mind to the comparative moderns—Carlyle, Emerson, Thoreau, and several others—and it was with a shock of joy he discovered that almost all of these light-bringers had *lived* with his little book. So queerly things happen.... However, the *Bhagavad Gita* gave him a brighter sense of the world under his feet, of a Force other than its own balance and momentum, and of its first fruits—the soul of man.... *In the beginning God created Heaven and Earth*—that morning star of Hebrew revelation was not at all dimmed; indeed, it shone with fairer lustre in the more spacious heavens of the Farther East.

Directly from his old Japanese teacher, and subtly from the *Bhagavad Gita* and the modern prophets, Bedient felt strongly urged to India. This culminated in 1903, when he was twenty-five years old. Hatred of Russia was powerfully fomenting through the Japanese nation at this time. Bedient grew sick at the thought of the coming struggle, but delayed leaving for several weeks, in the hope of seeing David Cairns, who, surely enough, was one of the first of the war-correspondents to reach Tokyo late that year. Cairns had put on pounds and power, and only Bedient knew at the end of certain fine days together, that the beauty of their first relation had not returned in its fullness.... They parted (a third time during five years) in the wintry rain on the water-front at Yokohama, Cairns remaining and Bedient taking ship for Calcutta.

Up into the Punjab he went with the new year; and there, all but lost trace of time and the world. *He seemed to have come home*—an ineffable emotion. When they told him quite seriously that the Ganges was sent from heaven, and had wandered a thousand years in the hair of Shiv before flowing down upon the plains with beauty and plenty and healing for sin-spent man—Bedient instantly comprehended the meaning of the figure: that the hair of Shiv was the Himalayas, whose peaks continually rape the rain-clouds. And the lotos—name, fragrance and sight of this flower—started a little lyrical wheel tinkling in his mind, turning off snatches of verses that sung themselves; and fluttering bits of romance, half-religious and altogether impersonal; and strange pictures, lovely, though all but effaced.

Indeed, he was one with the Hindus in a love for the bees, the silence, the mountains, rivers, the moon, and the heaven-protected cattle, in whose great soft eyes he found the completion of animal peace.... The legend that the bees had come from Venus, with the perfect cereal, wheat, as patterns of perfection from that farther evolved planet—fascinated, became the *leit-motif* of his thoughts for weeks. Earth had earned a special dispensation, it was said, and bright messengers came with a swarm and a sheaf, each milleniums advanced beyond any species of its kind here.

From a little boy he had loved the bees. Afternoons long ago (this was clear to him as the memory of that sinister hall-way of yellow-green light which returned on the afternoon of the great wind) he had lain upon the grass somewhere, and heard the hum of the honey-gatherers in thistle and clover. The hum was like the far singing of a child-choir, and the dreamings it started then were altogether too big for the memory mechanism of a little boy's head; but the vastness and wonder of those dreamings left a kind of bushed beauty far back in his mind. He had loved the bees as he had loved the *Bhagavad Gita*, thinking it peculiarly his own attraction, but when the world's great poets and prophets became known to him through their writings, he discovered, again with glad emotion, that bees had stirred the fancy of each, stimulated their conceptions of service and communistic blessedness; furnished their symbols for laws of beauty and cleanliness, brotherhood, race-spirit, the excellence of sacrifice—a thousand perfect analogies to show the way of human ethics and ideal performance.... But beyond all their service to literature, he perceived that these masters among men had *loved* the bees. This was the only verb that conveyed Bedient's feelings for them; and he found that they literally swarmed through Hindu simile in its expressions of song and story and faith.

Northward, he made his leisure way almost to the borders of Kashmir, before he found his place of abode—Preshbend, a little town of many Sikhs, which clung like a babe to the sloping hip of a mountain. He was taken on by the English of the forestry service, and liked the ranging life; liked, too, the rare meetings with his fellow-workers and superiors, quiet, steady-eyed men, quick-handed and slow of speech. With all his growth and knowledge of the finer sort, Bedient carried no equipment for earning a living—except through his hands. There was no hesitation with him in making a choice—between patrolling a forest, and the columns of a ledger. All the indoor ways of making money that intervene between the artisan and artist were to him out of the question. When asked his occupation, he had answered, "Cook."

One week in each month he spent in the town, and he came to love Preshbend and the people; the tall young men, many taller than he, and the great lean-armed, gaunt-breasted Sikh women. The boys were so studious, so simple and gentle, compared with the few others he had known, and the women such adepts at mothering! Then the shy, slender girls, impassable ranges between him and any romantic sense; yet, he was glad to be near them, glad to hear their voices and their laughter in the evenings.... He loved the long shadow of the mountains, the still dusty roads where the cattle moved so softly that the dust never rose above their knees; the smell of wood-smoke in the dusk, the legends of the gods, scents of the high forest, the thoughts which nourished his days and nights, and the brilliant stars, so steady and eternal, and so different from the steaming constellations of Luzon;—he loved it all, and saw these things, as one home from bitter exile.

And then with the cool dark and the mountain winds, after the long, pitiless day of fierce, devouring sunlight, the moon glided over the fainting world with peace and healing—like an angel over a battle-field.... The two are mystic in every Indian ideal of beauty, and alike cosmic—woman and the moon.

There was a certain trail that rose from Preshbend, and ended after an hour's walk in a high cliff of easy ascent. Bedient often went there alone when the moon was full—and waited for her rising. At last through a rift in the far mountains, a faint ghost would appear, and waveringly whiten the glacial breast of old *God-Mother*—the highest peak in the vision of Preshbend. Just a nucleus of light at first, like a shimmering mist, but it steadied and brightened—until that snowy summit was configured in the midst of her lowlier brethren on the borders of Kashmir—and Bedient, turning from his deep reflections, would find the source of the miracle, trailing her glory up from the South.

Often he lost the sense of personality in these meditations. His eyes turned at first upon that dead, dark mountain, which presently caught the reflection of the moon (in itself a miracle of loveliness); then the moon which held the reflection of the hidden sun, which in its turn reflected the power of All; and he, a bit of suppressed animation among the rocks of the cliff, audaciously comprehending that chain of reflections and adding his own! The marvel of it all carried him a dimension beyond the responsiveness of mere brain-tissue, and for hours in which he was not Bedient, but *one* with some Unity that swept over the pageant of the universe, his body lay hunched and chill in the cold of the heights.... That was his first departure, and he was in his twenty-eighth year.

Another time, as he watched old *God-Mother*, he suddenly felt *himself* an instrument upon which played the awful yearning of the younger peoples of Europe and America.

Greatly startled, he saw them hungering for this vastness, this beauty and peace; yet enchanted among little things, condemned to chattering and pecking at each other, and through interminable centuries to tread dim hot ways of spite and weariness, cruelty and nervous pain. He, Bedient, had found peace here, but it was not for him to take always. He seemed held by that awful yearning across the world; as if he were an envoy commissioned to find Content—to bring back the secret that would break their enchantment.... No, he was not yet detached from his people; he could only accept tentatively these mighty virtues of wonder and silence, gird his loins with them and finally take back the rich tidings.... Was he dwelling in silence to walk in power over there? This excited and puzzled him at first. Bedient as a bearer of light was new....

Yet hunger was growing within for his own people; a passion to tell them; rather to make them see that all their aims and possessions were not worth one moment, such as he had spent, watching the breast of old *God-Mother* whiten, with the consciousness of God walking in the mountain-winds, the scent of camphor, lotos, sandal and wild-honey in His garments. A passion, indeed, grew within him to make his people see that real life has no concern with wrestlings in fetid valleys, but up, up the rising roads—poised with faith, and laughing with power—until through a rift in the mountains, they are struck by the light of God's face, and shine back—like the peaks of Kashmir to the moon.

And another night it came to him that he had something to say to the women of his people. This thought emerged clean-cut from the deeps of abstraction, and he trembled before it, for his recent life had kept him far apart from women. And now, the thought occurred that he was better prepared to inspire women—because of this separateness. He had preserved the boyish ideal of their glowing mystery, their lovely cosmic magnetism. India had stimulated it. All the lights of his mind had fallen upon this ideal, all the colors of the spectrum and many from heaven—certain swift flashes of glory, such as are brought, in queer angles of light, from a butterfly's wing. He had been mercifully spared from moving among the infinitudes of small men who hold such a large estimate of the incapacity and commonness of women.... Even among the Sikh mothers (Bedient did not dream how his spirit prospered during these Indian years) his ideal was strengthened. He found among the mothers of the Punjab a finer courage than ever the wars had shown him—the courage that bends and bears—and an answering sweetness for all the good that men brought to their feet....

So one night at last he found himself thanking God in the great silence—that he could see the natural greatness of women; that he was alive to help them; that he could pity those who knew only the toiling, not the mystic, hands of women; pity those—and tell them—who knew her only as a sense creature.... And swiftly he wanted to tell women—how high he held them—that one man in the world had kept his vision of them brighter and brighter in substance and spirit. He had the queer, almost feminine, sense, of their needing to know this, and of impatience to give them their happiness. Perhaps they did not continually hold this in mind; perhaps the men of their world had taught them to forget.... They would be happier for his coming. He would put into each woman's heart—*as only a man could do*—a quickened sense of her incomparable importance; make her remember that mothering is the loveliest of all the arts; that only in the lower and savage orders of life the male is ascendant; that as the human race evolves in the finer regions of the spirit— when growth becomes centred in the ethereal dimension of the soul—woman, invariably a step nearer the great creative source, must assume supremacy.... Among the dark mountains the essence of all these thoughts came to him during many nights.

He would make women happier by restoring to them—their own. He must show how dreadful for them to forget for an instant—that they are the real inspirers of man; that they ignite his every conception; that it is men who follow and interpret, and the clumsy world is to blame because the praise so often goes to the interpreter, and not to the inspiration. But praise is a puny thing. Women must see that they only are lovely who remain true to their dreams, for of their dreams is made the spiritual loaf, the real vitality of the race; that by remaining true to their dreams, though starved of heart, the sons that come to them will be the lovers they dream of—and bring the happiness *they* missed, to the daughters of other women. For love is spirit—the stuff of dreams—and love is Giving.... He must bring to women again, lest they forget, this word: that never yet has man sung, painted, prophesied, made a woman happy, nor in any way woven finer the spirit of his time, but that God first covenanted with his mother for the gift—and, more often than not, the gift was startled into its supreme expression by the daughter of another.... All in a sentence, it summed at last, to Bedient alone,—a flaming sentence for all women to hear: *Only through the potential greatness of women can come the militant greatness of men.*

And so things appeared unto him to do, as he watched the miracle of the moon bringing forth the lineaments of the old *God-Mother*; and so the cliff became his Sinai. On this last night, for a moment at least, he felt as must an immortal lover who has seen clearly the way of chivalry—the task which was to be, as the Hindus say, the fruit of his birth.... Thus he would go down, face glowing with new and luminous resolves.... And once dawn was breaking as he descended, and the whir of wings aroused him. Looking upward he saw (as did Another of visions), in the red beauty of morning—a flock of swans flying off to the South.

*   *   *   *   *

Gobind must not be forgotten—old Gobind, who appeared in Preshbend at certain seasons, and sat down in the shade of a camphor-tree, old and gnarled as he; but a sumptuous refuge, as, in truth was Gobind in the spirit. The natives said that the austerities of Gobind were the envy of the gods; that he could hold still the blood in his veins from dusk to dawn; and make the listener understand many wonderful things about himself and the meaning of life.

The language had come to Bedient marvellously. Literally it flowed into his mind, as in the rains a rising river finds its old bed of an earlier season.

"This is your home, Wanderer," Gobind told him. "Long have you travelled to and fro and long still must you wander, but you will come back again to the cool shadows, and to these—" Gobind lifted his hand to point to the roof of the world. The yellow cloth fell away from his arm, which looked like a dead bough blackened from many rains. "For these are your mountains and you love these long shadows. All Asia and the Islands you have searched for these shadows, and here you are content, for your soul is Brahman.... But you are not ready for Home. You are not yet tired. Long still must you wander. Some sin of a former birth caused you to sink into the womb of a woman of the younger peoples. You have yet to return to them—as one coming down from the mountains, after the long summer, brings a song and a story for the heat-sick people of the plains to hear at evening—"

This was the substance of many talks. It was always the same when Gobind shut his eyes.

"You say I shall come back here, good Gobind?" Bedient asked.

"Yes, you will come back here to abandon the body—"

"Alone?"

"Yes."

Bedient was filled with grave questions. One can always put a mystic meaning to the direct saying of a Hindu holy man, but there seemed no equivocation here. The young man was slow to believe that all his dreaming must come to naught. It seemed as if his whole inner life had been built about the dream of a woman; and of late she had seemed nearer than ever, and different from any woman, he had ever known— the mate of his mind and soul and flesh. For a long time he progressed no farther than this, for falling into his own thoughts, he would find only the aged body of Gobind before him—the rest having stolen away on night-marches of deep moment, while he, Bedient, had tried to realize his life loneliness. At last he could think of nothing else throughout the long day, and he went early in the semi-light and sat before the holy man. The dusk darkened, and a new moon rose, but Gobind did not rise to mere physical consciousness that night, though Bedient sat very still before him for hours. The bony knees of the old ascetic, covered with dust, were moveless as the black roots of the camphor-tree; and a dog of the village sat afar off on his haunches and whined at intervals, waiting for the white man to go, that he might have the untouched supper, which a woman of Preshbend had brought to Gobind's begging-bowl.

And again the next night Bedient came, but Gobind was away playing with the gods of his youth—just the old withered body there—and the dog whining.

But the third night, the eyes of Gobind filled with his young friend—

"You say, good father Gobind," Bedient said quickly, "that I shall come back here alone to die?"

"Yes," the *Sannyasin* answered simply, but a moment later, he shivered, and seemingly divined all that was in the young man's mind, for he added: "You will learn to look *within* for the woman.... You would not find favor—in finding her without.... It is not for you—the red desire of love!"

* * * * *

It was during these years in India that Bedient began to put down the thoughts which delighted him during the long rides through the forest; and something of the thrill of his reflections, as he watched old *God-Mother* from his cliff. He found great delight in this, and his mind was integrated by expression. He recalled many little pictures of the early years—not the actions, but the reflections of action. It was fascinating. He found that his journal would bulk big presently, so he took to polishing as he went along; chose the finest, toughest Indian parchment—and wrote finely as this print—for it was clear to him that he had entered upon what was to prove a life-habit.

The letters from Captain Carreras had become more frequent in late years; in fact, there was almost always a letter en route either from Preshbend or Equatoria.... The Captain wanted him to come; stronger and stronger became the call. So far as money was concerned, he had done extraordinarily well. He always wrote of this half-humorously.... At last when Bedient was beginning his seventh year in the Punjab, there came a letter which held a plaint not to be put aside.

Bedient was in his thirty-second year; and just at this time old Gobind left his body for a last time beneath the camphor-tree. The young man had sat before him the night before, and the holy man had told him in symbolism—that the poor murky river of his life had made its last bend through the forests, and was swiftly flowing into the sea of time and space. Though he sat long after silence had settled down, Bedient did not know (so softly and sweetly did the old saint depart) that the *Sannyasin* was tranced in death instead of meditation. It was not until the next morning, when he heard the Sikh women of the village weeping—one above all—that he understood. It was not a shock of grief to these women, for such is their depth that the little matters which concern all flesh and which are inevitable, cannot be made much ado of. Still it was feminine and beautiful to him, their weeping; and possibly the one who wept loudest had mothered old Gobind in her heart, and there was emptiness in the thought that she could not fill his begging-bowl again. Bedient, as well as others of the village, knew that to Gobind, death was a long-awaited consummation; that he was gone only from the physical eye of the village. *That* missed him—as did Bedient, who had loved to sit at the fleshly feet of the holy man.... But he loved all Preshbend, too.

And at length, he set out on foot for Lahore—often looking back.

SIXTH CHAPTER

THAT ISLAND SOMEWHERE

ALL these impressive years, from seventeen to thirty-two, had brought Andrew Bedient nothing in the civilized sense of success. It is quickly granted that he was a failure according to such standards. He had never been in want nor debt, nor so poor that he could not cover another's immediate human need if presented; yet the reserve energy of all these years, in fact, of his whole life, as represented in gold, amounted to less than three hundred dollars. Probably, outside of Asia, there was not a white man who had accumulated three hundred dollars with less thought; certainly in Asia there was none, white or black, who carried this amount with less vital concern. Up the years, he had given no thought to the oft-expressed eagerness of Captain Carreras to help him in a substantial way. He had always felt that he would go to his friend—at times had hungered for him—and now he answered the call.

Fifteen years since he had taken the hand of Captain Carreras and laughingly refused to share the other's fortunes! Bedient remembered how bashfully, but how genuinely, that had been suggested. Then the Captain's manner had become crisp and nervous to hide his heart-break, and the order was given with all the authority of the quarter-deck, that Bedient must never fail in any extremity to make known his need. But there had been no need—save for the friendship....

Strange old true heart that could not forget! Bedient felt it in every letter. Thousands of acquaintances, but not a friend nor relative! He thought about Bedient every day; an old man's heart turned to the boy whose hands had suddenly fallen upon him with such amazing power. Occasionally in the letters, there was an obvious effort to cover this profundity of affection with a surface of humor, but it always broke through before a page was blotted.... Equatoria, and his really remarkable acquisitions there, were invariably matters for light touches. He had picked up big lands for almost nothing; and he found himself presently in strong favor with what was probably the most stable government Equatoria had ever known. The Captain's original purpose of acquiring the mineral rights of certain rich rivers had greatly prospered. Yes, there was gold in the river-beds.... Incidentally, to keep his hands "from mauling the natives," he had caused to be planted at different times, several thousand acres of cacao trees, all of which were now bearing. The Captain explained naively that these had turned out rather handsomely, since the natives harvested the nuts for him at a ludicrously low figure, and Holland sent ships twice a year for the product. "Just suggest anything to this soil, and the answer is perennials. We can't bother with stuff that has to be planted more than once," he observed. Bedient returned many times to the letter that told about the goats. Part of it read:

"There was a rocky strip of land in the fork of two rivers—several thousand acres—that almost shut itself off, so narrow and rocky was the neck.... For a long time this big bottle of land troubled me—couldn't think of any use to put it to—until somebody mentioned goats. In a fit of industry, I shipped over a few goat families from Mexico, turned them loose in the natural corral—and forgot all about them for a couple of years. You see, the natives are fruit-eaters, and it's too hot for skins. My men occasionally brought me word that the goats were doing well. Finally, I sent a party over to pile a few more rocks at the mouth. They came back pale and awed, begging me to come and look. I went. I tell you, boy, there were parades, caravans, pageants of goats in there—all happy in the stone-crop.... I haven't dared to look for a year or more, but with a good marine-glass from the upper window of the *hacienda*, you can see a portion of the tract. They're hopping about over there—thick as fleas!... That's the way everything multiplies. Come and extricate me from the goat problem!... Dear lad, I do need you—not for goats, nor for fruit, nor mining, nor chocolate interests, not to be my cook—forgive the mention of a delightful memory—but as a lonely old man needs a boy—his boy."

*　*　*　*　*

Only a half-day in New York on the way down to Equatoria, or the alternative of waiting over a ship, meaning eight days later with Captain Carreras. Bedient could not bring his mind to the latter delay at this stage of the journey, though the metropolis called to him amazingly. Here he had been born; and here was the setting of many early memories, now seen through a kind of faery dusk. With but an hour or so in lower Manhattan, he swept in impressions like a panorama-film, his mind held to no single thought for more than an instant. The finest outer integument had never been worn from his nerves, so that nothing of the pandemonium distressed; but what his oriental training called the illusion of it all—really dismayed. It seemed as if the millions were locked in some terrible slavery, which they did not fully understand, only that they must hurry, and never cease the devouring toil. In the hideous walled cities of China, the same thought had often come to Bedient—that these myriads had been condemned by the sins of their past lives, blindly to gather together and maim each others' souls.

Still there was some big meaning for him in New York. Bedient realized that sooner or later he would return. Toward the end of the afternoon, as he looked back from the deck of the Dryden steamer *Hatteras*, he realized that New York had dazed him; that something of the grand gloom, something of the granite, had entered his heart. Perhaps it was well for him to have these glimpses, and to hurry away to adjust himself in the silence—before he took up his place in New York again.

A week later the *Hatteras* awaited dawn, sixty miles off the northern coast of Equatoria. Treacherous coral reefs extend that far out to sea, and the lights of the passage into port are few. This is an ugly part of the Caribbean in high seas. Moreover, the coral has a way of changing its ramifications; its spires build rapidly in the warm surface water.

All the forenoon the liner crawled in toward the harbor, and at last through the blazing noon, Bedient saw Coral City in a foreground of palm-decked hills. Certain fresh-tinned roofs close to the water-front reflected the sun like a burning-glass. Nearer still, a few white buildings on the seaward slopes shone through the heat haze with the vividness of jewels— whitened walls gleaming among the palms and colorful turrets of pure Spanish line. The strip of beach, white as a road of shells, lost itself on either side of the city in its own dazzling light. Films of heat danced upon the painted roofs. The sky was a blinding azure that tranced the hills and harbor with its brilliance, silence and magic.

Clouds of yellow mud boiled up from the bottom of the oozy harbor as the *Hatteras* dropped her hook; and the sharks moved about, all the more shuddery in their tameness. Two launches were making for the steamer, and Bedient, sheltering his eyes from the light, discovered the little Captain standing well-forward on the nearest—a puffy, impatient face, pathetically unconscious of its own workings in anxiety. Bedient's uplifted hand caught the other's eye as the launch neared. The old adventurer needed a second or two to take in the tall figure and the changed countenance— then a look of gladness, full, deep and tender with embarrassment, crowned the years and the long journey.

Bedient had to remember hard, after dozens of fluent and delightful letters, that he must encounter the old bashfulness again.... Plainly the Captain showed the years. There was the dark dry look of some inner consuming, and the trembling mouth was lined and assertive where formerly it was unnoticed in the general cheer. There was a break in rotundity. Perhaps this, more than anything else, put a strange hush upon the meeting. Bedient was glad he had not delayed longer; and he saw he must break through the embarrassment, as the boy and the cook of years ago would not have thought of doing. The old perfume sought his nostrils delicately with a score of memories.

The Captain seemed to have an absurd number of natives at his disposal. Bedient's small pieces of baggage were prodigiously handled. A carriage was provided, and the two drove up the main thoroughfare, *Calle Real*. The little city was appointed and its streets named by the Spanish. Parts of it were very old, and Bedient liked the setting, which was new to him—the native courtesy and the mellowness of architecture which that old race of conquerors has left in so many isles of the Western sea.

At the head of the rising highway shone a gilded dome, a sort of crown for the city. Bedient had seen it shining from the harbor, and supposed it to be the capitol. The building stood upon an eminence like a temple. *Calle Real* parted to the right and left at its gates. Their carriage passed to the right, and within the walls were groves of palms, gardens of rose, rhododendron, jasmine, flames of poinsettia, and a suggestion of mystic glooms where orchids breathed—fruit, fragrance, fountains.

"The Capitol?" laughed the Captain. "No, my boy, those little rain-rotted, stone buildings near the water-front are the government property. However, you never can tell about Equatoria. There are folks who believe that this stone palace of Senor Rey is fated to become the Capitol. It might happen in two ways. Senor Rey might overturn the government and move headquarters to his own house. You see, he loves fine things too well to reside back yonder. Or, the government overturning Celestino Rey—would ultimately move up here on the hill."

Bedient laughed softly. It was all delightfully young to him. "Then Senor Rey aspires?"

"That's the idea—only we put it 'conspires' down here.... It is really a remarkable institution—this of Senor Rey's," Carreras went on. He forgot himself in a narrative. "Now, if you were in New York and had a hundred thousand dollars of another man's money, and wanted to relax—you would come here to Equatoria, and put up with Celestino Rey. To all appearances, *The Pleiad* is a hotel, but in reality it's just a club for those who have taken the short cut to fortune—the direct and amiable way of loot. There's so much red tape in Equatoria that a New York warrant for arrest would be about as compelling in our city as a comic valentine.

"So you see, Andrew, those who used to fly to Mexico now come here. This is the most interesting colony of crime-cultured gentlemen in the world—ex-cashiers, penmen, promoters and gamblers, all move in those great halls and gardens. There are big games. Senor Rey is an artist in many ways, not only as a master of gambling chances. His palace is filled with art treasures from all lands. He was a pirate in these waters—yes, within your years. I heard of him in Asia as the most murderous pirate the Caribbean had ever known—and this was the Spanish Main. Of course, stories build about a picturesque figure. The Senor must be seventy years old now, but a man of mystery, fabulously rich.... Just a little while ago, he brought over a fresh bride from South America. They say she's a thriller to look at. The Spaniard calls her his 'Glow-worm'—"

"Truly a honeymoon name," Bedient observed.

"You see," the Captain concluded, "I can speak of *The Pleiad* only from the outside. That's the Senor's name for his establishment, possibly because there are seven wings to his castle, but others say it was the name of a gold-ship that he took in the early days. Anyway, Rey and I don't neighbor. He's becoming formidable, I'm told, in the politics of the Island. He's at the head of a very powerful colony nevertheless, and no matter what its inter-relations are, it hangs together against the law and the outside world. Rey wants more say back yonder at headquarters, and our Dictator, Jaffier, all things considered, is a very good man, but old and stubborn and impolitic. He won't be driven even by Celestino Rey, who in turn is not a man to be denied. He is probably richer than Equatoria, and then Coral City lives off this institution as Monaco lives off Monte Carlo. He doubtless commands the whole lower element of the town. The word is, Celestino Rey intends to run the Island first-hand—if he can't run it through the powers that are."

All of which Bedient found of interest, inasmuch as he was passing through the heart of these strange affairs. Having any part in them seemed unearthly remote. The carriage was taking the gradual rise behind a pair of fine ponies, and the view behind, over *The Pleiad* to the sapphire water, was noble. The horizon, beyond the harbor distances, was a blazing intensity of light that stung the eyes to quick contraction. The Captain sat back in the cushions, weary from talking, but his face was happy, and he took in the exterior, and something of the inner proportions, of the young man, with a sense of awe. He did not try to explain yet—even to himself.

The *hacienda* was slightly over twenty miles interior. Bedient was entranced by the sunset from the heights. Then the slow ride to the Carreras House through the darkened hills: the smell of warm earth from the thick growths by the trail-side; little stars slipping into place like the glisten of fireflies in a garden, or gems in a maiden's hair; a scandalously-naked new moon lying low, like an arc of white-hot wire in the purple twilight, and always behind them, a majestic splash of jewel-edged crimson which showed the West.

And presently, from a high curve in the road, they saw the lights of the *hacienda* bold upon its eminence—and a dark valley between. Into this night they descended, for the last course of the journey; and as the ponies clattered upward again, white-coated natives came forth to meet them. Bedient was further astonished at their volubility and easy laughter. They spoke a debased Spanish, which the Captain had fallen into,—as difficult of understanding for one whose medium was pure Castilian as for one who spoke English. There was that mystery upon the environs that always comes to one who reaches his destination in the darkness. And to Bedient the sensation was not wholly of joy. These were wild hills, not without grandeur, but there was something of chaos, too, to him who came from the roof of the world. He missed the peace of the greater mountains. His heart hungered to go out to the natives crowding around—white-toothed men and women of incessant laughter—but the tones of their voices checked the current. It was emptiness—but nothing he had to give seemed able to enter.

The Captain was ill with fatigue. His face—the weakness expressed in the smiling mouth—remained before Bedient's mind, as he followed a giggling native boy to the large upper room which was for him. Rows of broad windows faced the South and East, while a corridor ran to the North for the cool wind at night. Electric lights and glistening black floors—the first effect came from these. Then the details: rugs that matched, by art or accident, as perfectly as a valley of various grain-fields pleases the eye from a mountain-side; a great teak bed, caned with bamboo strips and canopied with silk net, yards of which one could crush in his hand, so nearly immaterial was this mosquito fabric; sumptuous steamer-chairs; a leather reading-couch that could be moved to the best breeze or light with a touch of the finger; a broad-side of books and a vast writing-table, openly dimensioned to defy litter—the whole effect was that of coolness and silence and room. Everything a man needed seemed to be there and breathing spaciously.... Turning through a draped door, the astonished wanderer found completeness again—everything that makes a bath fragrant and refreshing—even to Carreras scent and a set of perfect English razors.... It was all new to Bedient. For an hour he *tried* things—and still there were drawers and cases of undiscovered novelties and luxuries—details of wealth which make delightful and uncommon the mere processes of living. Very much restored in his fresh clothing, and eagerly, he went down to dinner.

The little man was waiting with expectant smile under a dome of sheltered lights in the dining-hall. Something of his dazed, ashen look brought back to Bedient the afternoon of

the great wind—the Captain expecting to stick to his ship....
The table was set for two, and on one corner was the fresh
handkerchief and the rose-dark meerschaum bowl. Bedient
took his old place at the other's chair until the Captain was
seated—and both were laughing strangely.... The ships from
Holland brought all manner of European delicacies. Fresh
meats and Northern vegetables arrived every eight days in
the refrigerators of the alternating Dryden steamers, *Hatteras*
and *Henlopen*, from New York. Most tropical fruits were
native to Equatoria—those thick, abbreviated red bananas,
and small oranges with thin skin of *suede* finish, so sharply
sweet that one never forgets the first taste. These were served
in their own foliage.

Much of the solid and comfortable furnishing of the
hacienda had come from the old English house of the
Carreras' in Surrey. The Captain's cook, Leadley, and his
personal factotum, Falk, were English. A dozen natives kept
the great house in order; and their white dress was as fresh
and pleasing as the stewards of an Atlantic liner. As a matter
of fact, Captain Carreras had softened in this kingly luxury,
the infinite resourcefulness of which was startling to Bedient,
who had known but simplicities all his years, and who even
in the Orient had been his own servant.

The Captain lit his pipe but forgot to keep it going. His eyes
turned to Bedient again and again, and each time with deeper
regard. Often he cleared his voice—but failed to speak. The
young man plunged into the heart of things—and finally with
effort, the other interrupted.

"You are not what I expected—forgive me, Andrew—"

"You mean I've disappointed you? Thinking a long time
about one—sometimes throws the mind off the main road of
reality—"

"Dear God, not disappointed.... The Man has come to you in a different way than I expected, that's all. What has India been doing to you?"

"It made New York very strange to me," said Bedient.

"You are like an Oriental," Carreras added. "Oh, they are all mad up in The States.... It's very good to have you back. I wonder why it was—that I never doubted you'd come?" Here the Captain swallowed some wine without adequately preparing his throat, and fell to coughing. Then he rose with the remark that he had experienced altogether too much joy for one old man, in a single day—and started for bed in confusion. Bedient sat back laughing softly, but noting the feeble movement of the other's limbs, quickly gave his arm. Up they went together.... In the big room alone, Bedient put on night garments; and unsatisfied, crossed after a time to the Captain's quarters. He found the old man sitting in the dark by the window, the meerschaum glowing.... It may have been the darkness altogether; or that Bedient as a man gave the other an affection that the boy could not; in any event that night, they found each other across the externals.

This was the cue for further grand talks—pajamas and darkness. Often, if it were not too late, they would hear the natives singing in their cabins. The haunting elemental melody of the African curiously blended with the tuneful and cavalierish songs of Spain and fitted into the majestic nights. The darkies sang to the heart of flesh. In such moments, Equatoria was at her loveliest for Bedient—but the clear impersonal meditations did not come to him. In a hundred ways he had been given understanding during the first fortnight, of that something he had missed the first night on the Island. These people were infant souls. They were children, rudimentary in every thought. Theirs were sensations, not emotions; superstitions, not faiths. Their consciousness was never deeper than the skin. And fresh from his spacious years in India, where everything is old in spirit, where more often than not the beggar is a sage,—to encounter in this land of beauty, a people who were but babes in the thought of God—gave to Bedient the painful sense that his inner life was dissipating. There was no Gobind to restore him. It was as if the Spirit had favored the East; that Africa and the Western Isles had been cast apart as unfit for the experiment of the soul.

Moments of poignant sorrow were these when Bedient realized he was not of the West; that he irrevocably missed the great inner *con*tent of India, and would continue to hunger for it, until he returned, or coarsened his sensibilities to the Western vibration. This last was as far from him as the commoner treason to a friend. There were moments when he feared Captain Carreras almost understood. That dear old seaman through his solitudes, his natural cleanness and kindness, his real love, and more than all, through those vague visions which come late to men of simple hearts—had seemed, from several startling sayings, to touch the very ache in the young man's breast. These approaches were under the cover of darkness:

"There was something about you then, Andrew," (meaning the long-ago days at sea,) "I haven't been able to forget.... Damme—I haven't done well here—"

Bedient bent forward, perceiving that "here" meant his earthly life, as well as Equatoria.

"I should have stayed over yonder and sat down as you did— before you did. Here"—now the Captain meant Equatoria alone—"I have thought of my stomach and my ease. My stomach has gone back on me—and there is no ease. Over there, I might have—oh, I might have thought more—but I didn't know enough, early enough. And you did—at seventeen, you did! That's what made you. They're all mad up in The States, and they're just little children down here.... I might have profited in India—"

That was a frequent saying of the Captain's about the States. Twice a year at least, he was accustomed to make the voyage to New York.... The truth was, the old man felt a yearning for something the years and India had given Bedient. He felt much more than he said, and often regarded the young man, as one rapt in meditation.... His interest in Gobind and the Himalayas was insatiable; much more eagerly did he listen regarding the Punjab than about the ports he had known so well—and the changes that had passed under the eyes of the young man in Manila and Japan.... When Bedient was relating certain events of days and nights, that had become happy memories through the little things of the soul, Captain Carreras would start to convey the indefinite desires he felt; then suddenly, the deep intimacy of his revelations would appear to his timid nature, and even in the mothering dark, the panic would strike home—and he would swing off with pitiful humor about goats or some other Island affair....

Bedient had an odd way of associating men whom he liked with mothers of his own imagining. Happily discovering fine qualities in a man, he would conjure up a mother to fit them.... Often, he saw the little Englishwoman whose boy had taken early to the seas.... She was plump and placid in her cap; inclined to think a great deal for herself, but still she allowed herself to be kept in order mentally and spiritually by her husband, whose orthodoxy was a whip. Perhaps she died thinking her tremulous little departures were sure attractions of hell and heresy. Bedient liked to think of her as vastly bigger than her mate, bigger than she dreamed—but alone and afraid.

SEVENTH CHAPTER

ANDANTE CON MOTO—FIFTH

For the first time in his life, Bedient learned what America liked to read.... All the finer expressions of the human mind and hand gave him deep joy. His love and divination for the good and the true were the same that characterized the rarest minds of our ancestors, who had access only to a few noble books in their formative years. And Bedient's was the expanded and fortified intelligence of one who has grown up with the Bible.

Each ship brought the latest papers, periodicals and certain pickings from the publishers' lists. India had not prepared Bedient for this. With glad welcome he discovered David Cairns here and there among short-story contributors, but the love of man and woman which the stories in general exploited, struck him of Indian ideals as shifty and pestilential. The woman of fiction was equipped with everything to make her as common as man. She was glib, pert, mundane, her mind a chatter-mill; a creature of fur, paint, hair, and absurdly young. The clink of coins was her most favorable accompaniment; and her giving of self was a sort of disrobing formality. The men who pursued her were forward and solicitous. There was something of sacrilege about it all. The minds and souls of real women—such were not matters for American story; and yet the Americans wrote with dangerous facility. Bedient, who worshipped the abstraction, Womanhood, felt his intelligence seared, calcined.... Only here and there was a bit of real literature—usually by a woman. The men seemed hung up to dry at twenty-five. There was no manhood of mind.

Bedient's sense of loneliness became pervasive. Apparently he was outside the range of consciousness—for better or worse—with the country to which he had always hoped to give his best years. His ideals of the literary art were founded upon large flexible lines of beauty into which every dimension of life fell according to the reader's vision. He felt himself alone; that he was out of alignment with this young race from which he had sprung, to wander so far and so long.

And yet there was a Woman up there for him to know. This was imbedded in his consciousness. Soon he should go to her.... He should find her. And as the Hindu poets falteringly called upon the lotos and the nectars; upon the brilliance of midday athwart the plain, and the glory of moonlight upon mountain and glacier and the standing water of foliaged pools; upon the seas at large, and the stars and the bees and the gods—to express the triune loveliness of woman (which mere man may only venture to appraise, not to know)—so should he, Bedient, envision the reality when the winds of the world brought him home to her heart.

*   *   *   *   *

There was much to do at the *hacienda*. The Captain was past riding a great deal, and the large hill and river property—the coffee, cacao, cotton, cane and tobacco industries profited much better with an overseer. Still Bedient slowly realized that the hundreds of natives in touch with Captain Carreras' plantations worked about as well for him as they knew.

Single-handed, Carreras had done great things, and was loved as a good doctor is loved. In spite of his huge accumulation of land, the Captain was the least greedy of men. He had been content to improve slowly. His incalculable riches, as he had early confided to Bedient, were in the river-beds. Only a few of these placer possibilities were operated. There was a big leak in the washings. Still, the natives were not greedy, either. They were home-keepers, and had no way to dispose of bullion.

Carreras had managed all his affairs so as to keep the government on his side, and his revenues were no little part of the support of the Capitol. This was his largest outlay, but in return he was protected.... Deep disorder brooded in the present political silence; all recalcitrants were gathering under Celestino Rey—but this situation was only beginning to be understood.

At certain times of year, Carreras had in his employ the heads of five hundred families, and had shown himself unique in paying money for labor. This was un-Spanish. It gave him the choice of the natives. He represented therefore a stable and prosperous element of the population. His revenues were becoming enormous. The Hollanders paid him a fortune annually for raw chocolate. This, with tree-planting and culture, would double, for the soil seemed to contain the miraculous properties of *alkahest*. The point of all this is, that Captain Carreras had come to be regarded as the right wing of the government. He arranged all his dealings on a friendly rather than a business basis; his good-will was his best protection.... Bedient had been in Equatoria for several months when Jaffier sent for the Captain.

"I don't feel like it, but I'd better go," the old man said. "Something amiss is in the air. Damme, I've got all delicate to the saddle since you came, sir.... I used to think nothing of the ride down town—and now it's a carriage.... Ah, well, you can try out a new symphony—and tell me what it says when I get back."

As it turned out, Bedient did exactly this thing.... Time could not efface the humor evoked by the sight or sound of the magnificent orchestrelle. During one of the Captain's New York trips, he had heard a famous orchestra. The effect upon him was of something superhuman. The Captain went again—followed the musicians to Boston and Philadelphia. The result was more or less the same. Soul flew in one direction; mind in another; and, inert before the players—a little fat man, perspiring, weeping, ecstatic. What came of it, he had told Bedient in this way:

"The *Hatteras* was to sail at night-fall, but on that morning I went into a music-store, not knowing what I wanted exactly,—but a souvenir of some kind, a book about orchestras. It appears, I told a man there how I'd been philanderin' with the musicians; how I had caught them in an off day at Springfield, Mass., and bought cornucopias of Pilsner until they would have broken down and wept had they not been near their instruments.... It was a big music-store, and he was a very good man. He sold me the orchestrelle that morning. You think I had an electric plant installed down here to light the house and drive my sugar-mill, don't you? It wasn't that at all, but to run the big music-box yonder. The man had smoothly attached a current, but he said I could just as well pump it with my feet. Then he called in a church organist—to drive the stops. Between them, they got me where I was all run down from that orchestra crowd. They said a child could learn the stops.... You should have heard my friends on the *Hatteras*—when the orchestrelle was put aboard that afternoon. They never forget that. Then we had a triple ox-cart made down in Coral City, and four span were goaded up the trail—and there she stands.

"Andrew, they finally left me alone with it and a couple of hundred music-rolls.... It was hours after, that I came forth a sick man to cable for power.... About those music-rolls—I had called for the best. One does that blind, you know. But the best in music matters, it appears, has nothing to do with retired sea-captains.... It's a pretty piece of furniture. The orchestra had died out of me by the time we had the electric-plant going.... I take it you have to be caught young to deal with those stops.... You go after it, Andrew. It scares me and the natives when it begins to pipe up. I had a time getting my household back that first time. Maybe, I didn't touch the right button—or I touched too many. You go after it, my boy—it's all there—*appassionato*—*oboe*—*'consharto'*—*vox humana* and the whole system—"

... It is hard for one to realize how little music Bedient had heard in his life. Just a few old songs—always unfinished—but they had haunted the depths of him, and made him think powerfully. Certain strains had loosed within him emotions, ancient as world-dawns to his present understanding, but intimate as yesterday to something deeper than mind. And so he came to ask; "Are not all the landmarks of evolution identified with certain sounds or combinations of sounds? Is there not an answering interpretation in the eternal scroll of man's soul, to all that is true in music?"

Long ago, one night in Korea, he had been wakened by the yammering of a tigress. His terror for a moment had been primal, literally a simian's helpless quaking. Earlier still, he had heard a hoot-owl, and encountered through it, his first realization of phantom horrors; he knew then there *was* an Unseen, and nether acoustics; here was a key to ghostly doors. A mourning-dove had brought back in a swift passage of consciousness the breast of some savage mother. Night-birds everywhere meant to him restless mystery.... Is sound a key to psychology? Is the history of our emotions, from monster to man, sometime to be interpreted through music—as yet the infant among the arts?

The answer had come—why the unfinished songs had the greater magic for him. So diaphanous and ethereal is this marvellously expressive young medium, music, that the composers could only pin a strain here and there to concrete form—as a bit of lace from a lovely garment is caught by a thorn. So they build around it—as flesh around spirit. But it was the strain of pure spirit that sang in Bedient's mind—and knew no set forms. So an artistic imagination can finish a song or a picture, many times better than the original artist could with tones or pigments. Too much finish binds the spirit, and checks the feeling of those who follow to see or hear.

These, and many thoughts had come to him from the unpretentious things of music.... *Ben Bolt* brought back the memory of some prolonged and desperate sorrow. The lineaments of the tragedy were effaced, but its effect lived and preyed upon him under the stress of its own melody. Once he had heard *Caller Herrin'* grandly sung, and for the time, the circuit was complete between the Andrew Bedient of Now, and another of a bleak land and darker era. In this case the words brought him a clearer picture—gaunt coasts and the thrilling humanity of common fisher folk.... Many times a strain of angelic meaning and sweetness was yoked to a silly effigy of words; but he rejoiced in opposite examples, such as that little lullaby of Tennyson's, *Sweet and Low*, which J. Barnby seemed to have exactly *tono*-graphed.... Once across infantry campfires, *Juanita* came, with a bleeding passion for home—to him who had no home. There was a lyrical Ireland very dear to him—songs and poems which wrung him as if he were an exile; Tom Moore's *Sunflower Song* incited at first a poignant anguish, as of a sweetheart's dead face; and *Lead Kindly Light* brought almost the first glimmer of spiritual light across the desolate distances of the world—like a tender smile from a greater being than man. And there were baleful songs that ran red with blood, as the *Carmagnole*; and roused past the sense of physical pain, like the *Marseillaise*. What heroic sins have been committed in their spell! By no means was it all uplift which the songs brought. There was one night when he heard *Mandalay* sung by some British seaman across the dark of a Japanese harbor. They were going out, and he was coming into port....

These were his sole adventures in music, but they had bound his dreams together. He had felt, *if the right person were near*, he could have made music tell things, not to be uttered in mere words; and under the magic of certain songs, that which was creative within him, even dim and chaotic, stirred and warmed for utterance.... So fresh a surface did Bedient bring to the Carreras music-room.

The time had come when his nature hungered for great music. The orchestrelle added to the Island something he needed soulfully. Experimenting with the rolls, the stops and the power, he found there was nothing he could not do in time. Music answered—trombone, clarionet, horn, bassoon, hautboy, flute, 'cello answered. Volume and tempo were mere lever matters. On the rolls themselves were suggestions. Reaching this point, his exaltation knew no bounds. He looked upon the great array of rolls—symphonies, sonatas, concertos, fantasies, rhapsodies, overtures, prayers, requiems, meditations, minuets—and something of that rising power of gratitude overcame him, as only once before in his life—when he had realized that the Bible was all *words*, and they were for him. From the first studious marvellings, Bedient's mind lifted to adoring gratefulness in which he could have kissed the hands of the toilers who had made this instrument answer their dreams. Then, he fell deeply into misgiving. It seemed almost a sacrilege for him to take music so cheaply; that he had not earned such joy. But he could praise them in his heart, and he did with every sound.

The orchestrelle unfolded to a spirit like this. Doubtless his early renderings of random choice were weird, but more and more as he went on, the great living things righted themselves in his consciousness, for he had ear and soul and love for them. Some great fissure in his nature had long needed thus to be filled. He sent for books about the great composers; descriptions of the classics; how the themes were developed through different instruments. Then he wanted the history of all music; and for weeks his receptivity never faltered. No neophyte ever brought a purer devotion to the masters. His first loves—the *Andante in F*, the three movements of the *Kreutzer Sonata*, a prayer from *Otello*, the *Twelfth Rhapsody,* the *Swan Song* and the *Evening Star*, and finally *Isolde's Triumph over Death*—these were ascendings, indeed—to the point of wings.

The stops so formidable at first became as stars in the dark.... Little loves, little fears and sins and hopes were all he had known before; and now he entered into the torrential temperaments of the masters—magnificent and terrifying souls who dared to sin against God, or die defying man; whose passions stormed the world; whose dirges were wrung from heaven. Why, these men levelled emperors and aspired to angels, violated themselves, went mad with music, played with hell's own dissonances, and dared to transcribe their baptisms, illuminations, temptations, Gethsemanes, even their revilings and stigmata.

The dirges lifted him to immensity from which the abysses of the world spread themselves below. Two marches of Chopin, and the death-march of Siegfried, the haunting suggestion of a soul's preparation for departure in Schubert's *Unfinished*; the *Death of Aase*, the *Pilgrim's Chorus*, one of Mozart's requiems, and that Napoleonic *funebre* from the *Eroica*—these, with others, grouped themselves into an unearthly archipelago—towering cliffs of glorious gloom, white birds silently sweeping the gray solitudes above the breakers....

It was during the four days while Captain Carreras remained in Coral City with Jaffier, that Bedient entered into the mysterious enchantment of the *Andante* movement of Beethoven's Fifth Symphony. He had played it all, forgetting almost to breathe, and then returned to the second movement which opens with the 'celli:

Again and again it unfolded for him, but not its full message. There was a meaning in it *for him*! He heard it in the night; three voices in it—a man, a woman and a soul.... The lustrous third Presence was an angel—there for the sake of the woman. She was in the depths, but great enough to summon the angel to her tragedy. The man's figure was obscure, disintegrate.... Bedient realized in part at least that this was destined to prove his greatest musical experience....

Captain Carreras found much to do in the city, but he did not tell Bedient that the real reason for his remaining four days was that he couldn't sooner summon courage for the long ride home. He spoke but little regarding the reasons Jaffier had called him.

"He's afraid of Celestino Rey, and likely has good reason," said the Captain wearily. "The old pirate is half-dead below the knees, but his ugly ambition still burns bright. He thinks he ought to be drawing all the Island tributes, instead of the government. Jaffier expects assassination. On this point, it would be well to watch for the death of Rey. These two old hell-weathered Spaniards are worth watching—each tossing spies over the other's fences, and openly conducting affairs with melting courtesy toward each other—but I don't seem to have much appetite for the game. There was a time when I would have stopped work and helped Jaffier whip this fellow. But I hardly think he'll take our harvests and the river-beds just yet—"

They talked late. The Captain alternated from his bed to a chair, seemed unwilling for Bedient to leave and unable to sleep or find ease anywhere. He was over-tired, he explained, and hearing about Bedient's experience with the *Andante con moto*, insisted upon it being played that night....

"It's very soothing," Carreras said, when Andrew returned to the upper apartment. "I think I can sleep now. Off to bed with you, lad."

So lightly did Bedient sleep, however,—for the music haunted his brain,—that he was aroused by the bare feet of a servant in the hall-way, before the latter touched his door to call him. Captain Carreras had asked for him. The glow of dawn was in the old man's quarters, and he smiled in a queer, complacent way from his bed, as if a long-looked-for solution to some grave problem had come in the night, and he wanted his friend to guess. A hand lifted from the coverlet, and Bedient's sped to it; yet he saw that something more was wanted. The Captain's shoulder nudged a little, and the smile had become wistful. He did not fail to understand the need, but other realizations were pressing into his brain. So the Captain nudged his shoulder again bashfully. Bedient bent and took him in his arms.

It was death. Bedient had known it from the first instant of entering, but he was not prepared. He could not speak—only look into the tender, glowing smile. Captain Carreras finally turned his eyes into the morning:

"You know it was very foolish of me—very—to think I could make you happy, Andrew, with all these riches," he said at last, not thickly, but very low, as if he had saved strength for what he wished to say.... "You were a long time coming, but I knew you would come—knew it would be just like this—in your arms. Queer, isn't it? And all the waiting years, I kept piling up lands and money, saying: 'This shall be his when he comes.'... It was a little hard at first to know you didn't care—you couldn't care—that one, and ten, were all the same to you. And last night, I saw it all again. Had I brought you word that Celestino Rey had the government and that confiscation of these lands were inevitable, you would never have compared it in importance with finding that part of the symphony. It's all right. I wouldn't have it changed...."

Andrew listened with bowed head, patting the Captain's shoulder gently, as he sustained.

"But I have given you more than money, boy. And this you know—as a man, who knew money better, could never understand. I have given you an old man's love for a son—but more than that, too,—something of the old man's love for the mother of his son.... I thought only women had the delicacy and fineness—you have shown me, sir.... It is all done, and you have made me very glad for these years—since the great wind failed to get us—"

Then he mingled silences with sentences that finally became aimless—seas, ships, cooks, and the boy who had nipped him from the post he meant to hold—and a final genial blending of goats and symphonies, on the borders of the Crossing. Then he nestled, and Bedient felt the hand he had taken, try to sense his own through the gathering cold.... It was very easy and beautiful—and so brief that Bedient's arm was not even tired.

An hour afterward, Falk came in for orders—and withdrew.

Bedient had merely nodded to him from the depths of contemplation.... At last, he heard the weeping of the house-servants. And there was one low wailing tone that startled him with the memory of the Sikh woman who had wept for old Gobind.

EIGHTH CHAPTER

THE MAN FROM *THE PLEIAD*

Bedient drew from Falk a few days afterward that the Captain had planned almost exactly as it happened. Since the beginnings of unrest in Equatoria, he had transferred his banking to New York; so that in the event of defeat in war, only the lands and *hacienda* would revert, upon the fall of the present government. Falk could not remember (and his services dated back fifteen years, at which time he left Surrey with the Captain) when the master did not speak of Bedient's coming.

"But for your letters, sir, Leadley and I would have come to think of you as—as just one of the master's ways, Mister Andrew."

Falk was a middle-aged serving-class Englishman, highly trained and without humor. Leadley, the cook, and a power in his department, dated also from Surrey, which was his county. These men had learned to handle the natives to a degree, and the entire responsibility of the establishment had fallen upon them during the absences of the Captain. As chief of house-servants and as cook, these two at their best were faultless, but the life was very easy, and they were given altogether too many hands to help. Moreover, Falk and

Leadley belonged to that queer human type which proceeds to burn itself out with alcohol if left alone. The latter years of such servants become a steady battle to keep sober enough for service. Each man naturally believed himself an admirable drinker.

Natives came from the entire Island to smoke and drink and weep for the Captain. Dictator Jaffier sent his "abject bereavement" by pony pack-train, which, having formed in a sort of hollow square, received the thanks of Bedient, and assurances that his policy would continue in the delightful groove worn by the late best of men. The reply of Jaffier was the offer of a public funeral in Coral City, but Bedient declined this, and the body of his friend was turned toward the East upon the shoulder of his highest hill....

Presently Bedient read the Captain's documents. Falk and Leadley were bountifully cared for; scores of natives were remembered; the policy toward Jaffier outlined according to the best experience; and the bulk, name, lands, bonds, capital and all—"to my beloved young friend, Andrew Bedient."... At the request and expense of the latter, the New York bankers sent down an agent to verify the transfer of this great fortune. A month passed—a foretaste of what was to come. Bedient, prepared for greater work than this, was lonely in the sunlight.

He knew that he must soon begin to live his own life. His every faculty was deeply urging. Equatoria had little to do with the realities for which he had gathered more than thirty years' equipment. He felt a serious responsibility toward his fortune, though absolutely without the thrill of personal possession. The just administration of these huge forces formed no little part of his work, and in his entire thinking on this subject, New York stood most directly in the need of service. It was there that the Captain's accumulated vitality must be used for good.

Early in the second month, Bedient came in at noon from a long ride across the lands, and reaching the great porch of the *hacienda*, he turned to observe a tropic shower across the valley. The torrent approached at express speed. It was a clean-cut pouring, several acres in extent. Bedient watched it fill the spaces between the little hills, sweep from crest to crest, and bring out a subdued glow in the wild verdure as it swept across the main valley. Sharp was the line of dry sunlit air and gray slanting shower. Presently he heard its pounding, and the dustless slopes rolled into the gray.... Now he sniffed the acute fragrance that rushed before it in the wind, and then it climbed the drive, deluged the *hacienda,* and was gone.... In the moist, sweet, yellow light that filled his eyes, Bedient, fallen into deeps of contemplation, saw the face of a woman.

He went inside and looked up the Dryden sailings. The *Hatteras* would clear, according to schedule, in ten days. That meant that the *Henlopen* was now in port. His eyes had looked first for the former, since it had brought him down, and was the Captain's favorite.... Yes, the *Henlopen* was due to sail to-morrow at daylight.... He told Falk he would go.... In that upper room across from his own, he bowed his head for a space, and the fragrance still there brought back the heaving cabin of the *Truxton*.... Then he rode down to Coral City in the last hours of daylight.

His devoirs were paid to Dictator Jaffier, who confided that he had purchased a gunboat and search-light on behalf of the government. Its delivery was but ten days off, and with it he expected to keep that old sea-fighter, Celestino Rey, better in order.... Bedient had the evening to himself. In one of the *Calle Real* cafes, he was attracted by the face and figure of a young white man, of magnificent proportions and remarkably clean-cut profile. The stranger sipped iced claret, watched the natives moving about, and seemed occasionally to forget himself in his thinking.

He looked more than ever a giant in the midst of the little tropical people, and seemed to feel his size in the general diminutive setting. Yet there was balance and fitness about his splendid physical organization, which suggested that he could be quick as a mink in action. He chaffed the native who waited upon him, and his face softened into charming boyishness as he laughed. His mouth was fresh as a child's, but on a scale of grandeur. Bedient found himself smiling with him. Then there was that irresistible folding about the eyes when he laughed, which is Irish as sin, and quite as attractive. Left to himself he fell to brooding, and his brow puzzled over some matter in the frank bored way of one pinned to a textbook. Bedient sat down at the other's table. Acquaintance was as agreeably received as offered.

The stranger's name was Jim Framtree. He had been on the Island for several weeks, and intended to stay for awhile. He liked Equatoria well enough—as well, in fact, as a man could like any place, when he was barred from the real trophy-room in the house of the world, New York.

"I'm sailing for New York in the morning," Bedient said.

Framtree shivered and fell silent.

"You've found work that you like here?" Bedient asked simply.

The other glanced at him humorously, and yet with a bit of intensity, too,—as if searching for the meaning under such an unadorned question.

"I seem to have caught on with Senor Rey at *The Pleiad*," he replied.

"Ah—"

"I'm afraid you're making a mistake, sir," Framtree added quickly. "I'm not barred from New York on any cashier matter. You know when something you want badly—and can't have—is in a town—that isn't the place for you.... Even if you like that town best on earth.... What I mean is, I'm not using *The Pleiad* as a hiding proposition."

"I wasn't thinking of that," Bedient said.

"I suppose it would be natural—down here—"

"But I *saw you first.*"

"Um-m."

"I was only thinking," Bedient resumed, "that if the establishment of Senor Rey palled upon you at any time, I'd like to have you come up and see me in the hills.... I'd be glad to have you come, anyway. I may not be very long in New York—"

*   *   *   *   *

"That's mighty good of you," Framtree declared, and yet it was obvious that he could not regard the invitation as purely a friendly impulse, even if he wished to. "I remember now. I've heard of your big place up there."

"Perhaps, I'd better explain that I wasn't thinking of Island politics—when I asked you.... Queer how one has to explain things down here. I've noticed that it's hard for folks to go straight at a thing."

Framtree laughed again, and tried hard to understand what was in the other's mind. Bedient's simplicity was too deep for him. They talked for an hour, each singularly attracted, but evading any subject that would call in the matters of political unrest. Each felt that the other wanted to be square, but Bedient saw that it would be useless to impress upon Framtree how little hampered he was by Jaffier.... At daybreak the next morning, the fruity old *Henlopen* pointed out toward the reefs, and presently was nudging her way through the coral passage, as confidently as if the trick of getting to sea from Coral City was part of the weathered consciousness of her boilers and plates.

II. NEW YORK

Andante con moto

NINTH CHAPTER

THE LONG-AWAITED WOMAN

Bedient went directly to the house-number of David Cairns in West Sixty-seventh Street, without telephoning for an appointment. It happened that the time of his arrival was unfortunate. Something of this he caught, first from the look of the elevator attendant, who took him to the tenth floor of a modern studio-building; and further from the man-servant who answered his ring at the Cairns apartment.

"Mr. Cairns sees no one before two o'clock, sir," said the latter, whose cool eye took in the caller.

Bedient hesitated. It was now twelve-forty-five. He felt that Cairns would be hurt if he went away. "Tell him that Andrew Bedient is here, and that I shall be glad to wait or call again, just as he prefers."

And now the servant hesitated. "It is very seldom we disturb him, sir. Most of his friends understand that he is not available between nine and two."

Bedient was embarrassed. The morning in the city had preyed upon him. Realizing his discomfort, and the petty causes of it, he became unwilling to leave. "I am not of New

York and could not know. I think you'd better tell Mr. Cairns and let him judge—"

The servant had reached the same conclusion. Bedient was shown into a small room, furnished with much that was peculiarly metropolitan to read.... He rather expected Cairns to rush from some interior, and waited ten minutes, glancing frequently at the door through which the servant had left.... His heart had bounded at the thought of seeing David, and he smiled at his own hurt.... A door opened behind him. The writer came forward quietly, with warm dignity caught him by both shoulders and smilingly searched his eyes. Bedient was all kindness again. "Doubtless his friends come in from Asia often," he thought.

"Andrew, it's ripping good to see you.... Why didn't you let me know you were coming?"

"I didn't want you to alter your ways at all."

"You see, I have to keep these morning hours—"

"Go back—I'll wait gladly, or call when you like."

"Don't go away, pray, unless there is something you must do for the next hour or so."

*   *   *   *   *

In waiting, Bedient did not allow himself to search for anything theatric or unfeeling at the centre of the episode. Cairns had moved in many of the world atmospheres, and had done some work which the world noted with approval. Moreover, he had called from Bedient bestowals of friendship which could not be forgotten.... "I have been alone and in the quiet so much that *I* can remember," Bedient mused, "while he has been rushing about from action to action. Then New York would rub out anybody's old impressions."

As the clock struck, Cairns appeared ready for the street. He was a trifle drawn about the mouth, and irritated. Having been unable to work in the past hour, the day was amiss, for he hated a broken session and an allotment of space unfilled. Still, Cairns did not permit the other to see his displeasure; and the distress which Bedient felt, he attributed to New York, and not the New Yorker....

The mind of David Cairns had acquired that cultivated sense of authority which comes from constantly being printed. He was a much-praised young man. His mental films were altogether too many, and they had been badly developed for the insatiable momentary markets to which timeliness is all. Very much, he needed quiet years to synthesize and appraise his materials.... Bedient, he regarded as a luxury, and just at this moment, he was not in the mood for one. Cairns drove himself and his work, forgetting that the fuller artist is driven.... Luzon and pack-train memories were dim in his mind. He did not forget that he had won his first name in that field, but he did forget for a time the wonderful night-talks. A multitude of impressions since, had disordered these delicate and formative hours. Only now, in his slow-rousing heart he felt a restlessness, a breath of certain lost delights.

It was a sappy May day. The spring had been late—held long in wet and frosty fingers—and here was the first flood of moist warmth to stir the Northern year into creation. Cairns was better after a brisk walk. Housed for long, unprofitable hours, everything had looked slaty at first.

"Where are you staying, Andrew?"

"*Marigold*."

"Why do you live 'way down there? That's a part of town for business hours only. The heart of things has been derricked up here."

"I'm very sure of a welcome there," Bedient explained. "My old friend Captain Carreras had Room 50, from time to time for so many years, that I fell into it with his other properties. Besides, all the pirates, island kings and prosperous world-tramps call at the *Marigold*. And then, they say—the best dinner—"

"That's a tradition of the Forty-niners—"

"I have no particular reason for staying down there, even if I keep the room. I'll do that for the Captain's sake.... I'm not averse to breezing around up-town."

"Ah—" came softly from Cairns.

"I'd like to know some *folks*," Bedient admitted.

Cairns was smiling at him. "You'll have to have a card at my clubs. There's *Teuton's, Swan's* and the *Smilax* down Gramercy way.... Perhaps we'd better stop in at the *Swan's* for a bite to eat. The idea is, you can try them all, Andrew, and put up at the one you fit into best—"

"Exactly," breathed Bedient.

"You won't like the *Smilax* overmuch," Cairns ventured, "but you may pass a forenoon there, while I'm at work. Stately old place, with many paintings and virgin silence. The women artists are going there more and more—"

"I like paintings," said Bedient.

They walked across *Times Square* and toward the Avenue, through Forty-second. Cairns waited for the quiet to ask:

"Andrew, you haven't found Her yet—The Woman?"

"No. Have you?"

"Did—I used to have one, too?"

"Yes."

"Andrew, do you think She's in New York?" Cairns asked.

"It's rather queer about that," Bedient answered. "I was watching a rain-storm from the porch of the *hacienda* seven or eight days ago, when it came to me that I'd better take the first ship up. I sailed the next morning."

This startled Cairns. He was unaccustomed to such sincerity. "You mean it occurred to you that She was here—the One you used to tell me about in Asia?"

"Yes."

Cairns now felt an untimely eagerness of welcome for the wanderer. A renewal of Bedient's former attractions culminated in his mind, and something more that was fine and fresh and permanent. He twinged for what had happened at the apartment.... Bedient was a man's man, strong as a platoon in a pinch—that had been proved. He was plain as a sailor in ordinary talk, but Cairns knew now that he had only begun to challenge Bedient's finer possessions of mind.... Here in New York, a man over thirty years old, who could speak of the Woman-who-must-be-somewhere. And Bedient spoke in the same ideal, unhurt way of twenty, when they had spread blankets together under strange stars... Cairns knew in a flash that something was gone from his own breast that he had carried then. It was an altogether uncommon moment to him. "So it has not all been growth," he thought. "All that has come since has not been fineness.".... He felt a bit denied, as if New York had "gotten" to him, as if he had lost a young prince's vision, that the queen mother had given him on setting out.... He was just one of the million males, feathering nests of impermanence, and stifling the true hunger for the skies and the great cleansing migratory flights....

All this was a miracle to David Cairns. He was solid; almost English in his up-bringing to believe that man's work, and established affairs, thoughts and systems generally were right and unimpeachable. He heard himself scoffing at such a thing, had it happened to another.... He stared into Bedient's face, brown, bright and calm. He had seen only good humor and superb health before, but for an instant now, he perceived a spirit that rode with buoyancy, after a life of loneliness and terror that would have sunk most men's anchorage, fathoms deeper than the reach of the longest cable of faith.

"I think I'm getting to be—just a biped.... I'm glad you came up.... Here we are at *Swan's*," said Cairns.

*　*　*　*　*

Like most writers, David Cairns was intensely interesting to himself. His sudden reversal from bleak self-complacence to a clear-eyed view of his questionable approaches to real worth, was strong with bitterness, but deeply absorbing. He was remarkable in his capacity to follow this opening of his own insignificance. It had been slow coming, but ruthlessly now, he traced his way back from one breach to another, and

　　　　Will Levington Comfort

finally to that night in the plaza at Alphonso, when he had been enabled to see service from a unique and winning angle, through the pack-train cook. That was the key to his catching on; that, and his boy ideals of war had lifted his copy from the commonplace. He remembered Bedient in China, in Japan, and in his own house—how grudgingly he had appeared in his working hours. He felt like an office-boy who has made some pert answer to an employer too big and kind to notice. Now and then up the years, certain warm thoughts had come to him from those island nights, but he had forgotten their importance in gaining his so-called standing.

Andrew Bedient was nothing like the man he had expected to find. He remembered now that he might have looked for these rare elements of character, since the boyhood talks had promised them, and power had emanated from them.... Still, Bedient had grown marvellously, in strange, deep ways. Cairns could not fathom them all, but he realized that nothing better could happen to him than to study this man. Indeed, his mind was fascinated in following the rich leads of his friend's resources. He consoled himself for his shortcomings with the thought that, at least, he was ready to see....

They talked as of old, far into the night. Cairns found himself endeavoring with a swift, nervous eagerness to show his *best* to Andrew Bedient, and to be judged by that best. He spoke of none of the achievements which the world granted to be his; instead, the little byway humanities were called forth, for the other to hear—buds of thought and action, which other pressures had kept from fertilizing into seed—the very things he would have delighted in relating to a dear, wise woman. Something about Bedient called them forth, and Cairns fell into new depths. "I thought it was pure sex-challenge which made a man bring these things to a woman." (This is the way he developed the idea afterward.) "But that can't be all, since

I unfolded so to Bedient.... He has me going in all directions like a steam-shovel."

Cairns was arranging a little party for his friend. In the meantime, his productive quantity sank from torrent to trickle. His secretary, who knew the processes of the writer's mind as the keys of his machine, and had adjusted his own brain to them through many brisk sessions, fell now through empty space. He had no resources in this room, where he had been driven so long by the mental force of another. Having suffered himself to be played upon, like the instrument before him, he died many deaths from *ennui*.... So Cairns and the secretary stared helplessly at each other across the emptiness; and New York rushed on, with its mad business, singing spitefully in their ears: "You for the poor-farms. You'll lose your front, and your markets. Your income is suffering; the presses are waiting; editors dependent...."

Cairns left the house on the third morning after Bedient's coming, having dictated two or three letters.... Bedient was across the street from the *Smilax Club* in the little fenced-in park—Gramercy. Cairns told his work-difficulty.

"Don't you think it would be good for you, David," Bedient asked, "to let the subconscious catch up?"

Cairns was interested at once. "What do you mean?"

"I've been thinking more than a little about you and New York. One thing is sure: New York is pretty much wrong, or I'm insane—"

"You're happy about it," Cairns remarked. "Tell me the worst."

"People here use their reflectors and not their generators,"

Bedient said. "They shine with another's light, when they should be incandescent. The brain in your skull, in any man's skull, is but a reflector, an instrument of his deeper mind. There's your genius, infinitely wiser than your brain. It's your sun; your brain, the moon. All great work comes from the subconscious mind. You and New York use too much moonshine."

Both men were smiling, but to Cairns, nevertheless, it seemed that his own conscience had awakened after a long sleep. This wanderer from the seas had twigged the brain brass which he had long been passing for gold value. He saw many bits of his recent work, as products of intellectual foppery. He recalled a letter recently received from an editor; which read: "That last article of yours has caught on. Do six more like it." He hadn't felt the stab before. He had done the six—multiplied his original idea by mechanical means....

All things considered, it was rather an important affair—the party that night at the *Smilax Club*. Cairns began with the idea of asking ten people, but the more he studied Bedient's effect upon himself, the more particular he became about the "atmosphere." Just the men he wanted were out of reach, so he asked none at all, but five women. Four of these he would have grouped into a sentence as "the most interesting women in New York," and the fifth was a romantic novelty in a minor key, sort of "in the air" at the Club.

So there were seven to sit down to the round table in the historic Plate Room. The curving walls were fitted with a lining of walnut cabinets. Visible through their leaded-glass doors, were ancient services of gold and silver and pewter. The table streamed with light, but the faces and cabinets were in shadow.... Directly across from Bedient sat Beth Truba, the most brilliant woman his visioning eyes ever developed.

The sight of her was the perfect stimulus, an elixir too volatile to be drunk, rather to be breathed. Bedient felt the door of his inner chambers swing open before fragrant winds. The heart of him became greatly alive, and his brain in grand tune. It is true, she played upon his faculties, as the Hindus play upon the *vina*, that strange, sensitive, oriental harp with a dozen strings, of which the musician touches but one. The other strings through sympathetic vibration furnish an undertone almost like an aeolian harmony. You must listen in a still place to catch the mystic accompaniment. So it was in Bedient's mind. Beth Truba played upon the single string, and the others glorified her with their shadings. And the plaint from all humanity was in that undertone, as if to keep him sweet.

She was in white. "See the slim iceberg with the top afire!" Cairns had whispered, as she entered. Other lives must explain it, but the Titian hair went straight to his heart. And those wine-dark eyes, now cryptic black, now suffused with red glows like a night-sky above a prairie-fire, said to him, "Better come over and see if I'm tamable."

"I can see, it's just the place I wanted to be to-night," she said, taking her chair. "We're going to have such a good time!"

And Kate Wilkes drawled this comment to Cairns: "In other words, Beth says, 'Bring on your lion, for I'm the original wild huntress.'"

Kate Wilkes was a tall tanned woman rather variously weathered, and more draped than dressed. She conducted departments of large feminine interest in several periodicals, and was noted among the "emancipated and impossible" for her papers on Whitman. The romantic novelty was Mrs. Wordling, the actress, and the other two women were Vina

Nettleton, who made gods out of clay and worshipped Rodin, and Marguerite Grey, tall and lovely in a tragic, flower-like way, who painted, and played the 'cello.

"Meeting Bedient this time has been an experience to me," Cairns said, toward the end of dinner. "I called together the very finest people I knew, because of that. He had sailed for ten years before I knew him. That was nearly thirteen years ago. Not that there's anything in miles, nor sailing about from port to port.... He has ridden for the English since, through the great Himalayan forests—years so strange that he forgot their passing.... We are all good friends; in a sense, artists, together, so I can say things. One wants to be pretty sure when one lets go from the inside. I didn't realize before how rarely this happens with us.

"The point is, Bedient has kept something through the years, that I haven't. I'm getting away badly, but I trust what I mean will clear up.... Bedient and I rode together with an American pack-train, when there was fighting, there in Luzon. He was the cook of the outfit, and he took me in, a cub-correspondent. I look back now upon some of those talks (with the smell of coffee and forage and cigarettes in the night air) as belonging to the few perfect things. And last night and the night before, we talked again—"

Cairns' eye hurried past Mrs. Wordling, but he seemed to find what he wanted in the glances of the others, before he resumed:

"Without knowing it, Bedient has made me see that I haven't been keeping even decently white, here in New York. I found out, at the same time, that I couldn't meet him half-way, when he brought the talk close. Back yonder in Luzon, I used to. Here, after the years, I couldn't. Something inside is green and untrained. It shied before real man-talk....

Bedient came into a fortune recently, the result of saving a captain during a long-ago typhoon. His property is down in Equatoria, where he has been for some months. So he has had a windfall that would be unmanning to most, yet he comes up here, just as unspoiled as he used to be—"

"David," Bedient pleaded, "you're swinging around in a circle. Be easy with me."

"You've kept your boy's heart, that's what I'm trying to get at," Cairns added briefly.

Kate Wilkes dropped her hand upon Bedient's arm, and said, "Don't bother him. It looks to me as if truth were being born. You'd have to be a city man or woman to understand how rare and relishable such an event is."

"Thanks, Kate," said Cairns. "It's rather difficult to express, but I see I'm beginning to get it across."

"Go on, please."

Cairns mused absently before continuing:

"Probably it doesn't need to come home to anyone else, as it did to me.... I've been serving King Quantity here in New York so long that I'd come to think it the proper thing to do. Bedient has kept to the open—the Bright Open—and kept his ideals. I listened to him last night and the night before, ashamed of myself. His dreams came forth fresh and undefiled as a boy's—only they were man-strong and flexible—and his voice seemed to come from behind the intention of Fate.... I wouldn't talk this way, only I chose the people here. I think without saying more, you've got what I've been encountering since Bedient blew up Caribbean way."

Cairns leaned back in his chair with a glass of *moselle* in his hand and told about the big lands in Equatoria, about the two Spaniards, Jaffier and Rey, trying to assassinate each other under the cover of courtesy; about the orchestrelle, the mines and the goats. Cleverly, at length, he drew Bedient into telling the typhoon adventure.

It was hard, until Beth Truba leaned forward and ignited the story. After that, the furious experience *lived* in Bedient's mind, and most of it was related into her eyes. When he described the light before the break of the storm, how it was like the hall-way of his boyhood, where the yellow-green glass had frightened him, Beth became paler if possible, and more than ever intent. Back in her mind, a sentence of Cairns' was repeating, "His voice seemed to come from behind the intention of Fate."... Finally when Bedient told of reaching Equatoria, and of the morning when Captain Carreras nudged bashfully—wanting his arm a last time—Beth Truba exclaimed softly:

"Oh, no, that really can't all be true, it's too good!" and her listening eyes stirred with ecstasy....

She liked, too, his picture of the *hacienda* on the hill.... The party talked away up into the top of the night and over; and always when Bedient started across (in his heart) to tame the wine-dark eyes—lo, they were gone from him.

TENTH CHAPTER

THE JEWS AND THE ROMANS

Kate Wilkes lived at the *Smilax Club*, as did Vina Nettleton, and, for the present, Mrs. Wordling. The actress was recently in from the road. Her play had not run its course, merely abated for the hot months. She was an important satellite, if not a stellar attraction. About noon, on the day following the party for Bedient, Mrs. Wordling appeared in the breakfast room, and sat down at the table with Kate Wilkes, who was having her coffee.

"What an extraordinary evening we had," the actress remarked. "David's party was surely a success."

"Rather," assented Miss Wilkes, who felt old and nettled. She seemed of endless length, and one would suppose that her clothes were designed so that not one bone should be missed. Mrs. Wordling was not an especial favorite with her.

"They made it up beautifully between them, didn't they?" the actress observed, as she squeezed orange-juice into her spoon.

"What?"

"That story."

"Who?"

"Why, that story—that friendship, storm-at-sea, Equatoria story—done jointly by Messrs. Cairns and Bedient."

"You think they rehearsed it, then?" Kate Wilkes asked softly.

"Why, of course. It unfolded like a story—each piling on clever enthusiasm for the other."

There was a slight pause.

"And so you think David Cairns simulated that fine touch, about discovering through his friend, what damage New York was doing him?" Kate Wilkes' manner was lightly reflective.

"Of course. Don't you remember how he stumbled until you helped him going?"

"You think—as I understand it—" Miss Wilkes had become queerly penetrative, and spoke in a way that made one think of a beetle being pinned through the thorax, "—that David Cairns merely used his artistic intelligence for our entertainment; that Andrew Bedient is merely an interesting type of sailor and wanderer who has struck it rich?"

"Why, yes, Kate, that's the way it got over to me. We all know David Cairns is selling everything he writes at a top-figure; that he is eminently successful, quite the thing in many periodicals, finely pleased with himself as a successful man—"

"Wordling," said Kate Wilkes, leaning toward her, "what kind of people do you associate with in your work?"

"The best, dear,—always the best. People who think, and who love their work."

Slowly and without passion the elder woman now delivered herself:

"People who *think* they think and who love themselves!... I have tried to make myself believe you were different. You are not different, Wordling. You are true to your kind, and not distinguished from them. David Cairns never rehearsed a part with Andrew Bedient. Men as full of real things as these two do not need rehearsals. Bedient came up from his Island, and all unconsciously made his old companion realize that he was not breathing the breath of life here in New York. Cairns wept over it, and made up his mind to try again; and fine chap that he is, he called a few of his friends together, to give us a chance to see the thing as he saw it. I call it an honor that he invited me. I see you do not. Unfortunately this is one of those differences of opinion which are at the base of things.... Luck to you, Wordling," she finished, rising. "I feel seedy and have a busy afternoon ahead."

Mrs. Wordling laughed delightedly, though boiling lava ran within and pressed against the craters. Alone, she asked herself what Kate Wilkes had done to get away with eccentricities, to which only those of stardom are entitled.

"Hag," she muttered, after such conning.

* * * * *

Bedient was early abroad in the city, having felt entirely above the need of sleep. He was less serene than usual, but with compensations. There was a peculiar fear in his mind that New York was laughing at him a bit. Perhaps, Cairns had pressed down a little too hard on the queer unhurt quality he was alleged to possess. In a word, Bedient sensed the humor of Mrs. Wordling, and could not yet know that she, of the entire company, monopolized the taint.

The *Smilax Club* pleased him, and he had permitted Cairns to put him up there.

That flame of a woman, Beth Truba, was the spirit of his every thought. Her listening had drawn the soul from him. The great thing had happened; and yet it was different from the way he had visioned it.... Never had a woman so startled him with the sense of the world's fullness—in that she was in the world. That he had found her was his first achievement, true reward of deathless faith; and yet it was all so different. She was different. She had not known him.

In the amplitude of his wanderings, one conception had grown slightly out of proportion. He saw this now, and smiled affectionately at the old thought: "When The Woman appears, I shall not be alone in the gladness of the moment."... Those were mountain-tops of dreaming upon which he strode without reckoning. It would have been absurd, had Beth Truba given him a sign. This was not India, nor the Dream Ranges.... She had faced life, lived it among the teeming elements of this vast city. The world had wrought upon her, while she wrought her place in the world. She was finished, an artist, a woman of New York, wise, poised, brilliant. It was the world's ideals, and not those of the silence and the spirit, altogether, that governed her manner and dress and movement. She had not lived in the silence; therefore that which was of the silence had been kept among the deep inner places of her life. The secrets of her heart were deeper than mere man's leaden fathomings. Even had he appeared unto her as an illumination—only Beth Truba would have known.

He did not come into great peace in her presence. No matter what she dreamed of, or desired, the lover could only come to her in the world's approved ways. So, all the accumulated beauty of idealism counted nothing in this first stage of Bedient's quest. Instead of the peace of her presence, he was filled with restless energies, past all precedent. Quite in a boyish way, he wanted to do things for her, huge and little things, forgetting not the least, and performing each succeeding action with a finer art.

Beth Truba was the first woman who ever appealed to Bedient, without recalling in some way the Adelaide passion. There was hardly a trace of that element in the new outpouring. If it is true that a woman calls from man a love-token in her own image, Beth Truba was marble cold. The larger part of his first giving was above the flesh, a passion to bestow beautiful things, the happiness of others. That she might ever have any meaning to him beyond receiving these gifts, scarcely entered, as yet, his thrilled consciousness. It *had* startled him that she was seemingly free; that she had reached full womanhood in solitary empire. He dared be glad of this, but he could not grasp it, unless she were vowed to spinsterhood by some irrevocable iron of her will; or perhaps some king of men had come, and she had given her word.... Bedient could not understand how any discerning masculine mind could look upon Beth Truba, and go his way without determining his chance. He felt (and here he was "warm," as they say in the children's game) that David Cairns must be one of the men who had seen Beth Truba and not conquered. Perhaps Cairns would tell him regarding these things, but they were altogether too sacred to broach, except in the finest possible moment.

He had returned to the club early in the afternoon, and was standing at one of the windows, his eyes turned toward the green square opposite. He was thinking of the enchantress, and how she would admire the shower-whipped hills of Equatoria and all that wild perfumed beauty.... His name was softly spoken by one of the regal shadows of the night before, Marguerite Grey.

"If I hadn't seen you or Mr. Cairns again," she began, "I'd have come to think of last night almost as a dream."

"That's queer, Miss Grey," he answered, taking her hand. "It's like a dream to me, too."

"I didn't feel like working to-day," she said. "The routine appalled me, so I came over to look in upon Vina Nettleton. Her studio is above. Have you seen her 'Stations of the Cross'?"

"No."

"Her four years' task—for the great Quebec cathedral?... You really must. It's an experience to watch her work, and Vina's worth knowing—pure spirit.... Would you like to go up with me?"

Alternating fascinations possessed Bedient, as the elevator carried them upward.... These were his real playmates, these people of pictures and statues. He had come a long way through different lights and darkness to find them. He did not know their ways of play, but well knew he should like them when he learned, and that their play would prove prettier than any he had ever known.... And this tall, still woman beside him—almost as tall as he, of rarest texture, and with a voice sensuously soft, having that quality of softness which distinguishes a charcoal from a graphite line—this woman seemed identified in some remoteness of mind with long-ago rainy days, of which there had been none too many.... Her voice seemed to lose direction in his fancy, loitering there, strangely enticing.... *"Would you like to go up with me?"*... And these were Beth Truba's friends....

A bell was touched in the high hall, and Vina Nettleton's plaintive tone trailed forth:

"Won't you come right in—please—into my muddy room?"

A large room opening upon a steel fire-frame, where two could sit, and a view of the city to the North. Commandingly near on the left arose the Metropolitan Tower. The studio itself had an unfinished look, with its step-ladders and scaffolding and plaster-panels. In the midst of such ponderous affairs, stood a frail creature in a streaky blouse, exhibiting her clayey hands and smiling pensively. It was only when you looked at the figures in the panels, and at the models in clay, that Vina Nettleton appeared to belong to these matters of a contractor. Marguerite Grey was saying:

"When I get too weary, or heart-sick, tired of my own work, in the sense of being bored by its commonness—"

"Wicked woman," murmured Vina.

"When the thought comes that I should be a cashier in a restaurant," the other went on, in her sadly smiling way, speaking altogether to Bedient, "I come to this place. Here is an *artist*, Mr. Bedient. Vina has been working at these things for two years. She has still two years to finish within her contract. These are her prayers; they will live in the transept of a great cathedral."

"Don't mind the Grey One, Mr. Bedient," Vina Nettleton said

lightly. "We are dear friends."

Bedient lost himself in the study of the veins which showed through the delicate white skin of Vina's temples. He was moved to personal interest by this woman's work. The room was intense with the figures about, and the artist's being. He was sure Marguerite Grey did not know all that concerned her friend, the full meaning, for instance, of the shadows that began at the inner corners of her eyes and flared like dark wings outward. There was something tremendous in the frail, small creature, an inner brightness that shone forth through her white skin, as light through porcelain. Bedient granted quickly that there was power here to make the world remember the name of Vina Nettleton; but he knew she was not giving *all* to these creatures of clay. He had never sensed such a mingling of emotions and spirit.... "Pure spirit," the Grey One had said. Possibly it was so to the world, but he would have said that the spirit of Vina Nettleton was fed by emotion—seas, woods, fields, skies and rivers of emotion—and that mighty energies, unused by the great task, roamed in nightly anguish.

Bedient moved raptly among the panels. He wondered how the artist had made the light fall upon the dull clay, always where the Christ stood or walked or hung.... "And how did you know He had such beautiful hands?" he asked.

Vina Nettleton looked startled, and the Grey One came closer, saying: "I'm glad you see that. To me the hands are a particular achievement. Do you notice the fine modelling at the outer edges of the palms, and the trailing length of the fingers?"

"Yes," said Bedient, "as if you could not quite tell where the flesh ended and the healing magnetism began."

Vina Nettleton sat down upon one of the steps of a ladder and stared at him. The Grey One added:

"And yet you cannot say they are overdone. They are the hands of an artist, but not assertively so."

"It is my limitation that I don't know," he said, "but how is that effect obtained, that suggestion of psychic power?"

"Part is your sensitiveness of eye and understanding," the Grey One answered, "and the rest comes from our little woman making a prayer of her work; from taking an image of Him and the Others into the dark; of light, ascetic sleep and putting away the dreams of women—"

Scarlet showed under the transparent skin of the Nettleton temples now—as if putting away the dreams of women were not an unqualified success.

"It is all interesting. I am grateful to you both for letting me come," Bedient said with strange animation, eager yet full of hesitancy. "More wonderful than the hands, is the Face, which Miss Nettleton has kept averted throughout her entire idea. That's the way the Face appears to me. The disciples and the multitudes must have seen it so, except on rare, purposeful occasions.... He must have been slight and not tall, and delicate as you see Him. It was not that He lacked physical endurance, but He was worn, as those about Him did not understand, with constant inner agony. That was His great weariness.... It was not an imposing Figure. Nothing about Him challenged the Romans. They were but abandoned boys who bowed to the strength that roars, and the bulk that makes easy blood-letting. Even in custody, He was beneath the notice of most Romans, so inflamed and brutish from conquest were they; and Pilate, though the Tragic Instrument, was among the least ignoble of them—'"

Bedient felt vaguely the interest of Vina Nettleton in what he was saying. It was a remarkable moment. His mind was crowded with a hundred things to say; yet he was startled, diffident, in spite of the joy of speaking these things aloud.

"What a hideous time of darkness!" he added in the silence. "The Jews were but little better than the Romans. They were looking for a king, a Solomon sort of king with temples and trappings and sizable authorities. Isn't it divine irony, that the Messianic Figure should appear in the very heart of this racial weakness of the Jews? And their lesson seems still unlearned. New York brings this home to-day.... So, to the Jews and the Romans, He was insignificant in appearance. His beauty was spiritual, which to be recognized, requires spirituality—a feminine quality.

"And among the disciples: Hasn't it occurred to you again and again how their doubting egos arose, when His face was turned away? Poor fellows, they were bothered with their stomachs and their places to sleep; they quarrelled with the different villagers, and doubtless wished themselves back a hundred times to their fishing-banks and kindred employments, when the Christ moved a little apart from them. I can see them (behind His back), daring each other to approach and make known their fancied injustices and rebellions. It was so with the multitudes before they looked upon His countenance.

"But when He turns, whether in sorrow or in anger, the look is invincible.... That is always true, whether the Face is turned upon one, or the Twelve, or the multitude—in the crowded market-place, or by the sea where the many were fed, or on the Mount—perfect tributes of silence answered His direct attention, and all spiteful, petty ego outcroppings vanished.... So there were two Figures: One, a man, slender, tired and tortured; and an Angel Countenance, before whose lustrous communications all men were abased according to their spirit."

He paused, but the women did not speak....

"Dear God, how lonely He was!" Bedient said after a moment, as he regarded a picture of the Christ alone on the Mount, and the soldiers ascending to make the arrest "There were two who might have sustained in His daily death agonies. I have always wished they could have been near Him throughout the Passion. *They* would not have slept, that darkest of nights while He prayed! I mean Saint Paul, who of course did not see the Jesus of history, and John the Baptist, who was given to know Him but an hour at the beginning. They were the greatest mortals of those days.... They were above the attractions of women of flesh. Do you see what I mean? They were humanly complete, beyond sex! Their grandeur of soul meant a *union within themselves* of militant manhood and mystic womanhood. Illumination really means that. They could have sustained and ministered unto the Christ with real tenderness.

"Invariably, I think, this is true: It is a woman, or *the woman in man* that recognizes a Messiah.... Look at those males of singing flesh—the ultra-masculine Romans—how blind and how torpid they were to Him; and the materialistic Jews, ponderously confronting each other with stupid forms and lifeless rituals, while their Marys and Magdalens and Miriams followed the Master and waited upon Him!... I always found a kind of soulful feminine in John, the apostle—not the Forerunner, but the brother of James. He was weak in those days of the Passion, but became mighty afterward, and divinely tender, the apostle whom Jesus loved, to whom he intrusted His Mother.... But look into the arch-feminine ideal of the Christ Himself—that night on the Mount of Olives, when all Earth's struggle and anguish passed through Him, clothing itself with His pity and tenderness, before it reached the eye of the Father. What ineffable Motherhood!"

The room wrought strangely upon Bedient. He had never spoken at such length before, nor so eagerly. Vina Nettleton spoke for the first time almost, since she had welcomed him. "You help me greatly," she said with difficulty. "I cannot tell you exactly. I didn't know why, but last night I hoped you would come here. Oh, it wasn't to help me with this—not selfishly in the work, not that—but I seemed to know you knew the things you have said just now."

Bedient was thrilled by her sincerity.... The low voice of the Grey One now repeated:

"Spirituality, a feminine quality?"

"To me, always," said Bedient, his eyes lit with sudden enthusiasm. "The Holy Spirit *is* Mystic Motherhood. It is divinely the feminine principle.... Look at the world's prophets, or take Saint Paul, for he is in finished perspective. Completely human he is, unconquerable manhood ignited by the luminous feminine quality of the soul. There he stands, the man born again of the Holy Spirit, or Mystic Motherhood.... Now look at Jesus, a step higher still, and beyond which our vision cannot mount. Here is the prophet risen to Godhood—the union of Two, transcendent through that heavenly mystery—the adding of a Third! Doesn't it clear for you startlingly now? It did for me. Here is the *Three in One in Jesus*—the Godhood of the Father, the manhood of the Son, and the Mystic Motherhood of the Holy Spirit. So in the radiance of the Trinity—Jesus arose—'the first fruits of them that slept.'"

There was a light knock at the door. The face of the Grey

One was like a wraith, motionless and staring at him. Vina Nettleton looked up from her soiled hands, which had streaked her face.... She moved suddenly to the door, but did not touch it.

"Go away," she said intensely. "I can see no one."

Her eyes seemed to burn along the frame. There was no answer from without, but a light step turning away.... Assured that the visitor was gone, Vina turned back to Bedient.

"We mustn't be interrupted—nor must you go yet," she said with effort. "I don't think anything ever happened to me so important. Oh, I don't mean for my work; believe me in *that*, won't you? Since a little girl, I have thought of these things. And here for two years they have been about me. To me the Third of the Trinity has been as a voice calling out of darkness. They told me when I was a bit of a girl that It was not for me to understand, and that terrible men committed the deadly sin of blasphemy through It—"

"Poor child," Bedient said, smiling at her. "They didn't know. Could anything be lovelier for one to think about? The Holy Spirit as the source of the divine principle in Woman, and Woman ever so eager to give the spiritual loaf to man! That's the richest thought to me. After *that* is realized, all one's thinking must adjust itself to it; as in Hindu minds, all thoughts adjust to reincarnation, and flow from it.... There is a tender glow of spirit, a sort of ignition of the narrative, in every instance where a woman approaches the Christ in His mission on earth. And men seem to find no meaning in these wonderful things.... The women of this world *are* the symbols and the vessels of the Holy Spirit. It is only through woman's love that It can be given to the race. I like to think of it this way: *As a woman brings a child to her husband, the father, so the Holy Spirit—Mystic Motherhood—is bringing the World to God, the Father. And Jesus is the first fruits."*

The women regarded each other in silence. Bedient stayed, until the tardy May dusk effaced the city, all but the myriad points of light.

ELEVENTH CHAPTER

TWO DAVIDS COME TO BETH

Beth Truba awoke late. Goliath of Gath had just fallen with obituary hiccoughs and a great clatter of armor.... She sat up, and reviewed recent events backward. The stone had sunk into the forehead. David came down to meet the giant smiling. There was no anger about it. The stone had been slung leisurely. Before that, the boy had been brought in from his sheep-herding to be anointed king. Samuel had seen it in a vision, and not otherwise.... David found Saul's armor irksome, took up his staff, and went to the brook for good, sizable stones, just as if he had spied a wolf slavering at the herds from the brow of the hill....

Beth laughed, and wondered why the Bible story had come back in her dream. There seemed no clue, not even when she contemplated the events of the rather remarkable evening preceding. Many minutes afterward, however, arranging her hair, she found herself repeating:

"Now he was ruddy, and withal, of a beautiful countenance." Finally it came to her, and she was pleased and astonished: Throughout the evening, Beth had felt that some Bible description exactly fitted in her mind to the new impression of Bedient, but she could not think of it then. Her effort had

brought it forth in the night, and the whole story that went with it.

Beth drank a bottle of milk, ashamed of the hour, though she had not slept long. She loved mornings; New York could never change her delight in the long forenoon. She was at work at two, and undisturbed for two hours. Beth's studio was the garret of an old mansion, a step from Fifth Avenue in the Thirties. Its effect, as one entered, was golden at midday, and turned brown with the first shadows.

Mrs. Wordling called at four. For a woman who had been scornfully analyzed by Kate Wilkes (who really could be vitriol-tongued) and ordered away from Vina Nettleton's door like an untimely beggar, Mrs. Wordling looked remarkably well. In point of fact, Mrs. Wordling was ungovernably pretty. Moreover, she knew Kate Wilkes well enough to understand that she was too busy to sketch the characters of other women except for their own benefit. As for Vina Nettleton, the cloistered, she could do as she liked, being great in her calling; besides, a woman who had a man-visitor so rarely as Vina Nettleton, might be expected to become snappy and excited. Bedient was proving a rather stiff drug. Mrs. Wordling now wished to observe his action upon Beth Truba. "I'll appear to regard it as a perfectly lady-like party, which it was," she mused, in the dingy interminable stairways,—the elevator being an uncertain quantity—"and run no risk of being thrown three nights."

"Beth, you're looking really right," Mrs. Wordling enthused.

"So good of you," said Beth. "Must be lovely out, isn't it?... The poster will be ready in three or four days.... Didn't we have a good time at David's party?"

"Such a good time—"

"Really must have, since we stayed until an unconscionable hour. Half-past two when we broke up—"

"All of that, Beth."

The artist looked up from her work. Mrs. Wordling's acquiescences seemed modulated. The "Beths" were no more frequent than usual, however. The artist had grown used to this from certain people. It appeared that her name was so to the point, that many kept it juggling through their conversation with her, like a ball in a fountain.... The poster, Beth had consented to do in a weak moment. It was to be framed for theatre-lobbies. People whom Beth painted were seldom quite the same afterward to her. She seemed to learn too much. She had greatly admired Mrs. Wordling's good nature at the beginning. There was no objection now; only the actress had given her in quantity what had first attracted, and quantity had palled. Beth often wished she did not discern so critically.... Just now she divined that her caller wanted to discuss Cairns' friend. The result was that Mrs. Wordling left after a half-hour, with Bedient heavier and more undeveloped than ever in her consciousness. Always a considerable social factor in her theatrical companies, Mrs. Wordling was challenged by the people of the *Smilax Club*. She was not getting on with them, and the thought piqued. Bedient, who had not greatly impressed her, had apparently struck twelve with the others. Therefore, he became at once both an object and a means. There was a way to prove her artistry....

Beth went on with her painting, the face of another whom she had found out. And painting, she smiled and thought. She was like a pearl in the good North light. Across the pallor of her face ran a magnetic current of color from the famous hair to the crimson jacket she wore, pinned at the throat by a soaring gull, with the tiniest ruby for an eye....

David Cairns called. He seemed drawn and nervous. Obviously he had come to say things. Beth knew his moods.

"David, we had a memorable time last night, you know that," she said. "You know, too, that I have been, and am, friendly to Mrs. Wordling. As the party turned out, I'm interested to know just how you came to choose the guests. We drew rather close together for New Yorkers—"

"That's a fact."

"But the Grey One is engaged to be married. In theory, Kate Wilkes is a man-hater. Dear little Vina is consecrated to her 'Stations' for two years more. Eliminate me as, forborne, a spinster.... Yet you told me two or three days ago that you wouldn't be surprised if your friend took his lady back—"

"That may be true, Beth," he interrupted. "But I spoke hastily. It sounds crude and an infringement now. I really didn't know Bedient—"

"When you invited your guests—Mrs. Wordling?"

"I should have consulted someone—"

"Not at all, David. It was eminently right. I am not criticising, just interested."

"I've been revoluting inside. Mrs. Wordling happened three days ago, when I was first thinking out the party. I didn't know we were to get into real things. 'Ah, here's a ripe rounding influence,' said I. 'Do come, Mrs. Wordling.' Maybe I *did* figure out the contrast she furnished. She's friendly and powerfully pretty and, why, I see it now, one of the Wordlings of this world would have taken Andrew Bedient into camp years ago, if he were designed for that kind of woman. Why, that's the kind of woman he doubtless knows—"

"Do you know what I think?" Beth inquired. "I think you should be punished for using Mrs. Wordling or anyone else as a foil. That's a Wordl—a woman's strategy."

"I know it, Beth," Cairns said excitedly. "But I didn't think of it until afterward. I wouldn't do it again."

She was startled, saw too late that this was no time for showing him his crudities.

"You're a dear boy—" she began.

"No, I'm not, Beth. Oh, it isn't the only thing—that has been rammed home to me.... *Me*; there's so much *me* mixed up in my mind, so much tiresome and squalid *me*, that I wonder every decent person hasn't cut me long since for a bore and a nuisance. Why, I had become all puny and blinded—*my* stomach, *my* desires, markets, memories, ambitions, doubts, rages, rights, poses and conceits. I really need to tell some one, to unveil before some one who won't wince, but treasure the little moral residuum—"

"You have done well to come to Beth," she said, leaning forward and patting his shoulder with the thin stem of her brush, though a woman always feels her years when a man brings woes such as these to her.... It was Beth's weakness (or strength) that she could never reveal the intimacies of her heart. Only sometimes in half-humorous generalities, she permitted things to escape, thinking no one understood.

"Thanks, Beth. I'm grateful," Cairns said. "I seem to have missed for a long time the bigger dimension in people, books, pictures, faces, even in the heart. It's a long time since

I set out this way, a down-grade, and the last few days, I've heard the rapids. I'm going back, as far and as fast as I can up-stream. And this is no lie; no pose."

"I repeat, you're a dear boy—"

"Oh, it's Bedient who jerked me up straight. I'd have gone on.... And to think I made him wait over an hour, when he first called.... He's the finest bit of man-stuff I've ever known, Beth."

She found herself relieved, that he had given to the stranger the praise.

"... And, Beth, if you want to dig for his views, you'll get them. He says New York plucks everything green; opinionates on the wing, makes personal capital out of another's offering, refusing to wait for the fineness of impersonal judgment. He asks nothing more stimulating than the capacity to say on occasion, 'I don't know,' flat and unqualified. He sees everywhere, the readiness to be clever instead of true. So many New Yorkers, he says, are like fishes, that, knowing water, disclaim the possibility of air.

"You know, Beth, Bedient never encountered what America was thinking and reading, until a few months ago down on his Island. We are editorialists in the writing game, he declares, what-shall-I-write-about-to-day-folks! We don't wait for fulness, but wear out brain thin bandying about what drops on it. If we would wait until we were full men, we would *have* to write, and not drive ourselves to the work—"

"Oh, I do believe that!" Beth said. "We need to be reminded of that."

"That *we* is very pretty, Beth," Cairns went on. "...Such a queer finished incident happened yesterday. I hunted up Bedient at noon, and we talked about some of these matters. And then we met Ritchold for luncheon. It was at *Teuton's*. I took Bedient aside and whispered with a flourish, 'One of our ten-thousand-a-year editors, Andrew.'... 'What makes him worth that?' he asked. 'He knows what the people want,' I replied. Can you see us, Beth?...

"The luncheon was interesting. Bedient and Ritchold got together beautifully. The talk was brisk and big, just occasionally cutting the edges of shop. Both men came to me afterward. 'Splendid chap, your friend,' Ritchold said. 'A man who has seen so much and can talk so well, ought to *write*. Thanks for meeting him.'

"'I was very glad to meet Mr. Ritchold,' Bedient remarked later—hours later—after I had given up hope of hearing on the subject. 'I think he shows where one trouble lies.... It's in *him* and his kind, David. His periodical sells to the great number. He is a very bright man, and his art is in knowing what the great number wants. Being brighter, and of finer discernment, than those who buy his product, he debases his taste to make his organs relish the coarser article. That's the first evil—prostituting himself.... Now a people glutted with what it wants is a stagnant people. Its only hope is in such men as Ritchold leading them to the higher ways. In refusing, he wrongs the public—the second evil.... Again, in blunting his own sensibilities and catering to the common, he stands as a barrier between the public and real creative energy. He and the public are one. A prostituted taste and a stagnant popular mind are alike repelled by reality. Rousing creative power glances from them both. So his third evil is the busheling and harrying of genius.... There he stands, forcing genius to be common, to appear, paying well and swiftly only for that which is common. Genius writhes a bit, starves a bit, but the terrible needs of this complicated life have him by the throat until he cries "Enough," and presently is common, indeed.'"

"He need not have spoken of writing only," Beth remarked. "*They* must have taught him to see things clearly in the Orient.... You know, David, I found it hard last night, and a little now, to fix his point of view and his power to express it, with the life of outdoor men, the 'enlisted,' as he says, rather than the 'commissioned' folk of this world."

"He has done much reading, but more thinking," Cairns declared. "He has been much alone, and he has lived. He sees inside. 'The great books of the world are little books,' he said recently, 'books that a pocket or a haversack will hold. You don't realize what they have given you, until you sit down in a roomful of ordinary books and see how tame and common the quantities are.' And it's true. Look at the big men of few books. They learned to look *inside* of books they had! He knows the Bible, and the *Bhagavad Gita*."

"Oh, I'm beginning to understand," Beth exclaimed. "Nights alone with the Bible and the *Bhagavad Gita*, and one's schooldays—a weathering from the open and seasoning from the seas. Men have such chances to learn the perils and passions of the earth, but so few do.... I see it now. It isn't remarkable that we find him poised and finished, but that he should have had the inclination naturally—a child among sailors—for the great little books of the world, and through them and his nights alone, to have kept his balance and builded his power."

"That's the point, Beth. New York is crowded with voyagers, and men of mileage to the moon, but what made this powerful unlettered boy *look* for the inside of things? What made him different from the packers and cooks and sailors around the world, boys of the open who never become men except physically?"

Beth answered: "I think we'll find that has to do with Mr. Bedient's mother, David."

"I know he'd be thrilled to hear you say that."

"Is she still living?"

"No, or he'd be with her.... He has never spoken to me of her. And yet I'm sure she is the unseen glow upon his life. I think he would tell *you* about her. Only a woman could draw that from him.... He saw no one but you last night; did all his talking to you, Beth."

"I'm the flaringest, flauntingest posy in the garden. I call the bees first," she said dryly, but there was a flitting of ghostly memories through her mind. "And then I'm an extraordinary listener."

"Beth," he said solemnly, "no one knows better than I, that it is you who send the bees away."

She laughed at him. "We found each other out in time, David.... Too much artist between us. We'd surely taint each other, don't you see?"

"I never could see that—"

"That's being polite; and one must be polite.... We are really fine friends, better than ever after to-day, and that's something for a pair of incomplete New Yorkers."

There was a pause.

"Beth," said Cairns. "Shall I bring Bedient over to-morrow?"

"No, please. At least not to-morrow."

He was surprised. Beth saw it; saw, too, that he had observed how Bedient talked to her last night. Mrs. Wordling had not missed comment here.... Cairns must not think, however, that she would avoid Andrew Bedient. She fell into her old resource of laughing at the whole matter.

"I can't afford to take any chances, David. He's *too* attractive. Falling in love is pure dissipation to one of my temperament, and I have too many contracts to fill. I'm afraid of your sailor-man. Think of the character you built about him to-day in this room. If he didn't prove up to that, what a pity for us all! And if he did, what a pity for poor Beth, if he started coming here!... Anyway, I've ceased to be a bachelor-girl. I'm a spinster.... That word hypnotizes me. I'm all ice again. I shall know Mr. Bedient ethically and not otherwise."

Cairns laughed with her, but something within hurt. His relation with Beth Truba had been long, and increasingly delightful, since the ordeal of becoming just a friend was safely past. He realized that only a beautiful woman could speak this way, even in fun to an old friend.... His work dealt with wars, diplomacy and politics; his fictions were twenty-year-old appeals, so that Beth felt her present depth of mood to be fathoms deeper than his story instinct.

"You know, David, I've said for years there were no real lovers in the world," she went on lightly. "But your friend was full of touches last night such as one dreams of: that colored pane in the hall-way, when he was a little boy somewhere, and the light that frightened him from it.... 'One of the Chinese knifed me, but he died.'... That big 'X' of the *Truxton* flung stern up, as she sank; ... and about the old Captain wriggling his shoulder bashfully for his young friend's arm at the last.... It is altogether enticing, in the light of what you have brought to-day. Really you must take him away. Red-haired spinsters mustn't be bothered, nor imprisoned in magic spring weather. When does he return to his Island?"

"He hasn't spoken of that, but I do know, Beth, that Bedient will never sink back into the common, from your first fine impressions. I've known him for years, you see—"

She put down her brush and said theatrically, "I feel the fatal premonitive impulses.... Spinster, spinster; Beth Truba, spinster!... That's my salvation."

"You're the finest woman I know," Cairns said. "You know best, but I doubt if Bedient will go back to Equatoria without seeing more of you—"

"Did he speak of such a thing?"

"That isn't his way—"

"I am properly rebuked."

... Cairns was at the door. "Did you say, Beth, that the Grey One is engaged to be married?"

"Pure tragedy. The man is fifty and financial.... She's a courageous girl, but I think under her dear smile is a broken nerve. She has about reached the end of her rope. The demand for her work has fallen off. One of those inexplicable things. She had such a good start after returning from Paris. And now with Handel's expensive studio, probably not less than three thousand a year for that, debt and unsought pictures are eating out her heart. There's much more to the story—I mean leading up. Help her if you can, or she must go to the arms and house of a certain rich man....

What a blithe thing is Life, and how little you predatory men know about it!"

They regarded each other, their thoughts poised upon an *If*. Beth spoke first:

"If your friend—"

"But Bedient didn't look into the eyes of the Grey One when he told his tale of the sea," Cairns said, leaving.

TWELFTH CHAPTER

TWO LESSER ADVENTURES

A few nights after the party, Bedient was left to his own devices, Cairns being appointed out of town. He attended the performance of a famous actress in *Hedda Gabler*.... Bedient was early. The curtain interested him. It pictured an ancient Grecian ruin, a gloomy, heavy thing, but not inartistic. Beneath was a couplet from Kingsley:

"So fleet the works of men, back to their earth again,
Ancient and holy things fade like a dream."

Sensitive to such effects, he sat, musing and contemplative, when suddenly his spirit was imperiously aroused by the orchestra. The 'celli had opened the *Andante* from the C Minor Symphony. For ten minutes, the music held his every sense.... It unfolded as of old, but not its full message. There was a meaning in it *for him*! He heard the three voices—man, woman and angel. It was the woman's tragedy. The lustrous Third Presence was for her. The man's figure was obscure, disintegrate.... Bedient was so filled with the mystery, that the play had but little surface of his consciousness during the first act. He enjoyed it, but could not give all he had. Finally, as *Hedda* was ordering the young writer to drink wine to get "vine-leaves in his hair," there was an explosion back of the scenes. Bedient, as did many others, thought at first it belonged to the piece. The faces of the players fell away in thick gloom, the voices sank into crazy echoes, and the curtain went down. Bedient's last look at the stage brought him the impression of squirming chaos. Fire touched the curtain behind, disfiguring and darkening the pictured ruin. Then a woman near him screamed. The back of a chair snapped, and now scores took up the woman's cry.

The crowd caught a succession of hideous ideas: of being trapped and burned, of inadequate exits, murderous gases, bodies piled at the doors—all the detailed news-horror of former theatre disasters. And the crowd did all it could to repeat the worst of these. Bedient encountered an altogether new strength, the strength of a frenzied mass, and to his nostrils came a sick odor from the fear-mad. The lights had not been turned on with the fall of the curtain. Untrained to cities, Bedient was astonished at the fright of the people, the fright of the men!... The lines of *Hedda* recurred to him, and he called out laughingly:

"Now's the time for 'vine-leaves in your hair,' men!"

He moved among the seats free from the aisle. A body lay at his feet. Groping forward, his hand touched a woman's hair. He smiled at the thought that here was one for *him* to help, and lifted her, turning to look at the glare through the writhing curtain. There were voices behind in that garish furnace; and now the lights filled the theatre again. Bedient quickly made his way with others to a side exit, the red light of which had not attracted the crowd.

The woman was light in his arms. She wore a white net waist, and her brown hair was unfastened. She had crushed a large bunch of English violets to her mouth and nostrils, to keep out the smoke and gas. A peculiar thing about it was, Bedient did not see her face. In the alley, he handed his burden to a man and woman, standing together at the door of a car, and went back. One of the actors had stepped in front of the stage, and was calling out that the fire was under control, that there was no danger whatever. The roar from the gallery passages subsided. Only a few were hurt, since the theatre was modern and the main exit ample.... Bedient returned to the side-door but the woman he had carried forth was gone, probably with the pair in the car. He decided to see the end of *Hedda Gabler* another time. The *Andante*, the Grecian ruin and vine-leaves were curiously blended in his mind....

Though several days had passed since the Club affair, he had not seen Beth Truba again. This fact largely occupied his thinking. He would not telephone nor call, without a suggestion from her. The moment had not come to bring up her name to David Cairns, who, since his talk with Beth, had of course nothing to offer. So Bedient revolved in outer darkness.... The morning after *Hedda Gabler* he found a very good chestnut saddle-mare in an up-town stable, and rode for an hour or two in the Park, returning to the Club after eleven. At the office, he was told that Mrs. Wordling had asked for him to go up to her apartment, as soon as he came in. Five minutes later, he knocked at her door.

"Is that you, Mr. Bedient?" she called. The voice came seemingly from an inner room; a cultivated voice, with that husky note in it which charms the multitude. Had he not a good mental picture of Mrs. Wordling, he would have imagined some enchanted Dolores.... "How good of you to come! Just wait one moment."

The door opened partially after a few seconds, and he caught the gleam of a bare arm, but the actress had disappeared when he entered. Bedient was in a room where a torrential shower had congealed into photographs.

"I can't help it," she said at last, emerging from the inner room, unhooked.... "I've been trying to get a maid up here for the past half-hour.... I think there's only three or four between the shoulder-blades—won't you do them for me?"

She backed up to him bewitchingly.... Mrs. Wordling was in the twenty-nine period. If the thing can be imagined, she gave the impression of being both voluptuous and athletic. There was a rose-dusk tone under her healthy skin, where the neck went singing down to the shoulder, singing of warm blood and plenteous. Hers was the mid-height of woman, so that Bedient was amusedly conscious of the length of his hands, as he stood off for a second surveying the work to do.

"What's the trouble; can't you?"

There was a purring tremble in her tone that stirred the wanderer, only it was the past entirely that moved within him. The moment had little more rousing for him, than if he were asked to fasten a child's romper.... Yet he did not miss that here was one of the eternal types of man's pursuit—as natural a man's woman as ever animated a roomful of photographs—a woman who could love much, and, as Heine added, *many*.

"I'll just throw a shawl around, if you can't," she urged, nudging her shoulder.

"Far too warm for shawls," he laughed. "I was only getting it straight in my mind before beginning. You know it's tricksome for one accustomed mainly to men's affairs.... There's one—I won't pinch—and the second—anytime you can't find a maid, Mrs. Wordling—I'm in the Club a good deal—there they are, if they don't fly open—" and his hands fell with a pat on each of her shoulders.

Facing him, Mrs. Wordling encountered a perfectly unembarrassed young man, and a calm depth of eye that seemed to have come and gone from her world, and taken away nothing to remember that was wildly exciting.... At least three women of her acquaintance were raving about Andrew Bedient, two artists with a madness for sub-surface matters having to do with men. Mrs. Wordling believed herself a more finished artist in these affairs. She wanted to prove this, while Bedient was the dominant man-interest of the Club.

And now he surprised her. He was different from the man she had pictured. Equally well, she could have located him— had he kissed her, or appeared confused with embarrassment. Most men of her acquaintance would have kissed her; others would have proved clumsy and abashed, but none could have passed through the test she offered with both denial and calm.... She wanted the interest of Bedient, because the other women fancied him; she wanted to show them and "that hag, Kate Wilkes," what a man desires in a woman; and now a third reason evolved. Bedient had proved to her something of a challenging sensation. He was altogether too calm to be inexperienced. Every instinct had unerringly informed her of his bounteous ardor, yet he had refrained. That which she had seen first and last about him—the excellence of his masculine attractions—had suddenly become important because no longer impersonal. Mrs. Wordling was fully equipped to carry out her ideas.

"You did that very well," she said, dropping her eyes before his steady gaze, "for one experienced only with men-matters. And now, I suppose you want to know why I took the pains to ask you here; oh, no, not to hook me up.... I didn't know you would get back so soon; I had just left word a few moments before you came.... Wasn't it great the way a dreadful disaster was averted at the *Hedda Gabler* performance last night?... Did you see the morning paper?"

"No," said Bedient. "I was out early."

"Why, it appears that after the explosion, when everyone was crushing toward the doors, some man in the audience took the words of *Hedda* and steadied the crowd with them, as men and women struggled in the darkness.... 'Now's the time for vine-leaves!' he called out. An unknown—wasn't he lovely?"

She placed the paper before him, and he read a really remarkable account of "the vine-leaf man" magnetizing the mob and carrying out a fainting girl. It was absurd to him, though Ibsen's subtlety, queerly enough, gave the story force.... No face of the audience had impressed him; none had appeared to notice him in the dark. He wondered how the newspaper had obtained the account.... There was a light, quick knock at the door.

"It isn't very often that a newspaper story is gotten up so effectively," Mrs. Wordling was saying. Apparently she had not heard the knock. Her voice, however, had fallen in a half-whisper, more penetrating than her usual low tones. "Do you suppose the hero will permit his name to be known?"

The knock was repeated in a brief, that-ends-it fashion. Mrs. Wordling with a sudden streak of clumsiness half overturned a chair, as she sped to the door. Bedient did not at once penetrate the entire manoeuver, but his nerve and will tightened with a premonition of unpleasantness.

Beth Truba was admitted. Quite as he would have had her

do, the artist merely turned from one to the other a quick glance, and ignored the matter; yet that glance had stamped him with her conception of his commonness.

"I could just as well have sent the poster over," Beth said, "but, as I 'phoned, it is well to see, if it suits exactly, before putting it out of mind—"

"Lovely of you, dear. I'm so glad Mr. Bedient is here to see it!" Mrs. Wordling's brown eyes swam with happiness.

Beth was in brown. Her profile was turned to Bedient, as she unrolled the large, heavy paper.... The work was remarkable in its effect of having been done in a sweep. The subtle and characteristic appeal of the actress (so truly her own, that she would have been the last to notice it) had been caught in truth and cleverly, the restlessness of her empty arms and eager breast. The face was finer, and the curves of the figure slightly lengthened; the whole in Beth's sweeping way, rather masterful.

"Splendid!" Mrs. Wordling exclaimed, and to Bedient added: "It's for the road. Isn't it a winner?"

"Yes, I do like it," Bedient said.

Beth was glad that he didn't enlarge.

"I must be on my way, then," she said. "I'm going into the country to-morrow for the week-end.... We're getting the old house fixed up for the winter. Mother writes that the repairs are on in full blast, and that I'm needed. Last Saturday when I got there the plumbers had just come. Very carefully they took out all the plumbing and laid it on the front lawn; then put it back.... Good-by."

"Good-by, and thank you, Beth."

"I am glad that it pleases you, Mrs. Wordling." Her tone was pleasantly poised.

Bedient missed nothing now. He did not blame Mrs. Wordling for using him. He saw that she was out of her element with the others; therefore not at her best trying to be one with them. In her little strategies, she was quite true to herself. He could not be irritated, though he was very sorry. Of course, there could be no explanation. His own innocence was but a humorous aspect of the case. The trying part was that look in Beth Truba's eyes, which told him how bored she was by this sort of commonness.

Then there was to-morrow and Sunday with her away. In her brown dress and hat, glorious and away.

Bedient went away, too.

THIRTEENTH CHAPTER

ABOUT SHADOWY SISTERS

Beth Truba hadn't the gift of talking about the things that hurt her. She had met all her conflicts in solitudes of her own finding; and there they had been consummated, like certain processes of nature, far from the gaze of man. She had found the world deranged from every girlish ideal. Full grown young men could be so beautiful to her artist's eyes, that years were required to realize that these splendid exteriors held more often than not, little more than strutting half-truths and athletic vanities.

Whistler, the master, had entered the class-room unannounced, where Beth was studying, as a girl in Paris. Glancing about the walls, his eyes fastened upon a sketch of hers. He asked the teacher for the pupil who did it, and uplifted Beth's face to his, touching her chin and forehead lightly.

Then he whistled and said: "Off hand, I should say that you are to become an artist; but now that I look closely into your face, I am afraid you will become a woman."

Tentatively, she was an artist; she would not grant more.... A little while before, she had been very close to becoming a woman. None but the Shadowy Sister knew how near. (The

Shadowy Sister was an institution of Beth's—her conscience, her spirit, her higher self, or all three in one. She came from an old fairy-book. A little girl had longed for a playmate, even as Beth, and one day beside a fountain appeared a Shadowy Sister. She could stay a while, for she loved the little girl, but confessed it was much happier where *she* lived.)... Shadowy Sisters for little girls who have no playmates, and for women who have no confidantes.

Under Beth's mirth, during the recent talk with David Cairns, had been much of verity. She was carrying an unhealed wound, which neither he nor the world understood. In Andrew Bedient she had discerned a fine and deeply-endowed nature—glimpses—as if he were some great woman's gift to the world, her soul and all. But Beth's romantic nature had been desolated so short a time ago, that she despised even her willingness to put forth faith again.... Such fruit must perish on the vine, if only common hands attend the harvest.

Women like Beth Truba learn in bitterness to protect themselves from possibilities of disillusionment. They hate their hardness, yet hardness is better than rebuilding sanctuaries that have been brutally stormed. For one must build of faith, radium-rare to those who have lost their intrinsic supply.

The Other Man had been a find of Beth's. He had come to her mother's house years ago—a boy. He had seemed quick to learn the ways of real people, and the things a man must know to delight a woman's understanding. In so many ways, the finishing touches of manhood were put upon him gracefully, that Beth gloried in the work of adding treasures of mind and character. She had even made his place in the world, through strong friends of her own winning.

Beth was a year or two older. The boy had grown splendid in appearance, when she discovered she was giving him much that he must hold sacredly, or inflict havoc upon the giver.... In moments when she was happiest, there would come a thought that something would happen.... The young man did not fully understand what caused the break. This may be the key to the very limitation which made him impossible—this lack of delicacy of perception. Certainly he did not know the greatness of Beth's giving, nor the fineness she had come to expect from him.... She did not exactly love him less, but rather as a mother than a maid, since she had to forgive.

A woman may love a man whom she is too wise to marry. There are man-comets, splendid, flashing, unsubstantial, who sweep into the zones of attraction of all the planet sisterhood; but better, if one cannot have a sun all to oneself, is a little cold moon for the companion intimate.... Something that the young man had said or done was pure disturbance to Beth, compatible with no system of development. She had sent him from her, as one who had stood before her rooted among the second-rate.

Only Beth knew the depth of the hurt. All the feminine of her had turned to aching iron. The Shadowy Sister seemed riveted to a hideous clanking thing, and all the dream-children crushed.

Her friends said: "Who would have thought that after making such a *man* of her protege, Beth would refuse to marry him? Ah, Beth loves her pictures better than she could love any mere man. She was destined to be true to her work. Only the great women are called upon to make this choice. Nature keeps them virgin to reveal at the last unshadowed beauty. This refusal is the signet of her greatness."

Beth heard a murmur of this talk and laughed bitterly.

"No," she said to her studio-walls. "It's only because Beth is a bit choosey. She isn't a very great artist, and if she were, she wouldn't hesitate to become Mrs. Right Man, though it made her falter forever, eye and hand."

In her own heart, she would rather have had her visions of happiness in children, than to paint the most exquisite flowers and faces in the comprehension of Art.... For days, for weeks, she had remained in her studio seeing no one. Some big work was rumored, and she was left alone with understanding among real people, just as was Vina Nettleton.... But she was too maimed within to work. She wanted to rush off to Asia somewhere, and bury herself alive, but pride kept her at home. As soon as she was able to move and think coherently, she sought her few friends again. Even her dearest, Vina Nettleton, had realized but a tithe of the tragedy.

*　*　*　*　*

Beth Truba reached her studio again Monday noon. Among the letters in her post-box, was one she felt instinctively to be from Andrew Bedient, though it was post-marked Albany. She hesitated to open the letter at first, for fear that he had attempted to explain his presence in Mrs. Wordling's room. This would affix him eternally to commonness in her mind. He had a right to go to Mrs. Wordling's room, but she had thought him other than the sort which pursues such obvious attractions. Especially after what Cairns had said, she was hurt to meet him there.... Beth found herself thinking at a furious rate, on the mere hazard that the letter was from Bedient....

Were there really such men in the world as the Bedient whom Cairns pictured, and believed in? Personally, she didn't care to experiment, but there was a strange reliance in the thought that there *were* such men.... The fine nature she wanted to believe in—wouldn't have written!... This one letter alone remained unopened—when the telephone rang.

It was Cairns, who inquired if she had heard aught of his friend.... "I reached town Saturday morning," Cairns went on, "and found a note that he would be away for the day and possibly Sunday; didn't say where nor why. He left no word at the Club. In fact, Mrs. Wordling called me just now to inquire, volunteering that Bedient had been in her world Friday. Excuse me for bothering you. I've an idea this is his way when a gale is blowing in his brain. He pushes out for solitude and sea-room."

Beth had not offered to assist. The Albany letter might not be his. It stared at her now from the library-table, full-formed black writing. There were no two ways about a single letter. It was the writing of a man who had not covered continents of white paper. "Miss Beth Truba" had been put there to stay, with a full pen, and as if pleasing to his sight. She was thinking—it would be well if Mrs. Wordling were always inquiring; and that the day would be spoiled if he had undertaken to explain things in this letter....

Beth crossed to the table, placed the paper-cutter under the flap and slit it across. Just at this moment, the door of the elevator-shaft opened on her floor—and her knocker fell. She tossed the letter under the leather cover of the table, and admitted Vina Nettleton.

FOURTEENTH CHAPTER

THIS CLAY AND PAINT AGE

A new light had come into the studio of Vina Nettleton; and only when at last the light became too strong, and the struggle too close, had she left it to seek her friend Beth Truba. She had not been sleeping, nor remembering to eat; but she had been thinking enough for seven artists, in the long hours, when the light was bad for work. And now the packing was worn from her nerve-ends, so that she wept easily, like a nervous child, or a man undone from drink.

The new force of Andrew Bedient had found in her a larger sensitiveness than even in David Cairns. That long afternoon which he had spent in her place of working and living was to her a visitation, high above the years. She had been amazed at the Grey One, for preserving a semblance of calm. The gratefulness that she had faltered was but a sign of what she felt.

The figures of Jesus in her room, she had been unable to touch. Bedient had made her see the *Godhood* of the Christ. John the Baptist, who had attained the apex of manhood and prophecy, had called himself unworthy to loose the latchet of His shoes, and this before Jesus had put on the glory of the Father.

All the others were amazingly nearer to her. She saw the bleak Iscariot as never before, and his darkened mother emerged a step out of the gloom of ages. The Romans moved, as upon a stage, before her, unlit battling faces, clashing voices and armor; and the bearded Jews heavily collecting and confuting. She saw the Eleven, and nearest the light, the frail John, the brother of James,—sad young face and ascetic pallor.... And in the night, she heard that great Voice crying in the wilderness, that mighty Forerunner, the returned Elias; next to Christ Himself, this Baptist, who leaped in the womb of the aged Elizabeth, when the Mother of the Saviour entered her house in the hill country! This cataclysmic figure, not of the "Stations," was dominant in the background of them all. She saw him second to the Christ (for was he not a prophet in the elder Scripture?) in being called to the Father's Godhood; and Saint Paul, of that nameless thorn in the flesh, following gloriously on the Rising Road!

There was a new and loving friendliness in the Marys. She could pray to *them*, and wait for greater purity to image the Saviour, as they saw Him.... And one night from her fire-frame, staring down into the lurid precipices of the city, the awful question preyed upon her lips, "Are you Jews and Romans that you must have again the blood of the Christ, to show you the way to God?"... She was weeping, and would have swooned, but something in her consciousness bade her look above. There were the infinite worlds, immensities of time and space and evolving souls; and urging, weaving, glorifying all, was the Holy Spirit, Mystic Motherhood.... And back in the dark of her studio, she turned among creations and visions and longings. Next morning she sat upon the floor and wept, because she could not have her child of soul, only children of clay.... Hours afterward she was fashioning a cross with her fingers, and was suddenly crushed with anguish because she had not been there to carry the cross for Him, to confront the soldiery and take the cruel burden, and hear His Voice, Whom she knew now to be the Son of God.

* * * * *

The women embraced in that rare way which is neither formal nor an affectation. They had long liked and admired each other.

"Why, Vina,—it has been weeks—how did you manage to leave?"

"I haven't done much—for days," Vina said, ducking from under her huge hat, and tossing it with both hands upon the piano-top. "Not since he came up with the Grey One and spoiled my little old ideas. Let's have some tea?"

Beth laughed at the other, until Vina moved into the circle of light, and her face showed paler and more transparent than ever. She sat down upon Beth's working-stool, elbows on knees, and stared trance-like at her friend.

"Why, you dear little dreamer, what's the matter?" Beth asked quickly. "Who is the destructive *he*?"

"The sailor-man David Cairns called us together to see. He's been in the shadows among the panels ever since. What he said I keep hearing again and again—"

Beth laughed at the remarkable way Bedient was besieging her own studio, without appearing in person. "But Vina, you've been living like a Hindu holy man, and no one can do that in New York, not even Hindus. I order you to eat thrice daily and tire yourself physically—"

"I eat," Vina said, looking bored and helpless at the thought. "I eat and I do enough physical work to tire a stone-mason—"

"But I can see through you to the bone! I think you only imagine you take nourishment. Oh, Vina, I know your life—handling huge hard things and making them lovely with pure spirit. I must take better care of you. Tell me all about it, if it will help."

"Beth, please don't talk about pure spirit, meaning me. I used to be able to stand it, but not any more. The Grey One does that. I seem to suggest it to flesh and blood people.... I'm sure he didn't see me so. He looked at me, as if to say, oh, I don't know what!... I wish I *were* fish-cold! I'm all overturned.... I just met Mary McCullom on the way over."

Beth had forgotten the name for the moment. She thought Vina was about to tell her of Bedient.

"Don't you remember Mary McCullom, who tried painting for awhile, painted one after another, discolored and shapeless children, wholly bereft and unfortunate children?"

"Oh, yes," said Beth. "I heard she had married—"

"That's just it.... Do you remember how she used to look—pinched, evaporated, as one looks in a factory blue-light? I remember calling upon her, as she was giving up her last studio. We sat on a packing-case, while they took out her pictures, one child after another, foundlings which had come to her, and which no one would take nor buy—"

"Vina, you're cruel to her!"

"Listen, and you'll see whom I'm cruel to.... I remember telling her that day what a fearsome, ineffectual thing art is anyway.... How spooky thin she looked, and her face was yellow in patches! My heart was wrung with her, the image of a little woman with no place, no heart to go to, all her dreams of girlhood turned to ghosts, fit only to run from. Then she admitted that she might marry, that a man wanted her, but her wail was that she was mean and helpless, a failure; as such it was cowardly to let the man have her, hardly a square thing for a girl to do. Well, I perked her up on that.... She took him; I don't even know him by sight, but he's a man, Beth Truba! Mind you, here was a woman who said she was so dismayed and distressed and generally bowled over by living twenty-seven years, that she hadn't the heart left to love anybody. But he took her, and he's a man—"

"That seems to charm you," Beth ventured. "'He took her, and he's a man.'"

"It does, for I just left her, and she's a wicked flaunt of womanly happiness. I tell you, she has been playing with angels, all daintily plumped out, eyes shining, hands soft and white, her neck all round and new, lips red, and her voice low and ecstatic with the miracle of it all. And 'Oh, Vina,' she whispered, 'I almost die to think I might have refused him! You helped me not to. He loves me, and oh, he's so wonderful!'... I kissed her in an awed way—and asked about him.... 'Oh, he's just a nurseryman—trees, you know, but he lo—we're so happy!'... Oh, Beth," Vina finished in a lowered voice, "something eternal, something immortal happens, when a man brings love to a thirsting woman!"

"Not tea, but strong tea," Beth observed. "Perhaps you think that's a pretty story—and perhaps it is," she added indefinitely.

Vina seemed hardly to hear. Many matters were revolving in her tired mind, and as soon as she caught a loose end, she allowed words to come, for there was some relief in thinking aloud.

"Hasn't the world done for us perfectly, Beth?" she demanded finally. "Everything is arranged for men, to suit men—it's a man's world—and we're foreigners. We're forced to stand around and *mind*, before we understand. If we speak our own language, we're suspected of sedition. And then we don't stand together. We're continually looking for some kind male native, and only now and then one of us is lucky.... Hideous and false old shames are inflicted upon us. We are hungry for many things, but appear shameless, if we say so... Beth, has it ever occurred to you that we come—I mean fair and normal women—we come from a country where there are lots of little children—?"

"The kingdom of heaven, you mean, Vina?"

"Possibly that's it. And when we get here we miss them— want them terribly. It's all *through* us—like an abstraction. We know the way better than the natives here, but they have laws which make us dependent upon them for the way.... It has not lifted to an abstraction with our teachers, Beth. A crude concrete thing to them, a matter of rules broken or not. We must submit, or remain lonely, reviled foreigners.... Sometimes we discover a native who *could* bring us back our own, but he's probably teaching the nearest...."

"We've got to stand together, we foreigners," Beth said laughingly. "All our different castes must stand together first—and keep the natives waiting—until in their very eagerness, they suddenly perceive that we know best—"

"It's not for us—that happy time," Vina added hopelessly. "We are the sit-tight, hold-fast pilgrims. We belong to the clay-and-paint age—"

"It's something to see that—"

"Oh, how truly *he* sees it!"

"Your Sailor-man, does he see that, too?"

"Has he been *seeing* other things—in your studio?" Vina asked hastily.

"Oh, no, he hasn't been here, but he has been telling David Cairns things about writing.... David has really been born again."

"Do you know, Beth," Vina declared with intensity, "he has been such an inspiration to me, that I'm afraid my 'Stations' will look like a repaired wall, half new and half old plaster."

"My work will stand an inspiration, too."

"Beth—"

"Yes."

"You know what I think of your work, but I believe the Sailor-man could give you that inspiration—"

"Perhaps I can get it through you and David Cairns," remarked Beth, who was beginning to see, and with no little amazement, that to Vina the inspiration was spiritual, impersonal. This made Bedient's influence all the more exciting.

"Oh, he'll come to you, right enough. I supposed he had.... You know I was making my James and Matthews, my Peters and Jews and Romans quite contentedly in that bleak way it has been done a thousand times. But he made me see them!

And the slopes of Calvary, and Gethsemane hunched in the darkness, and the Christ kneeling in a faint starry light; he made me see Him kneeling there, His Spirit, like a great mother's loving heart, standing between an angry Father and the world, a wilful child—"

"Yes," came softly from Beth.

"And it's almost too much for me now—the Passion, the Agony, the Crime and the Night—too much for me and clay. It would be, if it were not for the glowing Marys. They're for *us*, Beth—"

"That's sweet of you, Vina.... It won't be too much. You're in the reaction now. After that passes you will do the 'Stations' as they have never been done. And God's poor people will pass before your work for years and years to come; and something, as much as they can bear of the thrilling anguish of this new light of yours, will come to them, as they pray before the Eternal Tragedy."

"But that isn't all, Beth!... There's another; a terrible side. I sort of had myself in hand until he came, sort of felt myself two thousand years old, back among them. But he has made me a pitiful modern again, a woman who has tried and refuses to try longer, to be happy with clay dolls. And Mary McCullom—"

"Is submerged in tea—past resuscitation.... That modern madness will pass, too, dear. 'Member how those Italian giants used to have periods of madness while they decorated the everlasting cathedrals? No modern man could come into your studio and break your work for long, Vina. You know we promised each other that none could." Beth shivered at her memory. Vina had made her forget for a moment.

"But we said in our haste then, that all men were just natives—"

"Many wise women say so at their leisure—"

"But Mary McCullom—"

"Taboo—"

"Well, then, *he* made me see there were real men in the world," Vina declared with slow defiance.

"Oh."

"You're sure to misunderstand. Please listen carefully. He is as far *to me*—from being that kind of a real man—as a mere native. Do you understand?... I could worship through him, as through a pure priest—"

"Vina, you're a passionate idealist!"

"You don't know him. I think he is beyond sex—or going beyond. Perhaps he doesn't know it.... Oh, we've been hurt a little, by boys who failed to grow into men, and so we took to our breasts painted and molded images, saying there *are* no real men. And here in our midst comes more than we ask or dream—a Prophet in the making. That's very clear to me, and you'll see it!... The result—a clearer vision into clay and its possibilities, and an expanded conception of my subjects—that's one point and a wonderful one. I'm grateful, but there's another.... Oh, Beth, I'm sick unto nausea with repression. Why, should I deny it; I want a real lover among men, and I want live dolls!"

A trenchant moment to Beth Truba. No one, so well as she, could perceive the tragedy of this gifted woman, whom the right man had missed in the crush of the world's women. A real artist, but a greater woman.... More than this was revealed to Beth. Her own Shadowy Sister was speaking to her with Vina Nettleton's tongue, as Beth Truba could never speak of another...

The Grey One, too, had her tragedy; and Kate Wilkes had hers long ago, a strong woman, whose cup of bitterness had overflowed in her veins; who had come so to despise men, as to profess disliking children. Indeed, that moment, Beth Truba seemed to hear the whispered affirmations of tragedy from evolved women everywhere....And whither was tending the race, if only the Wordlings of the world were to be satisfied—if Wordlings were all that men cared for? What was to become of the race, if the few women who loved art, and through art learned really to love their kind, were forever to be denied? And here was Vina Nettleton with the spiritual power to concentrate her dream into an avatar (if into the midst of her solitary labors, a great man's love should suddenly come)!... Did the Destiny Master fall asleep for a century at a time, that such a genius for motherhood should be denied, while the earth was being replenished with children of chance, branded with commonness and forever afraid?

Beth Truba shook herself from this crippling rush of thoughts, and started to her feet.

"Vina, you've been drinking deep of power. You're a giantess reeking with mad contagions. Also, you're a heretic. Allow me to remind you that we are spinsters; born and enforced, and decently-to-be-buried *spinsters*. It isn't the Sailor-man, but the spring of the year, that makes us a bit feverish. We should go to the catacombs for this season, when this devil's rousing is in the air.... If you have anything further to say, purely in regard to artistic inspirations, you may go on—"

Vina sat rigidly before her, wan and white-lipped as if her emotions were burned out. Presently she began to talk again in her trailing pensive way:

"I had been working deep and doggedly for days, hardly noticing who came in or out. When the Grey One entered with him, I felt myself bobbing, whirling up into light surface water. I hardly spoke the first half hour. I remembered the night before, when he told that fine story straight into your eyes. I thought him wonderful then, and it occurred to me that you were in for it. But it was different when he came into my shop—something intimate and important. His eyes roved from one 'Station' to another, while the Grey One exploited me in her absurd, selfless fashion. She's a third in our trouble Beth.

"Presently he asked me how I knew the Christ had such wonderful hands; then he talked of the Forerunner and Saint Paul, who could have done so much, had they been there during the Passion, and of the women who *were* there. It was strange to have him come into the studio—to me—with all these pictures developed through silent years. It seems to me something tremendous must come of it... Someone knocked, and frenziedly I ordered the intruder away, without opening the door."

And now Vina repeated the belief of Bedient that impressed her so deeply: that the Holy Spirit is the source of the divine principle in woman; that the Marys of this world are the symbols of that Mystic Motherhood—the third of the Trinity—which will bring the races of the world to God, as a woman brings children to her husband.

"Everything he said glowed with this message," she went on. "His every thought brought out that women are the holders of the spiritual loaf; that prophets are the sons of strength of great spiritual mothers; that artists and poets are prophets in the making, and that unto the purest and greatest of the prophets must come at last Godhood—the Three in One; and of this Jesus is the Exemplar; His life and death and rising, His whole Mission, should make us see with *human* eyes, the Way of Truth."

"I see, dear girl," Beth said softly, "*why* you could not open the door to anyone... Then the, Mission of Jesus was vicarious? I had about given up hope of comprehending that."

"Yes. He lived and moved and bled and died and rose before the eyes of common men!" Vina exclaimed. "One has to *bleed* for such eyes! Without the living sacrifice, only the rare souls here and there, with the highest prophetic vision, could have risen clearly to understand these things.... Thus the growth of spirituality was quickened among the lowly multitudes. The coming of the Christ is the loveliest manifestation of the divine feminine principle within Him— the Holy Spirit. Did he not become a Spiritual Mother of the world? Was not Godhood the next step for such a finished Spirit? His awful agony was that these tremendous mysteries of His illumination were enacted in the hideous low pressures of human understanding. That he could endure this for the world's eye, is his greatness, his Godhood!"

"And Mr. Bedient comes out of India with this Christian conception?"

"Beth," Vina said solemnly, "I believe there is meaning in that, too. The beauty and simplicity of that Sacrifice has been husked in dogmas for centuries, and we here have not torn them all away. He had just the Book and the Silence, and his own rare mind!"

*   *   *   *   *

"But, Vina, how could these things of pure religious fervor and beauty bring about that other rebellion of yours—the Mary McCullom one?"

"Oh, in a hundred ways; I'm all tired out now, but they'll come back. In a hundred ways, Beth, he spoke of women— with that same fervor and beauty. Just as he cleared and made exalted the Mystic Motherhood of the Christ, he pointed out how it works among *us*. Why, he says that there is nothing worth reading nor regarding nor listening to in the world of art, that has not that visioning feminine quality. The artist must be evolving through spirit, before his book or painting or symphony begins to live. All the rest of art is a mere squabbling over the letter of past prophecies, as the Jews did with the living Christ in their streets!... What a mother he must have had! I seemed to see her—to sense her—beside him. It was as if *she* looked into my heart and the Grey One's heart, and with her hand on her big boy's head, said to us, smiling and happily: 'This is *my* art—and he lives! You have but to look into your own hearts, you listening women, to know that he lives!'... Oh, Beth, her work does live to bless her! Can't you see how dead-cold the clay felt to my fingers after that?"

"Did he speak of his mother?"

"No."

Beth arose. "Vina," she said, "we are absolutely detached from the centres of sanity. We shall now walk Broadway, not the Avenue, but Broadway, to get back to markets and mere men. You're too powerful for this poor little room—"

"You always talk and laugh, Beth, but you're confronted and you know it. Confronted—that's the thing! Woman or artist—there's no word so naked and empty to me as just *artist*—"

"Only *spinster*," Beth suggested, shivering.

Vina stretched out her frail arms wearily, and her eyes suddenly fastened upon a fresh heather-plant on the corner of the writing-table. "Oh, please, drop a veil over that little bush," she pleaded. "It's arrayed like a bride—"

"A bridal veil, dear?"

"'No, no, a shawl, a rug!"

*　*　*　*　*

Beth returned alone at dusk. In some ways the afternoon was memorable. It was hard for her to keep her doubts about Bedient. Most of all that impressed her was Vina's sense of the mother's nearness to the man. She had thought of that at once, as she listened to his story. And he had not told Vina nor the Grey One about his mother... She sat down at her table and drew forth the opened but unread letter from Albany.

"Woman or artist," she whispered bitterly, "as if one could not be both!...It is only because a woman-and-artist requires a man who can love artistically. Few men can do that—and anything else beside.... Can you, Sailor-man?... Not if you explain to me why I found you at Wordling's.... Perhaps I can forgive you, after all the lovely things you've said. Anyway I shall tell no one...."

"Dear Miss Truba: I want to have a portrait painted of myself. I'm convinced that you can do it very well. Will you undertake the work? I shall be back in New York shortly after this letter reaches you Monday, and will wait at the Club until I hear from you. Yours, Andrew Bedient."

There was an instant in which she was conscious of something militant, something of the quiet power of the man who does not go home empty-handed. In his leaving the city Saturday, she perceived one who wishes to avoid the appearance of evil, and is content to leave his movements unexplained, trusting to another's perception.

"Vina is right," she said slowly. "'Confronted' is the word."

FIFTEENTH CHAPTER

THE STORY OF THE MOTHER

Andrew Bedient had entered the company of lovers.... There have been great lovers who were not otherwise great men, but never a great man who was not a great lover.... On the night he had first seen Beth Truba across the table, deep within there had been a swift ignition of altar-flames that would never cease to burn. Often in his reading and thinking, in pictures he had seen, and in his limited adventures into music; wherever, in fact, man had done well in the arts, the vision of some great woman was behind the work for his eyes; famous and lovely women long-dead, whose kisses are imperishable in tone or pigment or tale; women who called to themselves for a little space the big-souled men of their time, and sent them away illustrious. And these men forever afterward brought their art to witness that such women are the way to the Way of Life.

Bedient had rejoiced to discover the two women in every great man's life: the woman who visioned his greatness in the mothering; and the woman who saw it potentially afterward—and ignited it. How often the latter loosed a landslide of love at the ignition, and how seldom she stepped aside to let it pass!

Will Levington Comfort

All this thinking for years upon the beauty and fineness of women was focussed now.... The depth of his humility, and the vastness of his appreciation were the essential beginnings of the love of this hour, just as they would be, if he were ready to perform some great creative expression in art. The boyhood of a genius is a wild turning from one passionate adoration to another among the masters of his art; often his gift of appreciation is a generation ahead of his capacity to produce. And love is the genius of mothering, the greatest of all the arts. The love that a man inspires in a woman's heart is *her* expression of the Holy Spirit. According to the degree and beauty of that love, does the woman's child lift its head above the brute; according to the greater or lesser expression of this Mystic Motherhood in the world, at a certain hour, must be determined the morality of the race.

A fortnight in New York had terrorized Bedient. He perceived that men had not humility, nor passionate appreciation for anything; that they were dazed with their own or other men's accumulations; that they destroyed every dream of woman, drove the kingdom of heaven from her heart, with their comings and their goings and their commonness. He came to believe that this was an age of impossible men, impossible lovers, artists, and critics, because they had not the delicacy and wisdom to accept the finer forces, which women bring into the world for men.

Indeed, he saw that this was woman's gray hour of restless hoping, pitiful dreaming and untellable pain; that out of these must come the new generation. Then it appeared to him with splendid cheer, that woman had not fallen to these modern miseries, but *risen* to them, from a millenium of serfdom, untimely outraging, hideous momentary loving, brute mastery, ownership and drudgery.... These of to-day were finer sufferings; this an age of transition in which she was passing through valleys of terrible shadow, but having preserved her natural greatness through the milleniums, she could not fail now with her poor gleanings of real love to give the world a generation of finer-grained men.

Women, then, he thought, have a natural greatness which man cannot destroy. If men were able to destroy it, the sources of the saving principle of the race would be shut off. But marvellously can man *inspire* this natural greatness, make it immense and world-swaying by bringing out the best of women, and yet how few have this chivalry! Here was the anguish, the failure. With his mind filled with these illimitable possibilities, Bedient was overcome with his insight of New York, the awfulness of ignorance and cruelty in the ordinary relations of man with woman.

Bedient firmly believed that if women were granted (a heavenly dispensation, it would have to be) a decade of happiness beginning now, a decade of lovers of their own choosing, men of delicacy and wisdom, that thirty years from now there would be that poise and sweetness in the world that dreamers descry in far future ages. And here and there would be a beyond-man, indeed; and here and there cosmic, instead of mere self-consciousness.

He believed that the greatest miracle for the unsealed eye in this day, was that woman had emerged from a degraded past with this powerful present vitality; the capacity to hope and dream and suffer and be aroused; that she had the fervor and power of visioning *left* to be aroused! Surely this was the Third of the Trinity sustaining her.... Bedient began to study with sympathy and regard those groups of women, willing to sacrifice the best of their natures and descend into man's spheres of action, there to wring from man on his own ground the privileges so doggedly withheld. He saw that their sacrifice was heroic; that their cause was "in the air"; that this was but one startling manifestation of a great feminist seething over the world; and yet every brightness of evolution depended, as he saw it, upon woman being herself, retaining first of all those stores of beauty and spirit which are designed to be her gifts to manhood and the race. In the eyes of the future, he believed, these women would stand as the inspired pioneers of a rending transition period.

The note that came from Beth Truba, saying that she would see him about the portrait at two on Tuesday, Bedient regarded as one of the happiest things that ever befell. It was delivered at the Club by messenger that Monday night. Very well he knew, that she gracefully might have declined, and would have, had she not been able to look above a certain misleading event.

There were moments in which he seemed always to have known Beth Truba. Had he come back after long world-straying?

There was a painting of Bernhardt in an upper gallery at the Club, that he had regarded with no little emotion during past days. The face of the greatest actress, so intensely feminine, in strangely effective profile between a white feathery collar and a white fur hat, had made him think of Beth Truba in a score of subtle ways. They told him that the painting had been done by a young Italian, who had shown the good taste to worship the creator of *La Samaritaine*.... Bedient wished he could paint the russet-gold hair and the lustrous pallor of ivory which shone from Beth's skin, and put upon the canvas at the last, what had been a revelation to him, and which had carried credentials to the Bedient throne, to the very crown-cabinet of his empire, the fine and enduring spirit in her brilliant eyes.

They met in the studio on the business basis. It was a gray day, one of those soft, misty, growing days. She was a trifle taller than he had thought. Something of the world-habit was about her, or world-wear, a professionalism that work had taught her, and a bit of humor now and then. The studio was filled with pictures, many studies of her own, bits of Paris and Florence, many flowers and heads. There was one door which opened into a little white room. The door was only partly open, and it was shut altogether presently. Bedient had only looked *within* it once, but reverently. Besides, there was a screen which covered an arcanum, from which tea and cakes and sandwiches came on occasion. An upright piano, some shelves of books, an old-fashioned mantle and fireplace; and the rest—pictures and yellow-brown hangings and lounges. He wondered if anyone ever saw Beth's pictures so deeply as he.... She was in her blouse. The gray light subdued the richness of her hair, but made her pallor more luminous. She was very swift and still in her own house.

A chair was placed for him, and Beth went back to her stool under the light. Occasionally she asked him to look at certain pictures in her room, studying him as he turned. She told him of adorable springtimes in Florence; how once she had asked a beautiful Italian peasant boy to help her with an easel, and some other matters, up a long flight of marble steps, and he had answered, with drowsy gentleness, "Please ask another boy, Signorina. I have dined to-day."... And Bedient watched, when her head was bowed over the board upon her knee. Her hair, so wonderful now in the shadows, made amazing promises for sunlit days. Uncommon energy was in his heart, and a buoyant activity of mind that formed, one after another, ideals for her happiness.

"Yesterday at this time," she said finally, "Vina Nettleton was here. She spoke of your great help in her work—"

"Her studio was thrilling to me.... Altogether, getting back to New York has been my greatest experience."

"You have been away very long?"

"So long that I don't remember leaving, nor anything about it, except the boats and whistles, the elevated railways and the Park, and certain strains of music. I remember seeing the animals, and the hall of that house—"

"Where the light frightened you?"

"Yes. And I remember the bees.... I have ridden through and about the Park several times, but I can't seem to get anything back. I felt like asking questions, as I did long ago, of my mother."

Beth wanted to tell him that she would ride with him sometime and answer questions, but he seemed very near the deep places, and she dared not urge nor interrupt.

"It was very clear to me then, that we needed each other," he added. "A child knows that. She must have answered all the questions in the world, for I was always satisfied. I wonder that she had time to think about her own things.... Isn't it remarkable, and I don't remember anything she said?"

Bedient seemed to be thinking aloud, as if this were the right place to talk of these things. They had been in the foreground of his mind continually, but never uttered before.

"It was always above words—our relation," he went on presently. "Though we must have talked and talked—it is not the words I remember—but realizations of truth which came to me afterward, from them. What a place for a little boy's hand to be!...

"I remember the long voyage, and she was always near. There were many strange things—far too strange to remember; and then, the sick room. She was a long time there. I could not be with her as much as I wanted. It was very miserable all around, though it seems the people were not unkind. They must have been very poor. And then, one night I knew that my mother was going to die. I could not move, when this came to me. I tried not to breathe, tried to die too; and some one came in and shook me, and it was all red about my eyes.

"They took me to her, but I couldn't tell what I knew, though she saw it. And this I remember, though it was in the dark. The others were sent away, and she made a place for me on her arm, and she laughed, and whispered and whispered. Why, she made me over that night on her arm!

"She must have whispered it a thousand times—so it left a lasting impression. Though I could not always see her, *she would always be near*! That remains from the night, though none of the words ever came back. I never lost that, and it was true.... Do you see how great she was to laugh that night?... And how she had to struggle to leave that message on such a little boy's mind?... More wonderful and wonderful it becomes, as I grow older. She was dying, and we had been such dependent lovers. She was not leaving me, as it *had* been with us, nor in any way as she liked....

"She must have grappled with all the forces that drive the world that night!... First, I was happy on her arm—and then, through the long hours, and mysteriously, she implanted her message.... And see what came of it—see her strength! The actual parting was not so terrible—she had builded a fortress around me against that—not so terrible as the hours before, when I tried not to breathe."

Beth did not raise her eyes as he paused. She could not speak. The little boy had come home to her mind—like a wraith-child of her own. She was shaken with a passion of pity.

"It seems it was meant for me to stay in that house, but I couldn't," Bedient went on. "They probably bothered a great deal after I stole away, and tried to find me. But they didn't.... And I went down where there were ships. I think the ships fascinated me, because *we* had come on one. I slipped aboard, and fell asleep below. The sailors found me after we had cleared. They were very good, and called me 'Handy.'... I think my mother must have taught me my letters, for when an old sailor, with rings in his ears, pointed out to me the name of the ship on the jolly-boat, the letters came back to me. I was soon reading the Bible. That was the book I cut my teeth on, as they say.... And one time, as we were leaving port, I thought I had better have a name. One of the men had asked me, you see, and I was only able to say, 'Handy.' And just then, we passed an old low schooner. She had three masts; her planking was gray and weathered, and her seams gaped. On her stern, I saw in faded sprawly letters, that had been black:

"ANDREW BEDIENT

"Of—somewhere, I couldn't make out. So I took that for my name. It fitted 'Handy' and the little boy's idea of bigness and actuality, because I had seen it in print.... I never saw the old schooner again. I don't know the port in which she lay at the time; nor the port where my mother died. You see, I was very little.... Everyone was good to me. And it is true that my mother was near.... There were places and times that must have put dull care into her eyes, but she was the true sentry. I only *knew* when I was asleep."

It was beautiful to Beth, the way he spoke. His heart seemed to say, "God love her!" with every sentence.

Her lips breathed the words, her eyes had long questioned:

"And your father?"

The room suddenly filled with her fateful words.

"My father?" he repeated. "He was never with my mother. I did not understand until long afterward, but she meant me to understand—that she was not married. She impressed it upon my consciousness *for* me to understand—when I was older."

Beth could have knelt in her humility that moment.

"Please forgive me for asking," she faltered.

"It was right. I intended to tell you."

Some strange, sustaining atmosphere came from him. His words lifted her. Beth saw upon his brow and face the poise and fineness of a love-child.... With all the mother's giving there had been no name for him; and he had told her with all the ease and grace of one who knows in his heart—a mother's purity of soul.... It was hard for Beth to realize, with Bedient sitting there, that the world makes tragic secrets of these things he had told her; that lives of lesser men have been ruined with the fear of such discoveries.... Nothing of so intense and intimate appeal had ever come to her studio, as the heroism of this mother, impressing upon her tortured and desperate child, that though taken from him, she would be near always.... The sensitive Vina had seemed to see the mother *near* him, her hand upon his head, saying with a laugh, "This is my Art—and he *lives!*"

Beth spoke at last: "You honor me, Mr. Bedient, in telling me these deep things."

"This seemed the place," he said, leaning forward. "It's extraordinary when I recall I have only been here an hour or so. It would seem absurd to some women, but the story knew where it belonged.... In fact, it is hard for me to remember that this is our first talk alone.... Perhaps you should know, that I've never spoken of my mother to anyone else.... I never could find the port where she died."

They learned that they could be silent together.... Beth knew that she would have extended conference with the Shadowy Sister when alone. Big things were enacting in the depths. There was another thing that Vina had said regarding the appeal of Bedient personally to her, which required much understanding.... Beth had found herself thinking (in Bedient's presence) that she might have been hasty and imperious in sending the Other away. She had been rather proud of her iron courage up to this hour. Of course, it was ridiculous that Bedient should recall the Other, and after months suggest her unreasonableness; yet these things recurred.... Moreover, a moment after Bedient's entering, there had been no embarrassment between them. Not only had they dared be silent, but they had not tried each other out tentatively by talking about people they knew. Then he had said it was hard for him to remember this was their first talk together alone. Beth realized that here was a subject who would not bore her before his portrait was finished.

"Does David Cairns know Miss Nettleton very well?" Bedient asked, as he was leaving.

She smiled at the question, and was about to reply that they had been right good friends for years, when it occurred that he might have a deeper meaning.

Bedient resumed while she was thinking: "I know that he admires her work and intelligence, but he never spoke to me of any further discoveries. Perhaps he wouldn't.... He's a singularly fine chap, finer than I knew.... I noticed a short essay in your stand that contains a sentence I cannot forget. It was about a rare man who 'stooped and picked up a fair-coined soul that lay rusting in a pool of tears.'"

"Browning," she said excitedly.

"Yes.... Good-by and thank you.... To-morrow?"

"Yes."

* * * * *

He left her in the whirl of this new conception. She was taking dinner with David Cairns that night. David, she felt, had arranged this for further urging in the matter of her seeing his friend. And now she smiled at the surprise in store for him; then for a long time, until the yellows and browns were thickly shadowed about her, Beth sat very still, thinking about the Vina Nettleton of yesterday, and the altered and humble David Cairns of the past fortnight.... In the single saying of Bedient's, that he had found Cairns finer than he knew, there was a remarkable, winsome quality for her perception. Bedient had started the revolution which was clearing the inner atmospheres of his friend; and yet, he refused any part.

David took her for dinner to a club far down-town—a dining-room on the twentieth floor, overlooking the rivers and the bay, the shipping and the far shores pointed off with lights.... They waited by a window in the main hall for a moment while a smaller room was being arranged. Forty or more business men were banqueting in a glare of light and glass and red roses—a commercial dinner with speeches. The talk had to do with earnings, per cents, leakages, markets and such matters. The lower lid of many an eye was updrawn in calculation.

Beth shivered, for she saw avarice, cunning, bluff, campaigning with humor and natural forces. "The starry night and the majestic rivers might just as well be plaster-walls," she whispered. "What terrible occupations are these to make our brothers so dull, bald and stodgy-looking?"

"It's their art," said Cairns. "They start in merrily enough, but it's a fight out in the centre of the current. You see them all of one genial dining-countenance, yet this day they fought each other in the streets below, and to-morrow again.... It's not only the sweep of the current, but each other, they have to fight.... Oh, it's very easy for an artist to look and feel superior, Beth, but we know very well how much is sordid routine in our own decenter games—and suppose we had been called to money-making instead. It would catch us young, and we'd either harden or fail."

... They were taken to a place of stillness and the night-view was restoring.... Though Cairns had just left Bedient, he had not been told about the portrait nor the first sitting. Beth wondered if Bedient foresaw that she would appreciate this. She was getting so that she could believe anything of the Wanderer. For a long time they talked about him.... Cairns already was emerging from the miseries of reaction; new ways of work had opened; he was fired with fresh growth and delights of service. Beth was charmed with him.... At last she said:

"Nor has Mr. Bedient missed those rare and subtle things which make Vina Nettleton the most important woman of my acquaintance."

The sentence was a studied challenge.

"You mean in her work?" he said, under the first spur.

"Did I say *artist*? I meant woman—'most important woman'—"

"That's what you said."

"Yes, I thought so—" Beth shaded the interior light from her eyes to regard the night through the open window. "It was misty gray all day, and yet it is clear now as a summer night."

"And so Bedient sees more than a remarkable artist in Vina?" Cairns mused.

"That much is for the world to see.... Why, those dollar-eating gentlemen in the big room could see that, if they interested themselves in her kind of work. But they are not trained to know real women. Their work keeps them from knowing such things. When they marry a real woman, it's an accident, largely. A diadem of paste would have caught their eyes quite as quickly. Sometimes I think they prefer paste jewels.... Only here and there a man of deep discernment reads the truth—and is held by it. What a fortune is that discernment! A woman may well tremble before that kind of vision, for it is her own, empowered with a man's understanding—"

"Why, Beth, that's Bedient's mind exactly!" Cairns exclaimed. "A woman's vision of the finest sort, empowered with a man's understanding—"

"Of the finest sort," Beth finished laughingly. "By the way, that's a good definition of a prophet, isn't it?"

"It does work out," he said, thinking hard.

Beth observed with interest at this point, that Bedient had confined his discussion of the visioning feminine principle to Vina. There were several approaches to his elevation.

"How glorious it is to see things, David!" she exclaimed happily. "Even to see things after they are pointed out. And you—I'm really so glad about you! You're coming along so finely, and putting away boyish things."

She reached across the table and dropped her hand upon his sleeve.

"It's so tonic and bracing to watch one's friend burst into bloom!... I needed the stimulus, too. You are helping me."

It was Cairns' turn to shade his eyes for a clearer view of the night.

SIXTEENTH CHAPTER

"THROUGH DESIRE FOR HER"

David Cairns left Beth at her elevator, and walked down the Avenue toward Gramercy. It was still an hour from midnight. As he had hoped, Bedient was at the Club. The library was deserted, and they sat down in the big chairs by the open window. The only lights in the large room were those on the reading table. The quiet was actually interesting for down-town New York.

"I've been out hunting up music," Bedient said. "There is a place called the *Columbine* where you eat and drink; and a little Hungarian violinist there with his daughter—surely they can't know how great they are! He played the *Kreutzer Sonata*, the daughter accompanying as if it were all in the piano, and she just let it out for fun, and then they played it again for me—"

Cairns laughed at his joy. Bedient suddenly leaned forward and regarded him intently through the vague light. "David," he said, "you're looking fit and happy, and I'm very glad to see you." This was a way of Bedient's at unexpected moments.... "Do you know, it's a marvellous life you live," he went on, "looking inward upon the great universe of ideas constantly, balancing thought against thought, seeking the best vehicle, and weighing the effects—for or against the Ultimate Good—"

"It appears that you had to come up here—to show me—"

"It's good of you to say so, David, but you had to be Cairns and not New York! A woman would have shown you—"

Cairns had met before, in various ways, Bedient's unwillingness to identify himself with results of his own bringing about. Beth had long realized his immaturity, yet she had not spoken. Cairns saw this now.

"A woman would have shown me—?" he repeated.

"That the way to heaven is always against the crowd," Bedient finished.... "A few days after I came to New York, you joined me at the Club. You said you couldn't work; that you found your mind stealing away from the pages before you. I knew you were getting closer to real work then. David, when you find yourself stealing mentally away to follow some pale vision or shade of remembrance, don't jerk up, thinking you must get back to work. Why, you're nearer real work in following the phantoms than mere gray matter ever will unfold for you. Creating is a process of the depths; the brain is but the surface of the instrument that produces. How wearisome music would be, if we knew only the major key! How terrible would be sunlight, if there were no night! Out of darkness and the deep minor keys of the soul come those utterances vast and flexible enough to contain reality."

"Why don't you write, Andrew?" Cairns asked.

"New York has brought one thought to my mind with such intensity, that all others seem to have dropped back into the melting-pot," Bedient answered.

"And that one?"

"The needs of women."

"I have heard your tributes to women—"

"I have uttered no tributes to women, David!" Bedient said, with uncommon zeal. "Women want no tributes; they want truth.... The man who can restore to woman those beauties of consciousness which belong to her—which men have made her forget—just a knowledge of her incomparable importance to the race, to the world, to the kingdom of heaven—and help woman to make men see it; in a word, David, the man who can make men see what women are, will perform in this rousing hour of the world—the greatest good of his time!"

"Go on, it is for me to listen!"

"You can break the statement up into a thousand signs and reasons," said Bedient. "We hear such wonderful things about America in Asia—in India. Waiting for a ship in Calcutta, I saw a picture-show for the first time. It ran for a half hour, showing the sufferings of a poor Hindu buffeted around the world—a long, dreary portion of starvation, imprisonment and pain. The dramatic climax lifted me from the chair. It was his heaven and happiness. His stormy passage was ended. I saw him standing in the rain among the steerage passengers of an Atlantic steamer—and suddenly through the gray rushing clouds, appeared the Goddess of Liberty. He had come home at last—to a port of freedom and peace and equality—"

"God have mercy on him," murmured Cairns.

"Yes," said Bedient, "a poor little shaking picture show, and

I wept like a boy in the dark. It was my New York, too....
But we shall be that—all that the world in its distress and
darkness thinks of us, we must be. You know a man is at his
best with those who think highly of him. The great world-
good must come out of America, for its bones still bend, its
sutures are not closed.... You and I spent our early years
afield with troops and wars, before we were adult enough to
perceive the bigger conflict—the sex conflict. This is on,
David. It must clear the atmosphere before men and women
realize that their interests are *one*; that neither can rise by
holding down the other; that the present relations of men and
women, broadly speaking, are false to themselves, to each
other, and crippling to the morality and vitality of the race.

"You have seen it, for it is about you. The heart of woman
to-day is kept in a half-starved state. That's why so many
women run to cultists and false prophets and devourers, who
preach a heaven of the senses. In another way, the race is
sustaining a tragic loss. Look at the young women from the
wisest homes—the finest flower of young womanhood—our
fairest chance for sons of strength. How few of them marry!
I tell you, David, they are afraid. They prefer to accept the
bitter alternative of spinsterhood, rather than the degrading
sense of being less a partner than a property. They see that
men are not grown, except physically. They suffer, unmated,
and the tragedy lies in the leakage of genius from the race."

Cairns' mind moved swiftly from one to another of the five
women he had called together to meet his friend.

"David," Bedient added after a moment, "the man who does
the great good, must do it *through* women, for women are
listening to-day! Men are down in the clatter—examining,
analyzing, bartering. The man with a message must drive it
home through women! If it is a true message, they will *feel*
it. Women do not analyze, they realize. When women realize

their incomparable importance, that they are identified with everything lovely and of good report under the sun, they will not throw themselves and their gifts away. First, they will stand together—a hard thing for women, whose great love pours out so eagerly to man—stand together and demand of men, Manliness. Women will learn to withhold themselves where manliness is not, as the flower of young womanhood is doing to-day.... I tell you, David, woman can make of man anything she wills—by withholding herself from him.... *Through his desire for her*!... This is her Power. This is all in man that electricity is in Nature—a measureless, colossal force. Mastering that (and to woman alone is the mastery), she can light the world. Giving away to it ignorantly, she destroys herself."

... So much was but a beginning. Their talk that night was all that the old Luzon nights had promised, which was a great deal, indeed.... It was not until Cairns was walking home, that he recalled his first idea in looking in upon Bedient that night—a sort of hope that his friend would talk about Vina Nettleton in the way Beth had suggested. "How absurd," he thought, "that is exactly the sort of thing he would leave for me to find out!"

SEVENTEENTH CHAPTER

THE PLAN OF THE BUILDER

New York had brought Andrew Bedient rather marvellously into his own. He awoke each morning with a ruling thought. He lived in a state of continual transport; he saw all that was savage in his race, and missed little that was beautiful. Work was forming within him; he felt all the inspiritings, all the strange pressures of his long preparation. He realized that his thirty-three years had been full years; that all the main exteriors of man's life had passed before him in swift review, as a human babe in embryo takes on from time to time the forms of the great stations of evolution. He had passed without temptation from one to another of the vast traps which catch the multitude; nor tarried at a single one of the poisoned oasis of sense. Mother Earth had taken him to her breast; India had lulled his body and awakened his spirit; he had gone up to his Sinai there.

He looked back upon the several crises in which he might have faltered, and truly it seemed to him that he had been guided through these, by some wiser spirit, by something of larger vision, at least, than his own intelligence. Humility and thankfulness became resurgent at the memory of these times. Books of beauty and wisdom had come to his hand, it seemed, at the certain particular instants when he was ready.

Exactly as he had been spared the terrible temptations of flesh in his boyhood years, so had he preserved a humble spirit in his intellectual attainments. It was not he, but the poise that had been given him, through which he was enabled to cry out in gratitude this hour; for the soul of man meets a deadlier dragon in intellectual arrogance than in the foulest pits of flesh. The Destiny Master can smile in pity at a poor brain, brutalized through bodily lusts, but white with anger is the countenance that regards a spirit, maimed and sick from being yoked together with a proud mind. Angels burst into singing when that spirit is free.

His health was a perfect thing; of that kind that men dream of, and boys know, but do not stop to feel. He could smell the freshness of pure water in his bath or when he drank; there was delight in the taste of common foods; at night in his high room, higher still than the studio of Vina Nettleton, there were moments when the land-wind seemed to bring delicacies from the spring meadows of Jersey; or blowing from the sea, he sensed the great sterile open. He was tireless, and could discern the finest prints and weaves at bad angles of light.

He moved often along the water-fronts and through abandoned districts; a curious sense of unreality often came over him in these night rambles, as if he were tranced among the perversions of astral light. He gave a great deal, but saw that if he gave his life nightly, even that would not avail. His money was easily passed into another hand; that would not do—little vessels of oil overturned upon an Atlantic of storm. These were but tentative givings; they denied him nothing. Bedient saw that he must give more than this, and waited for the way.... The most poignant and heart-wringing experience for him in New York was suddenly to find himself in the midst of the harried human herd, when it was trying to play. One can best read a city's tragedy at its pleasure-places.

...Beth Truba was his great ignition. His love for her overflowed upon all things.... The hour or more in her studio became the feature of his day. Bedient was not shown the work on the portrait. Beth didn't altogether like the way it progressed. Sometimes, she talked as she worked (sitting low beneath the skylight, so that every change of light was in her hair, while the spring matured outside). Deep realities were often uttered thus, sentences which bore the signet of her strong understanding, for they passed through the stimulated faculties of the artist, engrossed in her particular expression. Thus the same intelligence which colored her work, distinguished her sayings.... Bedient daily astonished her. Again and again, she perceived that he had come to New York, full of power from his silences apart. She wanted him to preserve his freshness of vision. His quiet expressions thrilled her.

"The women I know, married or unmarried, are nearly all unhappy," she said, one day. "My younger friends, even among girls, are afraid. They see that men are blinded by things they can taste and see and touch—speed, noise and show. The married women are restless and terrified by spiritual loneliness. The younger women see it and are afraid."

"'Had I but two loaves of bread, I should sell one to buy white hyacinths,'" Bedient quoted; "I like to think of that line of Mahomet's.... Women are ready for white hyacinths—the bread of life.... But this spiritual loneliness is a wonderful sign. The spirit floods in where it can—where it is sought after—and the children of women who are hungry for spiritual things, are children of dreams. They must be. They may not be happy, but they will feel a stronger yearning to go out alone and find 'the white presences among the hills.'"

Beth was silent.

"Yearning is religion," Bedient added. "Hunger of the heart for higher things will bring spiritual expansion. Look at the better-born children to-day. I mean those who do not have *every* chance against them. I seem to catch a new tone in the murmur of this rousing generation. They have an expanded consciousness. It is the spiritual yearnings of motherhood."

"But what of the woman who will not take the bowl of porridge that ordinary man gives her?" Beth demanded. "So many women dare not—cannot—and then their dreams, their best, are not reflected in the consciousness of the new race."

Bedient smiled, and Beth regarded her work intently, for an echo of the confessional had come back to her from her own words.

"That is a matter so intensely individual," he replied. "We are at the beginning of the woman's era, and with every transition there are pangs to be suffered by those who are great enough. These great ones are especially prepared to see how terrible is their denial from the highest privileges of woman. And yet they may be spiritual mothers, centres of pure and radiant energy. Every work of genius has been inspired by such a woman. And if, as sometimes happens, a true lover does come, the two are so happy that the temperature of the whole race warms through them."

"What an optimist!" she said, but when alone, it came to her that he had been less certain than usual in this answer. Perhaps, he had felt her stress upon realizing the personal aspect; perhaps he had too many things to say, and was not ready. It *was* a matter intensely individual. However, this was the only time he had failed to carry her critical attention.

Bedient saw that the years had locked one door after another about the real heart of Beth Truba. His work was plain—to unlock them one by one. How the task fascinated; he made it his art and his first thought.

"You change so," she complained laughingly, after there had been several sittings. "I'm afraid I shall paint you very badly because I am trying so hard. You don't look at all the same as you did at first. Therefore all the first must be destroyed."

Bedient knew if his work prospered, all that had been before would be redeemed.

One morning—it was one of the first of the May mornings—there was something like heart-break in the room. Up on the skylight, the sparrows were debating whether it would rain or not. There was tension in the air which Bedient tried to ease from every angle. Consummately he set about to restore and reassure, but she seemed to feel her work was faring ill; that life was an evil thing. All the brightness that had suffused her mind from his presence, again and again, had vanished apparently, leaving not the slightest glow behind.

"Don't bother to work on this to-day," he said. "I am not in the slightest hurry and you are to do it wonderfully. Please be sure that I know that.... Will you go with me to the Metropolitan galleries to-day?"

Beth smiled, and went on deliberating before the picture. Presently, the tension possessed her again. She looked very white in the North light.

"Did you ever doubt if you were really in the world?" she asked after a moment, but did not wait, nor seem to expect an answer.... "I have," she added, "and concluded that I only thought I was here—queer sense of unreality that has more than once sent me flying to the telephone after a day's work alone—to hear my own voice and be answered. But, even if one proves that one is indeed here, one can never get an answer to the eternal—*What for?*... I shall do a story, sometime, and call it *Miss What For*.... A young girl who came into the world with greatness of vitality and enthusiasm, alive as few humans are, and believing in everything and everybody. Before she was fully grown, she realized that she was not sought after so much as certain friends whose fathers had greater possessions. This was terrible. It took long for her to believe that nothing counted so much as money. It made the world a nightmare, but she set to work to become her own heiress.... In this struggle she must at last lose faith. This can be brought about by long years, smashing blows and incredible suffering, but the result must be made complete—to fit the title."

"But, why do you try to fit such a poor shivering little title?"

She smiled wearily. "I was trying, perhaps, to picture one of your spiritual mothers, centres of pure and radiant energy, in one of the *other* moments, that the world seldom sees. The power is almost always turned on, when the world is looking."

She had made him writhe inwardly, as no one else could.

"But there *are* many such women," she went on, "victims of your transition period, caught between the new and the old, helpers, perhaps, of the Great Forces at work which will bring better conditions; but oh, so helpless!... They may bring a little cheer to passing souls who quickly forget; they may even inspire genius, as you say, but what of themselves when they, all alone, see that they have no real place in the world, no lasting effect, leaving no image, having no part in the plan of the Builder?"

Bedient arose. Beth saw he was not ready to answer.

"A visit to the galleries is tempting," she said. "It may give me an idea.... I never had quite such a patron. You are so little curious to see what I have done, that I sometimes wonder why you wanted the portrait, and why you came to me for it.... I wonder if it's the day or my eyes—it's so much easier to talk aimlessly than to work—"

"It's really gray, and the sparrows have decided upon a shower."

She regarded him whimsically.

"And you look so well in your raincoat," he added.

They took the 'bus up the Avenue.... She pointed out the tremendous vitalities of the Rodin marbles, intimated their visions, and remarked that he should hear Vina Nettleton on this subject.

"She breaks down, becomes livid, at the stupidity of the world, for reviling her idol on his later work, especially the bust of Balzac, which the critics said showed deterioration," Beth told him, "As if Rodin did not know the mystic Balzac better than the populace."

"It has always seemed that the mystics of the arts must recognize one another," Bedient said.... "I do not know Balzac—"

"You must. Why, even Taine, Sainte Beuve, and Gautier didn't *know* him! They glorified his work just so long as it had to do with fleshly Paris, but called him mad in his loftier altitudes where they couldn't follow."

It was possibly an hour afterward, when Bedient halted before a certain picture longer than others; then went back to another that had interested him. Moments passed. He seemed to have forgotten all exteriors, but vibrated at intervals from one to another of these—two small silent things—*Le Chant du Berger* and another. They were designated only by catalogue numbers. Beth, who knew them, would have waited hours.... Presently he spoke, and told her long of their effects, what they meant to him.

"You have not been here before?" she asked.

"No."

"You don't know who did those pictures?"

"No."

"Puvis de Chavannes."

"The name is but a name to me, but the work—why, they are out of the body entirely! I can feel the great silence!" he explained, and told her of his cliff and *God-mother*, of Gobind, the bees, the moon, the standing pools, the lotos, the stars, the forests, the voices and the dreams.... They stood close together, talking very low, and the visitors brushed past, without hearing.

"If not the greatest painter, Puvis de Chavannes is the greatest mural painter of the nineteenth century," Beth said. "Rodin, who knew Balzac, also knew Puvis de Chavannes.... *'The mystics of the arts know one another,'*" she added. "I saw Rodin's bust and statue of these men in Paris."

To Beth, the incident was of inestimable importance in her conception of Bedient.... A Japanese group interested him later—an old vender of sweetmeats in a city street, with children about him—little girls bent forward under the weight of their small brothers. Beth regarded the picture curiously and waited for Bedient to speak.

"It's very real," he said. "The little girls are crippled from these weights. The boy babe rides his sister for his first views of the world.... Look at the sweet little girl-faces, haggard from the burden of their fat-cheeked, wet-nosed brothers. A birth is a miss over there—a miss for which the mother suffers—when it is not a boy. The girls of Japan carry their brothers until they begin to carry their sons. You need only look at this picture to know that here is a people messing with uniforms and explosives, a people still hot with the ape and the tiger in their breasts."

Beth was thinking that America was not yet aeons distant from this Japanese institution, the male incubus of the girl child. She did not speak, for she was thinking of what she had said in the studio—of the edginess of her temper. "Spinsters may scold, but not spiritual mothers," she thought. She might have been very happy, but for a mental anchor fast to that gloomy mood of the morning.... Hours had flown magically. It was past mid-afternoon.... There was one more picture that had held him, not for itself, but like the Japanese scene, for the thoughts it incited.... An aged woman in a cheerless room, bending over the embers of a low fire. In the glow, the weary old face revealed a bitter loneliness, and yet it was strangely sustained. The twisted hands held to the fire, would have fitted exactly about the waist of a little child— which was not there.

"I would call her *The Race Mother*," Bedient said reverently. "She is of every race, and every age. She has carried her brothers and her sons; given them her strength; shielded them from cold winds and dangerous heats; given them the nourishment of her body and the food prepared with her hands. Their evils were her own deeper shame; their goodness or greatness was of her conceiving, her dreams first. Her sons have turned to her in hunger, her mate in passion, but neither as their equal. For that which was noble in their sight and of good report, they turned to men. In their counsels they have never asked her voice; they suffered her sometimes to listen to their devotions, but hers were given to them.

"They were stronger. They chose what should become the intellectual growth of the race. Having no part in this, her mind was stunted, according to their standards. She had the silences, the bearing, the services for others, the giving of love. She loved her mate sometimes, her brothers often, her sons always,—and served them. Loving much, she learned to love God. Silences, and much loving of men, one learns to love God. Silences and services and much loving of her kind—out of these comes the spirit which knows God.

"So while her men, like children with heavy blocks, were passing their intellectual matters one to the other, she came to know that love is giving; that as love pours out in service, the Holy Spirit floods in; that spaciousness of soul is immortality; that out of the spaciousness of soul, great sons are born.... And here and there down the ages, these great sons have appeared, veered the race right at moments of impending destruction, and buoyed it on."

He had not raised his voice above that low animate tone, which has not half the carrying quality of a whisper. Beth had hoped for such a moment, for in her heart she knew that Vina Nettleton had felt this power of his. With her whole soul, she listened, and the look upon his face which she wanted for the portrait lived in her mind as he resumed:

"I ask you to look how every evil, every combination of hell, has arisen to tear at the flanks of the race, for this is history. Yet a few women, and a few men, the gifts of women, have arisen to save.... Do you think that war or money, or lust of any kind, shall destroy us *now*, in this modern rousing hour, with woman at last coming into her own—when they have never yet in the darkest hour of the world, vanquished a single great dream of a pure woman? And now women *generally* are rising to their full dreams; approaching each moment nearer to that glorious formula for the making of immortals...."

He smiled suddenly into her white face. "I tell you, Beth Truba," he said, "there isn't a phase, a moment, of this harsh hour of transition, that isn't majestic with promise!... It's a good picture.... Dear old mother, in every province of the soul, she is a step nearer the Truth than man. The little matters of the intellect, from which she has been barred for centuries, she shall override like a Brunhilde. Even that which men called her sins were from loving.... Gaunt mother with bended back—she has stood between God and the world; she has been the vessel of the Holy Spirit; she *is* the Holy Spirit in the world; and when she shall fully know her greatness, then prophets of her bearing shall walk the earth."

They wound through the park in the rainy dusk, emerging in Fifty-ninth Street; and even then, Beth did not care to ride, so they finished the distance to her studio in the Avenue crowd.

EIGHTEENTH CHAPTER

THAT PARK PREDICAMENT

More May days had passed. Bedient came in from one of his night-strolls, just as an open carriage stopped in front of the Club, and Mrs. Wordling called his name. He waited while she dismissed her driver familiarly.... The Northern beauty of the night was full of charm to him. A full moon rode aloft in the blue. He had been thinking that there was cruelty and destruction wherever crowds gathered; that great cities were not a development of higher manhood. He thought of the sparcely tenanted islands around the world, of Australian, Siberian and Canadian areas—of glorious, virgin mountain places and empty shores—where these pent and tortured tens of thousands might have breathed and lived indeed. All they needed was but to dare. But they seemed not yet lifted from the herd; as though it took numbers to make an entity, a group to make a soul. The airs were still; the night serene as in a zone of peace blessed of God. The silence of Gramercy gave him back poise which the city—a terrible companion—had torn apart.

"That's old John, who never misses a night at my theatre door, when that door opens to New York," Mrs. Wordling said. "He only asks to know that I am in the city to be at my service night or day. And who would have a taxicab on a night like this?... Let's not hurry in.... Have you been away?"

"No, Mrs. Wordling."

"Don't you think you are rather careless with your friends?" she asked, as one whom the earth had made much to mourn. "It is true, I haven't been here many times for dinner (there have been so many invitations), but breakfasts and luncheons—always I have peeked into the farthest corners hoping to see you—before I sat down alone."

"I have missed a great deal, but it's good to be thought of," he said.

"You didn't mean, then, to be careless with your friends?"

"No."

"I thought you were avoiding me."

"If there were people here to be avoided, I'm afraid I shouldn't stay."

"But supposing you liked the place very much, and there was just one whom you wished to avoid—"

He laughed. "I give it up. I might stay—but I don't avoid— certainly not one of my first friends in New York—"

"Yes, I was a member of the original company, when David Cairns' *Sailor-Friend* was produced.... How different you seem from that night!" she added confidentially. "How is it you make people believe you so? You have been a great puzzle to me—to us. I supposed at first you were just a breezy individual, whom David Cairns (who is a very brilliant man) had found an interesting type—"

"So long as I don't fall from that, it is enough," Bedient answered. "But why do you say I make people believe—?"

Mrs. Wordling considered. "I never quite understood about one part of that typhoon story," she qualified. "You were carrying the Captain across the deck, and a Chinese tried to knife you. You just mentioned that the Chinese died."

"Yes," said Bedient, who disliked this part of the story, and had shirred the narrative.

"But I wanted to hear more about it—"

"That was all. He died. There were only a few survivors."

Mrs. Wordling's head was high-held. She was sniffing the night, with the air of a connoisseur. "Do you smell the mignonette, or is it Sweet William? Something we had in the garden at home when I was little.... Are you afraid to go across in the park—with *me*?"

"Sailors are never afraid," he said, following her pointed finger to the open gate.

They crossed the street laughingly. There had been no one at the Club entrance.... They never determined what the fragrance was, though they strolled for some time through the paths of the park, among the thick low trees, and finally sat down by the fountain. The moonlight, cut with foliage, was magic upon the water. Bedient was merry in heart. The rising error which might shadow this hour was clear enough to him, but he refused to reckon with it. He was interested, and a little troubled, to perceive there was nothing in common in Mrs. Wordling's mind and his. They spoke a different language. He was sorry, for he knew she could think hard and suddenly, if he had the power to say the exact thing. And that which he might have taken, and which her training had designed her both to attract and exact, Bedient did not want. All her sighs, soft tones, suddennesses and confidences fell wide; and yet, to Mrs. Wordling, he was too challenging and mysterious for her to be bored an instant. Their talk throughout was trifling and ineffectual, as it had begun. Mrs. Wordling was not Bedient's type. No woman could have dethroned Beth Truba this hour. Bedient was not sorry (nothing he had said seemed to animate) when Mrs. Wordling arose, and led the way to the gate... which had been locked meanwhile.

Mrs. Wordling was inclined to cry a little. "One couldn't possibly climb the fence!" she moaned.

"They have keys at the Club, haven't they?" Bedient asked.

"Yes. All the houses and establishments on the park front have keys. It's private—that far.... I should have known it would be locked after midnight. Our talk was so interesting!... Oh, one will die of exposure, and the whole Club will seethe."

Bedient patted her shoulder cheerfully, and led the way along the fence through the thick greenery, until they were opposite the Club entrance. He had not known the park was ever locked. He saw disturbance ahead—bright disturbance —but steadily refused to grant it importance. He was sorry for Mrs. Wordling.

"Let the Club seethe, if it starts so readily," he observed.

The remark astonished his companion, who had concluded he was either bashful to the depths, or some other woman's property, probably Beth Truba's.

"But you men have nothing to lose!" she exclaimed.

"I ask you to pardon me," Bedient said quickly. "I had not thought of it in that way."

They were watching the Club entrance. One o'clock struck over the city. Mrs. Wordling had become cold, and needed his coat, though she had to be forced to submit to its protection. At last, a gentleman entered the Club, and Bedient called to the page who appeared in the doorway. The boy stepped out into the street, when called a second time. Bedient made known his trouble. The keys were brought and richly paid for, though Bedient did not negotiate. The night-man smiled pleasantly, and cheered them, with the word that this had happened before, on nights less fine.

*   *   *   *   *

David Cairns had stepped into a telephone-booth in the main-hall of the *Smilax Club* the following afternoon, to announce his presence in the building to Vina Nettleton. Waiting for the exchange-operator to connect, he heard two pages talking about Bedient and Mrs. Wordling. These were bright street-boys, very clever in their uniforms, and courteous, but street-boys nevertheless; and they had not noted the man in the booth. A clouded, noisome thing, David Cairns heard. Doubtless it had passed through several grades of back-stair intelligence before it became a morsel for Cairns' particular informers. Having heard enough to understand, he kicked the door shut, and Vina found him distraught that day....

It was in the dusk of that afternoon when Cairns met Bedient, whose happiness was eminent and shining as usual. Cairns gave him a chance to mention the episode which had despoiled his own day, but Bedient seemed to have forgotten it remotely. It was because such wonderful things had been accomplished in his own life that Cairns was troubled. In no other man would he have objected to this sort of affair, though he might have criticised the trysting-place as a matter of taste. He had to bring up the subject.

Bedient's face clouded. "How did you hear?"

Cairns told, but spared details.

"I hoped it wouldn't get out on account of Mrs. Wordling," Bedient said. "I should have had the instinct to spare her from any such comments. I didn't know the laws of the park. It was a perfect night. We talked by the fountain. She was the first to suggest that we recross the street—and there we were—locked in."

Cairns asked several questions. Once he started impatiently to say that Mrs. Wordling had nothing to lose, but he caught himself in time. He saw that Bedient had been handled a bit, and had only a vague idea that he was embroiled in a scandal, the sordidness of which was apt to reach every ear but the principals'. At all events, the old Bedient was restored; in fact, if it were possible, he was brightened at one certain angle. Cairns had been unable to forbear this question:

"But, Andrew, who suggested going across to the park?"

"I can't just say," Bedient answered thoughtfully. "You see we smelled mignonette, and followed a common impulse. You should have seen the night to understand.... I say, David, can I do anything to straighten this out for Mrs. Wordling?"

"Only ignore it," Cairns said hastily. "I'll nip it—wherever it comes up. And the next time a woman asks—"

"But I didn't say—"

"The next time you smell mignonette, think of it as a soporific. Just yawn and say you've been working like a fire-horse on the Fourth.... You see, it isn't what happens that gets out to the others, including those we care about, but what is imagined by minds which are not decently policed."

"Crowds are cruel," Bedient mused.

Cairns had found it hard not to be spiteful toward one whom he considered had abused his friend's fineness.... They dined at the Club. The talk turned to a much fairer thing. Bedient saw (with deep and full delight) that Cairns had sighted his island of that Delectable Archipelago, and was making for it full-sailed. An enchanting idea came to Bedient (the fruit of an hour's happy talk), as to the best way for Cairns to make a landing in still waters....

Bedient was detailing the plan with some spirit, when Cairns' hand fell swiftly upon his arm.... At a near table just behind, Mrs. Wordling was sitting with a gentleman. Neither had noticed her come in. Mrs. Wordling turned to greet them. She was looking her best, which was sensational.

NINETEENTH CHAPTER

IN THE HOUSE OF GREY ONE

Bedient went one morning to the old Handel studio in East Fourteenth Street. The Grey One had asked him to come. Bedient liked the Grey One. He could laugh with Mrs. Wordling; Vina Nettleton awed him, though he was full of praise for her; he admired Kate Wilkes and had a keen relish for her mind. The latter had passed the crisis, had put on the full armor of the world; she was sharp and vindictive and implacable to the world; a woman who had won rather than lost her squareness, who showed her strength and hid her tenderness. He had rejoiced in several brushes with Kate Wilkes. There was a tang to them. A little sac of fiery acid had formed in her brain. It came from fighting the world to the last ditch, year after year. Her children played in the quick-passing columns of the periodicals—ambidextrous, untamable, shockingly rough in their games, these children, but shams slunk away from their shrill laughter. In tearing down, *she* prepared for the Builder.

Bedient was not at all at his best with Kate Wilkes; indeed, none of the things that had aroused Vina and Beth and David, like sudden arraignments from their higher selves, came to his lips with this indomitable veteran opposite; still he would go far for ten minutes talk with her. She needed nothing that he could give; her copy had all gone to the compositor, her last forms were locked; and yet, he caught her story from queer angles on the stones, and it was a transcript from New York in this, the latest year of our Lord....

Bedient's "poise and general decency" disturbed the arrant man-hater she had become; she called him "fanatically idealistic," and was inclined to regard him at first as one of those smooth and finished Orientalists who have learned to use their intellects to a dangerous degree. But each time she talked with him, it seemed less possible to put a philosophical ticket upon him. "He's not Buddhist, Vedantist, neo-Platonist," she declared, deeply puzzled. Somehow she did not attract from him, as did Vina Nettleton, the rare pabulum which would have proved him just a Christian. Finally, from fragments brought by Vina, the Grey One, and David Cairns, she hit upon a name for him that would do, even if intended a trifle ironically at first: *The Modern*. She was easier after that; became very fond of him, and only doubted in her own thoughts, lest she hurt his work with the others, the good of which she was quick to see.... "He does not break training," she said at last. "He cut out a high place and holds it easily. Suppose he is *The Modern*?" she asked finally. "If he is, we who thought ourselves modern, should laugh and clap our hands!" This was open heresy to the Kate Wilkes of the world. "I thought I was past that," she sighed. "Here I am getting ready to be stung again."

Certain of her barbed sentences caught in Bedient's mind: "Women whom men avoid for being 'strong-minded' are apt to be strongest in their affections. You can prove this by the sons of clinging vines."... "Beware of the man who discusses often, and broods much, upon his spiritual growth, when he fails to make his wife happy."... "A man's courage may be just his cowardice running forward under the fear of scorn from his fellows."... "The most passionate mother is likely to be the least satisfied with just passion from her husband. Wedded to a man capable of real love, this woman, of all earth's creatures, is the most natural monogamist."... "A real woman had three caskets to give to a man she loved. One day she read in his eyes that he could take but the nearest and lowest; and that moment arose in her heart the wailing cry: 'The King is dead!'"... "The half-grown man never understands that woman is happiest, and at her best in all her services to him, when he depends upon her for a few of the finer things."...

Also Kate Wilkes had a way of doing a memorable bit of criticism in a sentence or two: Regarding MacDowell, the American composer, "He left the harvest to the others, but what exquisite gleanings he found!"... As to Nietschze; "He didn't see all; his isn't the last word; but he crossed the Forbidden Continent, and has spoken deliriously, half-mad from the journey."... And her beloved Whitman, "America's wisest patriot."...

*   *   *   *   *

Bedient liked the Grey One. He liked her that afternoon, when she asked if he cared to come up to Vina Nettleton's with her. There was real warmth in her manner from the first.... Always that illusion of having played with her long ago, stole into mind with her name or presence. (Once he had found her sobbing, about something she wouldn't tell. She had always been ready to give up things. The smile she had for *him*, would remain upon her lips, while she thought of something else. She would leave the others and wait for him to come and find her.) These things were altogether outside of human experience, a sweet and subtly attractive run of vagaries which had to do with a tall yellow-haired maid, now Marguerite Grey.... From something Cairns had said, Bedient knew she was unhappy. He saw it afresh when he entered the big still place where she was. She had been working, but dropped a curtain over the easel as he entered.

"Did I come at a wrong time?" he asked. "I can just as well come again."

"I don't know of any time so good. You may not want to come again."

She had not been weeping. He saw that with a quick look. It was deeper than that—something cold and slow and creeping, that made her reckless with hatred, and writhing. Answering Bedient's swift glance, she perceived that he had seen deeply, and was glad. It eased her; she hoped he had seen all, for she was sick with holding her own.... Meanwhile, her soft voice was telling him about her house. The pictures of her own here and there, were passed over quickly. Children, these, that the world had found wanting; badly-brought-up children that the world had frightened back to the parent roof where they warred with one another.

Back of all, Bedient saw a most feminine creature in the Grey One, naturally defenceless in her life against the world; a woman so preyed upon by moods that many a time she gladly would have turned devil, but was helpless to know how to begin; again and again plucked to the quick by the world. She had put on foreign scepticisms, and pitifully attempted to harden herself; but the hardening, try as she would, could not be spread evenly. It didn't protect her, as Kate Wilkes' did, only made her the more misunderstood. She did not have less talent than Vina or Beth; indeed, she had been considered of rather rich promise in Paris; but she had less developed energies and balance to use them, less physique. She lacked the spirit of that little thoroughbred, Vina Nettleton, and the pride and courage of Beth Truba. The Grey One had been badly hurt in that sadly sensitive period which follows the putting away of girlish things—when womanhood is new and wonderful. She was slow to heal. Few men interested her, but she needed a man-friend, some one to take her in hand. She had needed such a one for years. He would have been of little use, had he not come at this time. Bedient's eager friendliness for this woman was one of the most interesting things he had encountered in New York, a sort of fellowship which no one else had evoked. The Grey One had felt something of this, but had learned to expect so little, that she had not allowed herself to think about it. Only she had felt suddenly easier, perceiving the comprehension in his glance.

They had talked an hour, and were having tea. He admired some of her pictures unreservedly. They were like her voice to him—lingering, soft, mysteriously of the long-ago. Their settings were play-places that he might have imagined. She believed what he said, but did not approve of his perception. She had lost faith. It was the sailor part of him that liked her pictures.

"I had great dreams when I came to New York three years ago," she said somewhat scornfully. "For a time in Paris, I did things with little thought, and they took very well. I must have been happy. Then when I came here, all that period was gone. I was to be an artist—sheer, concentrated, the nothing-else sort of an artist. And things went so well for a time. That's queer when you think of it. The papers took me up. They gave me an exhibition at the *Smilax Club*, and not a few things were disposed of. In fact, when I learned that this studio was to be let, I was so prosperous as to consider it none too adequate for Margie Grey herself—

"Since then these things and others have been done, and they haven't struck the vogue at all. First, I thought it was just one of those changing periods which come to every artist, in which one does badly during the transition. I have continued to do badly. It was not a change of skin. I have become sour and ineffectual, and know it—"

"You won't mind if I say you are wrong?" Bedient asked quietly.

"No," she laughed. "Only please don't tell me that I'm only a little ahead of my time; that presently these things will dart into the public mood, and people will squabble among themselves to possess them—"

"I might have told you just that—if you hadn't warned me.... I like your woods; they're the sort of woods that fairies come to; and I like your fields and afternoons—I can hear the bees and forget myself in them. I *know* they're good."

The Grey One whipped out a match and cigarette from the pocket of her blouse, lit it and stared at her covered easel. "You have your way, don't you?" she asked, and her lips were tightened to keep from trembling.

"It isn't a way," he said. "It's a matter of feeling. I never judge a book or picture, but when I *feel* them, they are good to me. I would have stopped before some of these in any gallery, because I feel them. They make me steal away—"

"I'm hard-hearted and a scoffer," she said, holding fast. "It isn't that I want to be—oh, you are different. I don't believe you were ever *tired*!... I see what David Cairns meant about your coming up here out of the seas with a fresh eye—and all your ideals.... Don't you see—we're all tired out! New York has made us put our ideals away—commercial, romantic—every sort of ideal.... Oh, it's harder for a woman to talk like this than for a man; she's slower to learn it. When a woman does learn it, you may know she carries scars—"

The Grey One arose. She looked tall and gaunt, and her eyes had that burning look which dries tears before they can be shed. He did not hasten to speak.

"It's crude to talk so to you, but you came *to-day*," she went on. "I had about given up. The race—oh, it's a race to sanctuary right enough—but so long!... In the forenoons one can run, but strength doesn't last."

With a quick movement, the Grey One tossed up the covering from the easel. He saw a girl in red, natty figure, piquant face. It was not finished. She was to stand at the head of a saddle-horse, as yet embryonic. She stepped hastily to a little desk and poked at a formidable pile of business-looking correspondence.

"Do these look like an artist's communications?" she asked in the dry pent way that goes with burning eyes.... "They are not, but letters to one who paints for lithographers' stones! See here—"

And now she lifted a couch-cover, and drew from beneath a big portfolio which she opened on the floor before him. It was filled with flaring magazine covers, calendars, and other painted products having to do with that expensive sort of advertising which packing-houses and steel-shops afford. *Girls*—girls mounted side and astride, girls in racing-shells and skiting motor-boats, in limousines and runabouts, in dirigibles and 'planes;—seaside, mountain and prairie girls; house-boat, hunting and skating girls; even a vivid parlor variety—all conventional, colorful and unsigned.

"Eight years in Europe for these," she said in a dragging, morbid tone. "And the letters on the table say I may do more, as the managers of shirt-waist factories might say to poor sewing-women when business is good. And they pay piece-work prices just the same; and they want girls, not real girls, but things of bright paint like these! Oh, they know what they want—and they must be common in order to suit—girls of just paint—"

"And women of just flesh," said Bedient. "New York has shown me that about so many men!"

This startled her—made her forget the sailor part. It was particularly in the range of her mood that moment, and seemed finished.

"You're going to feel a lot better, and soon," he went on. "It's going to be much better than you think—"

She drew suddenly back, hatred altering her features as a gust of wind on the face of a pool.

"You mean my marriage?" she asked, clearing her voice.

"I did not know that you were to be married," he said quickly. "I'm sorry not to have been clearer. I meant the days to come through your work—and nothing more."

"A few have heard that I'm to be married," she said. "I thought you had heard. As a matter of fact, it is not settled. Oh, I have croaked to you terribly—please forgive me!"

"That first night, I felt that we were old friends at once," he added, rising and standing before her. "The next day, you said it was just like a dream—the night before—and it was the same to me. We went up to Miss Nettleton's on the minute, just as if we were old playmates, and you had said, 'Let's—'... So to-day, you have only told an old friend things—trying things—exactly as you should. And I—I think you're brave to have done so well—for so long. I like

New York better. I'm coming again. I like your pictures. They are not just paint.... Hasn't anyone told you—don't you know—that it wouldn't hurt you at all to do the others—if your real pictures were just paint? And since you are driven to do them, and don't do them out of greed, nor through commonness, nor by habit, they can't hurt your real work? I really believe, too, that it is what you have done that will help you, and bring the better times, and not what anyone else will do.... I seem to be talking a great deal—as I could not at all, except for the sense of an old friend's authority, and to one I have found rare and admirable. Believe me, I have very good eyes,—New York has not printed its metal soul upon you."

The Grey One had listened with bowed head. A tall woman is at her loveliest, standing so. She regarded his face searchingly for an instant, smiled, and turned away.

*   *   *   *   *

Bedient asked no one. He did not know that the race Marguerite Grey was running was with American dollars, and that the sanctuary she meant was only a debtless spinsterhood. He did not know that she dared not give up the Handel studio while she held a single hope of her vogue returning. Only the great, who are permitted eccentricities, dare return to their garrets. Nor did Bedient know that her marriage meant she had failed utterly, and that another must square her debts; that only out of the hate of defeat could she give herself for this price.... Still, Bedient knew quite enough.

It was a little later, after he had been truly admitted into the circle he loved so well, that Beth told him the story of the Grey One's first collision with the man world. It was a rainy afternoon; they were together in the studio he always entered with reverence.

"She is different from Vina," Beth said, speaking of Marguerite Grey. "She has been working fearfully and she's not made for such furious sessions as Vina Nettleton can endure. Vina seems replenished by her own atmosphere. She told me once that when her work is coming well, her whole body sings, all the functions in rhythm. Aren't people strange? That little soft thing with baby hands! Why, her physical labor alone some days would weary a strong man— and that is the thoughtless part.

"But I was telling you about the Grey One. Sometimes I think she is more noble than we understand—one of those strange, solitary women who love only once. At least, she seems to ask only success in her work, and what that will bring her." Beth thought a moment of the horrible alternative which she did not care to explain to Bedient. "A few years ago in Europe—just a young thing, she was, when she met her hero. He was a good man, and loved her. I knew them both over there. In the beginning, it was one of those really golden romances, and in Italy. One day, a woman came to the Grey One, and in the lightest, brassiest way, asked to be congratulated on her engagement, mentioning the man whose attentions Marguerite had accepted as a heavenly dispensation. This was in Florence. The woman hurried away that day for London. The Grey One, just a gullible girl, was left half dead. When her lover came, she refused to see him. He wrote a letter which she foolishly sent back, unopened. And she returned to Paris—all this in the first shock.... She did not hear from him again for two years. Word came that he was married—no, not to that destroyer, but to a girl who made him happy, let us hope. The Grey One penetrated then to the truth. He had only a laughing acquaintance with the other woman to whom he was one of several chances. Leaving Florence, she had crippled the Grey

One. This is just the bare fact—but it is enough to show how the lie of a worthless woman—kept Marguerite from happiness. And she has remained apart.... It is said that the Grey One encountered the destroyer here in New York a few months ago, the first time since that day in Florence. So natural was evil to this woman, that she did not remember, but came forward gushingly—and would have kissed her victim...."

TWENTIETH CHAPTER

A CHEMISTRY OF SCANDAL

Beth had seen Andrew Bedient almost daily for three weeks. Many wonderful moments had been passed together; indeed, there were moments when he reached in her mind that height he had gained at once in the ideals of Vina Nettleton. But he was sustained in Vina's mind, while Beth encountered reactions.... "I believe he is beyond sex—or fast going beyond—though he may not know it," Vina had said in effect.... On the contrary, the Shadowy Sister had sensed a lover in the room. Beth had perceived what Vina meant—the mystic who worshipped woman as an abstraction—but it had also come to her, that he could love *one*.

Beth would not trust the Shadowy Sister, but was determined to judge Bedient according to world standards. Plainly she attracted him, but could not be sure that her attraction was unique, though she always remembered that he had told of his mother only to her. He had a different mood, a different voice almost, for each of the other women of their acquaintance. His liking for the Grey One mystified Beth; Vina Nettleton had charmed him, brought forth in a single afternoon many intimate things from his depths. He spoke pleasantly of Mrs. Wordling.

The Shadowy Sister was bewitched. To her a great lover had come—a lover who had added to a boy's delicacy and beauty of ideal, a man's certainty and power. This was the trusting, visionary part of Beth, that had not entered at all into the other romance. Beth refused now to be ruled by it. The world had hurt her. The fault was not hers, but the world's. The only profit she could see to be drawn from her miseries of the past was to use her head to prevent repetition. Hearts were condemned.

And yet, the contrasting conduct of the Shadowy Sister in this and that other romance, was one of the most astonishing things in Beth's experience. (Sailor-man had but to enter and speak, for Shadowy Sister to appear in kneeling adoration.)

Often Bedient was allowed to stay while she worked at other things. His own portrait prospered slowly, a fact in which the world might have found humor. And often they talked together long after the slanting light had made work impossible; their faces altered in the dim place; their voices low.... There were moments when the woman's heart stirred to break its silence; when the man before her seemed bravely a man, and the confines of his nature to hold magnificent distances. If she could creep within those confines, would it not mean truly to live?... But the years would sweep through her mind—grim, gray, implacable chariots—and in their dusty train, the specific memories of fleshly limitation and untruth. To survive, she had been forced to lock her heart; to hold every hope in the cold white fingers of fear; cruelly to curb the sweep of feminine outpouring, lest its object soften into chaos; and roused womanhood, returning empty—overwhelm. This is the sorriest instinct of self-preservation.

She would have said at this time that Andrew Bedient had not aroused the woman in her as the Other had done. Indeed, she paled at the thought that the Other had exhausted a trifle, her great force of heart-giving. There had been beauty in such a bestowal—pain and passion—but beauty, too.... Another strange circumstance: Bedient had made her think of the Other so differently. She had half put away her pride; she might have been too insistent for her rights. The Other really had improved miraculously from the poor boy who had come to their house. And to the artist's eye, he was commandingly masculine, a veritable ideal.... Bedient was different every day.

The visit to the gallery, too, had given Beth much to think over. What he had said about the pictures, especially before the one he had called *The Race Mother*, had revealed his processes of mind, and made her feel very small for a while. She saw that all her own talk had not lifted from herself, from her own troubles, and certain hateful aspects of the world; while his thoughts had concerned the sufferings of all women, and the fruitage that was to come from them. She had talked for herself; he for the race. But he had merely *observed* the life of women, while she had lived that life.

Why did Andrew Bedient continue to show her seemingly inexhaustible sources of fineness, ways so delicate and wise that the Shadowy Sister was conquered daily, and was difficult to live with? It is true that Bedient asked nothing. But if the hour of asking struck, what should she say to him? (Here Shadowy Sister was firmly commanded to begone.) Beth had not been able to answer alone.... Could Vina Nettleton be right? Was her studio honored by a man who was beyond the completing of any woman? If so, why did Shadowy Sister so delight in him? Or was this proof that he was not designed to be the human mate of woman? These were mighty quandaries. Beth determined to talk about prophets when he came again.... Her friends told her she hadn't looked so well in years.

Beth drew forth at length a picture of the Other Man, that she had painted recently from a number of kodak prints. The work of a miniature had been put upon it. A laughing face, a reckless face, but huge and handsome. Before her, was the contrasting work of the new portrait. The two pictures interested her together.... Bedient was at the door. It was his hour. Beth placed the smaller picture upon the mantle, instead of in its hidden niche—and admitted the Shadowy Sister's Knight....

"I saw Vina yesterday," she observed, after work was begun. "She was still talking about prophets and those other things you said—"

"What a real interest she has," Bedient answered. "She has asked me for a *Credo*—in two or three hundred words—to embody the main outline of the talk that day. Perhaps it can be done. I'm trying."

"How interesting!"

"If one could put all his thinking into a few pages, that would be big work."...

After a pause, Beth said:

"Don't think I'm flippant if I ask: How do these men who, in their maturity, become great spiritual forces, escape being caught young by some perceiving woman?"

"I'm not so sure the question could be put better," Bedient said. "There is often a time in the youth of men, to whom illumination comes later, when they hang divided between the need of woman and some inner austerity that commands them to go alone."

"If they disobey, does the light fail to come?" Beth asked.

"It is less likely to come. But then, often the youth of such men is spent in some great passion for an unattainable woman, a distant star for the groping years. In other cases, women have divined the mystic quality, and instead of giving themselves, have held the young visionaries pure. Again, poverty, that grim stepmother of the elect, often intervenes. And to common women—such lovers are absurd, beyond comprehension. That helps.... Illumination comes between the age of thirty and forty. After that, the way is clear. They do not grope, they see; they do not believe, they feel and know."

Beth found these things absorbing, though she accepted them only tentatively. She saw they were real to him—as bread and wool and paint.

"There is an impulse, too, among serious young men to live the life of asceticism and restraint," Bedient added. "It comes out of their very strength. This is the hasty conclusion of monasteries—"

"Hasty?"

"Well—unfledged saints fall.... Their growth becomes self-centred. The intellect expands at the expense of soul, a treacherous way that leads to the dark.... And then—a man must father his own children beautifully before he can father his race."

"That sounds unerring to me," Beth said.

"Why, it's all the Holy Spirit driving the race!" Bedient exclaimed suddenly. "You can perceive the measure of it in every man. Look at the multitude. The sexes devour each other; marriage is the vulgarest proposition of chance. Men and women want each other—that is all they know. They have no exquisite sense of selection. In them this glorious driving Energy finds no beautiful surfaces to work upon, just the passions, the meat-fed passions. Here is quantity. Nature is always ruthless with quantity, as cities are ruthless with the crowds. Here is the great waste, the tearing-down, and all that is ghastly among the masses; yet here and there from some pitiful tortured mother emerges a faltering artist—her dream."

"You never forget her, do you,—that figure which sustains through the darkness and horror?"

"I cannot," he smiled. "No race would outlast a millenium without her. Such women are saviors—always giving themselves to men—silently falling with men."

"But about the artist?" Beth asked. "What is his measure of the driving Energy? How does it work upon him?"

"He has risen from the common," Bedient replied. "He feels the furious need of completion, some one to ignite his powers and perfect his expression. It is a woman, but he has an ideal about her. He rushes madly from one to another, as a bee to different blooms. The flesh and the devil pull at him, too; surface beauty blinds him, and the world he has come from, hates him for emerging. It is a fight, but he has not lost, who fails once. The women who know him are not the same again. The poor singer destroys his life, but leaves a song, a bit of fastidiousness. The world remembers the song, links it with the destroyed life, and loves both.

"But look at the mother-given prophets standing alone, militant but tender, the real producers! The spirit that sparks fitfully in the artist is a steady flame now. Their giving is to all, not to one. What they take of the world is very little, but through them to the world is given direct the Holy Spirit. Saint Paul and the Forerunner are the highest types, and in perspective. Their way is the way of the Christ, Who showed the world that unto the completed union of Mystic Womanhood and militant manhood, is added Godhood.

"There are immediate examples of men maturing in prophecy," Bedient concluded. "Men in our own lives almost —Whitman, Lincoln, Thoreau, Emerson, Carlyle, Wordsworth. See the poise and the service which came from their greater gifts. Contrast them with the beautiful boys who searched so madly, so vainly, among the senses—Burns, Byron, Shelley, Keats, Poe. What noble elder brothers they are! More *con*tent, they have, more soul-age, more of the visioning feminine principle.... And see how flesh destroys! In the small matter of years they lived, the prophets more than doubled the age of the singers. Their greatest work was done in the years which the lyric-makers did not reach.... The great masses of the world have not yet the spark which shows itself in the singing poetic consciousness. Such men are mere males, leaning upon matter, soldiers and money-makers, pitifully unlit, chance children, without fastidiousness, but all on the road."

"There will be plenty, yes, more than plenty," said Beth, "to take the places of those, who confine their parenthood to the race."

Bedient was gone, and though his incorruptible optimism was working more than ever in her heart, that which she had sought to learn, had not come. Prophet or not, his smile at the door had left something volatile within her, something like girlhood in her heart. He had not overlooked the picture upon the mantel. Twice she had looked up, and found him regarding it.... It was the late still time of afternoon. Beth felt emotional. She ran over several songs on the piano, while the dusk thickened in the studio. One was about an Indian maiden who yearned for the sky-blue water; another about an Irish Kathleen who gave her lover to strike a blow for the Green; and still another concerned a girl who would rather lie in the dust of her lord's chariot than be the ecstasy of lesser man. Beth Truba's face was upturned to the light—to the last pallor of day. She was like a wraith singing and communing with the tuneful tragedies of women world-wide. But there was gaiety in her heart.... Then the knocker, the scurrying of dreams away, and the voice of Marguerite Grey in the dark.

"Most romantic—song, hour and all," she said, while Beth turned on the lamps.

"Beth Truba is naturally so romantic—"

"Possibly the piano could tell tales; I know my 'cello could," said the Grey One. "Beth, dear, I am touching wood, and praying to preserve 'an humble and a contrite heart,' but reeking with commerce. Sold three pictures—real pictures. The one that was hanging at Torvin's so long was sold four days ago, and Torvin immediately took two more—"

"Margie Grey, there are few things you could tell to make me happier," Beth exclaimed, coming forward with both hands out.

"I know it. That's why I came."

"With Torvin interested, anything is liable to happen. He's one of the few in New York who know, and those who buy carefully know he knows. Really we should celebrate.... Let's get Vina to go with us, and we three set out in search of an absurd supper—"

Beth phoned at once. Her part was utterly disconnected. She put up the receiver, smiling.

"What have you to say—about those two going out to dinner?"

"Vina and David Cairns?"

"Exactly."

A long, low talk followed, but Beth did not tell that she had spurred David to look deeply into Vina's case, through a remark made by Andrew Bedient.... The Grey One was emancipated, restless. She bloomed like a lily as she moved about the studio, above the shaded reading-lamps. Beth felt her happiness, the intensity of it, and rejoiced with her. Bedient came in for discussion presently, and the park episode. Beth, who had not heard, grew cold, and remembered her own call at Mrs. Wordling's apartment, with the poster.... The Grey One was speaking as if Beth had heard about the later park affair:

"... Sometimes that woman seems so obvious, and again so deep."

"I have failed to see the deep part," Beth ventured, turning her face from the light.

"Evidently she interests Mr. Bedient."

"I wonder if she really does?" Beth said idly. The Grey One was not a tale-bearer. She would not have spoken at all, except granting Beth's knowledge.

"I don't like to see him lose caste that way," the Grey One went on. "He's too splendid, and yet she's the sort that twirls men. She knows he has interested all of us, and doubtless wants to show *her* strength. Possibly he hasn't thought twice about it. That's what Vina says. And then Mrs. Wordling was one of those first asked to meet him. I wish David Cairns hadn't done that—"

"David's idea was all right," Beth said slowly. "He thought one of her kind would set us all off to advantage. Then, I was painting her poster—"

"It would have been only a little joke in a man's club, but the *Smilax* took to it as something looked and yearned for long.... Two things appear funny to me. Mrs. Wordling has lived at the Club part of the year for three years, and yet didn't know the Park was locked at midnight. And she, who has done all the crying about consequences, was the one who told me—"

Beth was beginning to understand. Here was an opening such as she had awaited: "What is her story?" she asked.

"Why, they met between eleven and twelve coming into the Club—one of those perfect nights. Wordling dismissed her carriage and talked a little while before going in. The Park looked inviting for a stroll—full moon, you know. They crossed. Wordling didn't know or had forgotten about midnight locking. 'His talk was so interesting,' she said.... It was after one, when Mr. Bedient hailed a page at the Club entrance."

"From inside the bars, across the street?" Beth asked.

"Of course. The boy came over with the keys."

"How clumsy and uninteresting, even innocence of that sort can be!" Beth remarked. "And Mrs. Wordling was so zealous for you to hear that she told you herself?"

"That *is* rather humorous, isn't it?" the Grey One agreed. "Of course she supposed I had heard, and wanted to be sure the truth came to me. I think, too, she wanted me to know that Mr. Bedient had invited her to go to the shore for a few days—later. She asked if I thought she had better go—"

"And you told her?" Beth managed to say.

"Just as you would, that she was an adult and must use her own judgment."

"Exactly," said Beth, and then a sentence got away from her, though she contrived to garb it in a laugh. "He won't go to the shore with Mrs. Wordling!... Wait until I get my hat."

*   *   *   *   *

In the little room alone, she saw that the long dark road must be traversed again; the chains had fallen upon her anew—their former wounds yet unhealed.... The old lies and acting; the old hateful garment for the world to see; suffering beneath a smile. She must hear the voice of Beth Truba lightly observing and answering, while *she*—the heart of her—was deathly ill.

Her throat tightened; it seemed her breast must burst with old and new agonies. Once more she had given her full faith. This was clear now. She had been a weakling again, and tumultuously, in spite of an ugly warning! Had she not called at Wordling's apartment with the poster? Had she not heard the whispers, the overturned chair and scornfully fathomed the delayed answering of the door?... And to think she had almost succeeded in putting that rankling incident away, though he had not been in New York a month. And the shame of it, the recent hours she had spent, with this visionary thing; that *he* was beyond mating with a woman of flesh—beyond her best—a forerunner with glad tidings for all women!... Forerunner, indeed, and twice caught in a second-rate woman's net of beguilings! Twice caught, and how many times uncaught?... And she had thought herself hard and sceptical in his presence.

The old romance looked clean and fair compared to this—the old lover, boyish and forgivable. He had not won by preaching.... Where was the Shadowy Sister now?

There was no quarter for Beth. She was a modern product, a twentieth century woman, an angry, solitary, world-trained woman, who could not make a concession to imperfect manhood. This was the key to all her agonies. She had asked manhood of mind, and could not accept less. The awful part was that she must do over again all the hateful strategies, all the concealing and worldliness—her body, mind and soul sorely crippled from before. That she must thus use her womanhood, her precious prime of strength. One experience had not hardened her enough. With what corrosion of self-hatred did she turn upon herself that moment!

Her intellect had faltered; the Shadowy Sister had betrayed; David Cairns had been consummately stupid; Vina Nettleton was soft with dreams, and not to be reckoned with in the world; Vina could tell her woes, but she, Beth Truba, must not scream nor fall. She must face the woman in the other room, sit across a lighted table for an hour, and talk and laugh. Her heart cried out against this, but pride uprose to whip—Beth's iron pride finished under the world's mastery. Slowly, rhythmically, the blows fell. Beth could not run away.

She stretched out her fingers, which were biting into her palms, drenched her face with cold water, breathed for a minute by the open window like a doe in covert.... There was ammonia, and she inhaled the potent fumes....

"*Pale hands I loved
Beside the Shalimar—*"

hummed the Grey One, from the open sheet on the piano.

Beth faltered at the door, for the song hurled her back to an hour ago with bruising force. She re-entered the little room—to fix her hat....

"You weren't long, Beth," the Grey One said.

"No?... I'm glad of that, but speaking of glad things, let us not forget Torvin."

Beth was already turning out the lights.

"You look a little tired, dear," the Grey One said in the elevator.

"It's the time of day," Beth responded readily. After being in all day, and suddenly deciding to go out, haven't you felt a tension come over you as if you could hardly wait a minute?"

"Many times, dear, as if one must snatch hat and gloves and get into the street at any cost."

* * * * *

Beth came in alone about ten, sighed as the latch clicked, and sat down in the dark. But she rose again in a moment, for she didn't like the dark. She was worn out, even physically; and yet it was different now from the first reaction. Bedient had not continued to fit so readily to commonness, as in those first implacable moments in the little room. He had never judged anyone in her presence; had spoken well of everyone, even of Mrs. Wordling. He was no intimidated New Yorker, who felt he must conduct himself for the eyes of others.

Mrs. Wordling had not shown the quality to hold the fancy position she aspired to, in the little circle of artists at the Club; and retaliated by showing her power over the lion of this circle. She had challenged him to cross the street, knowing they would be locked in and that the Club would hear. She had desired this, having nothing to lose. For fear the Grey One had not heard, she had told the story. The recent agony in the little room was great, above the Wordling's expectations.... And now Beth faltered. Had Andrew Bedient asked her to join him somewhere on the shore? She could not see him asking this; and yet, regarded as a fiction plunge, it seemed bigger and more formidable than Wordling could devise.

This must wait. This must prove. If he went away—enough! She had been hasty and implacable once—this time she would wait.

Beth would have liked to talk with David Cairns, but she could not bring up such a subject. This was not her sort of talk-material with him. Plainly he would not mention it, in the hope that her ears had missed it entirely.

She had even felt a rage against the Grey One for bringing the news. This helped to show how maddened and unjust she was, in those first terrible moments. Piece by piece she had drawn the odious thing from her caller, who was by no means inclined to spread and thicken the shadow of an evil tale. Marguerite Grey was not a weigher of motives, nor penetrative in the chemistry of scandal. So many testimonies had come to her of the world's commonness that she had become flexible in judgment. What had been so terrible at first was to identify Andrew Bedient with these sordid things, so obvious and shallow. But was he identified with them? Rather, did he not feel himself sufficiently an entity to be safe in any company? Did he not trust her, and worthwhile people, to grant him this much?.... This was the highest point in the upsweep of her thoughts.

So the story extracted from the Grey One was held free from its fatal aspect, until time should dissolve the matter of the shore.... After all, the lamplight, usually soft and mellow in the gold-brown room, held an alien, unearthly glitter for Beth's strained eyes.... Was it that which kept the Shadowy Sister afar, as the light from the colored pane in the hall of his boyhood had frightened *him*?

Will Levington Comfort

TWENTY-FIRST CHAPTER

THE SINGING DISTANCES

David Cairns was coming along. He had ridden his ego down stream, until he heard the rapids. Now he was towing it back. He planned to go just as far and as fast up stream as he could. The current, to him, had become the crowd. One can see the crowd as it brushes past, as one can never see it from the ruck.... Sometimes it came to him in a flash, that this new David Cairns was but another lie and pose—but this couldn't hold. It was a bit of deviltry that wouldn't stand scrutiny. There had been too much unfolding o' nights; too many gifts found upon the doorstep of his mind in the morning, revealing the sleepless activity of something identified with him, but wiser than he; too much cutting down of false cultures, and outpourings of sincere friendship, and general joy of giving. Then, there was some real clean-cut thinking that expressed itself with brevity and finish; and also, the wonder-working in his heart—the happiest thing that had ever befallen—his conception of the genius of woman in Vina Nettleton.

Cairns' experience with women was not nearly so large as it looked. He had known many women, but impersonally. He was late to mature, and all his younger energies were used for what he had believed to be the world's work, but what he now perceived were the activities of a vain, ego-driven intellect, that delighted to attract the passing eye by the ring of the anvil and a great show of unsleeved muscle. Much of this early work had kept him afield, and his calls home to New York had inflicted upon him the fatal stimulus for quantity. His still earlier years were passed in a home where a placid mother reigned, and a large family of sisters served. He, therefore, met the world's women without that mighty tang of novelty which features the young manhood of the unsistered.

He had undergone his mannish period of treason to women generally. These were the days when he believed in using force—punishing with words—"punch," he called it. This is a mental indelicacy which the ordinary man seldom outgrows. His crowning fact is that dynamite will loosen stumps and break rock. Therefore, all that is not dynamite is not proper man-stuff. Woman, to this sort, is something between "an angel and an idiot." She must be guarded from herself in all that has to do with thought and performance. As panderer and caterer, she emphatically belongs. Young men grasp this. If they reach middle age with it, only an angel can roll the stone away.

Cairns now realized he had been near to missing one of the greatest moments that come into the life of man. What chance has the ordinary male—half-grown, except physically—of ever glowing with real chivalry? To him women are easy, common, plentiful, without mystery or lofty radiance. How can the valor of humility brighten his quest? How can *he* be a lover—who does not realize his poverty, his evil, the vastness of his need? What does it mean to the mere male, this highest of earthly gifts, the glance from a woman which ends his quest of her, the gift of herself? To be great and a man, and a lover, he must reach that point of declaration which holds: *Without her, I am an outcast; with her I can alter worlds!* A transcendent moment of conquest is the winning of a woman, to such a spirit....

A frightful void stretches between mere man and reality.... Mere man must be baptized in spirit to feel the anguish that is woman's, to give her *real* treasures to some male. Which are the greater artists and producers, the saviors of the race? Those heroines who survive the heart-break of man's indelicacy, and manage alone to give their treasures to their children. The art of such women lives, indeed. David Cairns was coming along.

The work that Andrew Bedient began in the Cairns mind and heart was being finished by Vina Nettleton. In great thirst of soul, he had come to her and been restored. He was very eager to leave all he had in the shelter of the palms.

"David," Bedient had said, "there is only one greater work for a man in the world than making a woman happy; and that—making *all* women happier! It seems that an avatar must come for that soon. To-day the great gifts of women are uncalled for by men. They cannot take each other, save in physical arms. There is a barrier between the sexes. Man has not learned, or has forgotten, the heart-language. What a need for lovers! If one could look into the secret places of women, across the world's table, into the minds of women who hate and are restless, and whose desires rove; even into the minds of those who actually venture beyond the man-made pale, he would see over all the need of lovers!... Give a woman love, and she will give the world lovers, and we shall have brotherhood singing in our ears.... David, I ask you only to look at the genius born of woman, in and out of wedlock, during the first days of her mating with a man whom she believes to be all that she has cried out for. He may have destroyed every hope afterward, sacked every sanctuary, but, if she trembled close to her great happiness in the beginning, the child of such a beginning has glory upon his brow!"

Cairns was ready to see; ready to read this in the history of men. More than this, he was ready to flood fresh dawns of light into the tired eyes of Vina Nettleton, and upon her pallor make roses bloom. Moreover, he could discern in her an immortal artist, the conception of which changed him from a male to a man.

And of this seeing came another needed conception: that intellectual arrogance is the true modern devil; that the ancient devil, desire of flesh, is obvious, banal, and common-place, compared to this.... He dared to bring his realizations to a woman, and found that she had a crown for each and every one. And he learned to talk to her about things vital to men and women, and found that this was the strangest, grandest and most providential hour in the world—this newest hour.

It was with a rich and encompassing delight that Cairns discovered Vina's fineness, endurance, delicacy, and intuition. He was humble before her spirit, for he had become sensitive to that which was mystic and ineffable. He saw through her, a sanction and authority for his own future years, her light upon the work he must do. The animation of his mind in her presence was pure with service. And Vina awakened, for she saw with trembling, what is a miracle to a modern woman's eyes, man's delight to honor that which is most truly woman's. So her girlhood crept back.

* * * * *

At first Vina thought he was using her for a study. They had long been friends; she was glad to be of assistance; so he was free to come and go, and she was free with him as only an old comrade can be—one who expects nothing. They had great talks about Bedient; both revered him, and were grateful for his coming. And Vina was not slow to see the change in David Cairns; that it was in nowise momentary, but sound and structural. She took a deep interest in his progress, mothered it, made him glad to show her its phases.

"Things are looking so differently to me," he said, one of the first days. "It makes me think of the American soldiers I met the first time afield—the time I met Bedient. I praised the officers for their own home papers. They looked so big and thrilling to me, as men. It was easy. I remember riding with a cavalry leader one rough day—a long day. He was hard and still with courage. He rolled a hundred cigarettes that day. I thought him the genius of an officer. Then I saw him afterward over here. It was the same with others. They seemed to have left their glory out there among the swamps and the hills.... It's the same way with the things I thought before Bedient came.... I can see *your* things a lot better."

It was true, he could. Vina had noted that. He could sense her atmosphere, and divine her intents. Formerly, he had taken the word of the others that she had power for her work.... Almost every afternoon now he tapped at her door. Entering, he would take a seat by the fire-frame, stare a bit at the city or the tower, or move about behind her, regarding the freshly done work; and presently they would find themselves talking. It was because David Cairns, as a lover, was out of the question from her point of view in the first days, that such a splendid companionship was established. He did not know that a woman could be such a companion; and her unconsciousness of his deeper quest, gave her an ease with him, that was one of the secrets of her great and growing charm.

Heretofore, all feminine aspirants for Cairns' admiration had ranged themselves in his mind against the paragon, Beth

Truba (with whom he had long comported himself with a rueful might-have-been manner, both pretty and pleasant). Beth had easily transcended. Whatever was great and desirable in woman was likely to wear a Beth Truba hall-mark for his observation. Now, that was changed, not that Beth suffered eclipse, nor that his admiration abated; indeed, his gratefulness for that word of Beth's at just the proper moment, which had caused him gallantly to take the road of Vina Nettleton, was a rare study; but another had risen, not of Beth, but of more intimate meaning to the man, David Cairns. Beth's great force of feminine energy and aspiration, he had been unable to attract. Beth had demanded more than virtue from him, and at a time when he was not finished enough to answer her many restless dreams.

Cairns and Vina Nettleton had in reality just met, and at one of the memorable crossings of eternity. To each, the other had just been brought forth from a sumptuous shadow of nature. In the brighter light they discerned each other. Cairns was first to see, for he had been told, and he brought to the meeting all the fresh inspirations of his maturity, and they rested upon the solid values earned through a life of hard-held decency.

Among the May days there was one afternoon in which the conception of summer was in the air. It was not the heat alone, but the stirring of the year's tremendous energy everywhere, even under pavements. The warmth of creation was kindly in old bones and old walls, and an imperious quickening in the elastic veins of youth. Vina (half-way up a step-ladder) turned about and sat down on one of the steps. Cairns had asked her what plans she had for the summer.

"Oh, I shan't be a great way from New York. Maybe a trip or two over to my beloved Nantucket."

This started her to thinking and presently to expatiating upon the dearest place on earth to her mind.... She told him how the villagers refused to have mail-service, as it threatened to destroy one of the important social features of the day, that of going to the post office for letters. Also he was informed that automobiles were forbidden in Nantucket, and that a train started daily across the Island, a nine-mile journey, and sometimes arrived. The conductor and engineer, both old seamen, were much more interested in a change of weather, a passing ship, or a school of fish, than in the immediate schedule or right of way.... And Cairns was given another glimpse of the enchantress that had been hidden so long in the workaday vesture of the little artist, as she unfolded:

"To me, there's real peace and silence away out there in the sea. Every thought is a picture.... You know the little gray shingle houses are built very close together, and many are flush with the sidewalk. They don't draw the shades at night, and everyone uses little muslin curtains which conceal nothing. One of my favorite things to do is to walk along Pleasant Street to Lily Lane, or through Vestal Street, just about dusk, and see the darling interiors of the spotless cottages. Not really to stop nor stare, just to go softly and slowly by.... One house has little heads around the tea-table with father and mother; another has company for supper; and the next—just old folks are left—but all so radiant as they shine out through the old-fashioned window-panes.... To have one of those places for one's own! It has seemed the happiest destiny for me, but only for the very fortunate and elect.... I wonder if they ever know of the night-birds that flutter at the window-panes to see the happiness within?"

Cairns might have taken this very lightly; even with a reservation that she knew realities did not fit the ideal; that such realities were not for the elect always;—but he chose to regard it instead, as an expression of Vina's yearning, which she felt safe in disclosing for the sake of the ingenious picture she made.... He looked about this remarkable studio in the heart of New York, where a really great task was being wrought to endure. Sometimes it seemed to him that the spirits of the saints came to rest in this place, where the woman worshipped them through her work.... And he knew she meant much that she said; that to her, work was not enough of the breath of life.... She had not completed her picture; rather life had not completed it for her.

Cairns confided in Bedient the Nantucket story, and an idea, occurred to the latter that delighted him. It was one of the evenings when they dined together at the Club.... Another day, Cairns inquired of Vina what took her to Nantucket in summer, curious as to the material arrangement.

"My own people used to go there summers when I was a little thing," she told him, "and of late—there are many friends who ask me over."

"Say, Vina, when you get over to Nantucket, would you be terribly disconcerted to discover some morning, down among the wharves there, with a copy of *Moby Dick,* and a distressed look from deciding whether breakfast should be of clam or cod chowder—*me*?"

"I should be glad of all things," she said with quiet eagerness. "There are so many ways to pass the hours—"

"Besides walking in Lily Lane in the dusk?"

"Yes.... There's the ride over the open moors. It's like Scotland in places, with no division or fences, and the sea away off in all directions. Then, we must go to the lighthouse, one of the most important of America, and the first to welcome the steamers coming in from Europe. And the Haunted House on Moor's End, the Prince Gardens and the wonderful old water-front—where I am to discover you—once so rich and important in the world, now forgotten and sunken and deserted, except for an old seasoned sea captain here and there, smoking about, dreaming as you imagine, of the China trade or the lordly days of the old sperm fishery, and looking wistfully out toward the last port.... Venice or Nantucket—I can hardly say which is more dream-like or alluring, or sad with the goneness of its glory.... I'd love to show you, because I know every stick and stone on the Island, and many of its quaint people."

"And when do you think you will go?" he asked.

"I don't know, David,—not before the last of June. And I won't be able to stay very long this year, because there is no place to work there. I ought to have a little change and rest, but I can't afford to 'run down' entirely—just enough to freshen the eye."

Cairns nodded seriously....

A day or two afterward he brought Bedient. To Vina he was like some tremendous vibration in the room. Her mind was roused as if by some great music.... It was in nothing that Bedient had said or looked, yet only a little while after the two men had gone, Vina realized she had a lover in David Cairns.

She was dismayed, filled with confusion and alarm, but this was the foreground of mind. She had the sense of glad singing in the distances. There was no sleep for hours this night, though of late, she had been sleeping unusually well.... Why had the realization been so slow in coming? An answer was ready enough: Because David was an old acquaintance. But another thought came: For years, except in rare reactionary hours, such as that afternoon in Beth's studio, she had put away the thought of man as a mate.... For years, she had tried to become a block instead of a battery; tried to give the full portion of her life to the thing called work, and hated herself because she couldn't. For years she had dreaded to go where men and women were, because the rare sight of human happiness brought upon her a torrent of dreams. The emptiness of her own life, together with the hatred of self, because she could not be glad for the simple object lesson of a man and woman happy in each other, made her miserable for hours. Late years she had not cared if she looked tacky. "What does it matter," she would ask, with a hateful glance into the glass, "when at best, I look like a water-nymph with hay-fever?"... A long and hard fight, but she had almost broken the habit of thinking what she might do with certain prerogatives of women, which were not granted to her. A bitter fight, and only she knew the hollowness of the honors her good work had brought. It was not the hard work that had left her at the end of many a long day—just a worn bundle of sparking nerve-ends.

And yet, this was the creature whom the new David Cairns had come to, again and again and again. This mighty fact arose from the vortex of confusion and alarm. "Ah, David," she thought, "is it not too late? Am I not too old and weathered a world-campaigner?... I am old, David. Older than my years. Older even than I look! I have warred so long, that I think all peace and happiness from now on would kill me. Oh, you don't want me. Surely you can't want me!"

But there were sad smilings upon the hundred hand-wrought faces in the room. The Marys, the Magdalens, and the Marthas were a strangely smiling Sisterhood.... "Child, you have been faithful in the little things," came to her. "You have thought of us and wept with us and loved us, and we have prevailed to bring you happiness."

And so the other side of the picture—Vina Nettleton's life picture—now turned. The "Stations" were like panels of fairies, after that. All the hidden shames and secrets of the years, the awful sense of being unwanted at the hearth of the human family, were taken from her, like the brittle and dusty packings from a glorious urn. Some marvel of freshness sped through her veins. She was not as yesterday—a little gray shade of an evil dream. Yesterday, and all the yesterdays, she had modelled alone, poor creatures of clay, and now the world suddenly called her to the academy of immortals....

Yes, he had come. He was brave and beloved.... She arose and knelt in the dark before that panel of greatest meaning—the Gethsemane. And long afterward, she stood by the open window. There were no stars, but the tired city was cut in light. And faint sounds reached her from below.... They were not Jews and Romans, but her own people, rushing to and fro for the happiness she had found.

TWENTY-SECOND CHAPTER

BETH SIGNS THE PICTURE

Bedient walked up the Avenue, carrying one of his small leather-bound books to Beth. It was the day after the call of the Grey One there. He had learned to give—which may be made an exquisite art—little things that forbade refusal, but which were invested with cumulative values. Thus he brought many of his rare books of the world to the studio. In them she came upon his marginal milestones, and girdled them with her own pencillings. So their inner silences were broken, and they entered the concourse of the elect together.

The wonder of the woman rose and rose in his mind. His joy, apart from her, was to give joy to others, and so he had moved about New York for days and nights, reflecting her in countless ways. When he thought of his money at all, it was to realize with curious amazement that there was quite enough for anything he wished to do. Things to do were so many in New York, that numberless times each day he sent a prayer of thankfulness to Captain Carreras, always with a warm delight in the memory. And he liked to think it was Beth's hand. She had told him of her pilgrimages during holiday time to the infinite centres of sorrow—and it became a kind of dream of his—the time when they would go together, not holidays alone, but always. The great fortune slowly became identified in his mind with the work he had to do; but Equatoria, the base, amusingly enough, sank away into vaster remoteness. There were moments in which Bedient almost believed there was a little garden of his planting in the heart of the lustrous lady; moments, even, when he thought it was extending broader and broader upon an arable surface. Again, some bitterness from the world seemed to blast the young growths—and the delicate fragrance was far-blown. It was these reactions, and his sensitiveness to the beauty of the romance, which put off from day to day the time for words.

Two or three days before, she had returned from a week-end in the country, and more than ever her presence was an inspiration. She must have been keeping holy vigils. There was animation in her hands, a note of singing in her laughter—the dawn of June in her eyes, the fresh loveliness of the country in her whole presence. She showed him that Monday morning, how good it was to see him again—after forty-eight hours. And he had gone about his work with renewed spirit—the silent siege. The strength of youth was in his attentions, but the fineness of maturity, as well. He cultured her heart as only a great lover could; but being the lover, he was slow to see the blooms that answered.

Only of words, he would have none of them yet. Deeply he understood that she had been terribly hurt—long ago or recently, he could not tell. Could the story she had suggested of the Grey One's lover be anything like her own?... Words—he was afraid. Words often break the sensitive new-forming tissues over old wounds of the heart. His was a life-work, to heal and expand her heart to hold the great happiness....

Beth felt herself giving away secrets, when Bedient looked at her early this afternoon. He glanced as usual into her face—

but then, a second time. She followed his eyes an instant later to the place on the mantel, where the small picture of the Other had rested for just one day. He started to ask a question, but she took the little book, and thanking him, held the talk to it.

Bedient grappled with an obstacle he could not master. In the silences of that day, something different from anything he had met before, closed in; a new order of atmosphere that altered the very tone and color of things. It seemed not in the studio alone, but in the world. Bedient fell into depths of thinking before it. A sudden turn for the worst in a well-established convalescence, held something of the same startling confrontation. There was no response to his willing it away. It was fateful, encompassing.

Beth moved about the room, not ready at once to touch the picture. She carried the little book in her hand.... Strong but mild winds were blowing. Sudden gusts fell upon the skylight with the sound of spray, and sparrows scurried across the glass, their clawed feet moving swiftly about Mother Nature's business. The East ventilator shook, as if grimly holding on.

"A day like this always touches my nerves," she said. "The wind seems to bring a great loneliness out of the sea."

"It's pure land weather," he answered, "damp, warm, aimless winds. Now, if there was a strong, steady and chill East wind—"

But she wouldn't discuss what that might do. "Loneliness," she repeated. "What a common lot! One scarcely dares stop to think how lonely one is.... How many people do you know, who are happily companioned? I've known only six in my life, and two of those were brother and sister. It's the dull, constant, ache at the human heart. What's the reason, do you suppose?"

"The urge to completion—"

"I suppose it is, and almost never satisfied. I think I should train children first and last for the stern trials of loneliness. It's almost necessary to have resources within one's self—"

"But how wonderful when real companions catch a glimpse of each other across some room of the world!" he said quietly.

"A tragedy more often than not," she finished. "One of them so often has built his house, and must abide. Real companions never build their house upon the ruins of another."

"That has a sound ring."

"What is the reason for this everywhere, this forever loneliness?" she demanded, without lifting her eyes from the work.

"Something must drive," he replied. "You call it loneliness this morning. It's as good as any. Great things come from yearning. People of the crowd choose each other at random, under the pressure of passionate loneliness. Greater human hearts vision their One. Once in a while the One appears and answers the need—and then there is happiness. There is nothing quite so important as the happiness in each other of two great human hearts. Don't you see, it can exist hardly a moment, until it is adjusted to *all time*—until its relation to eternity is firmly established? When that comes, the world has another beautiful centre of pure energy to look at and admire and aspire to. And the spirit of such a union never dies, but goes on augmenting until it becomes a great river in the world.

"It is very clear to me," he went on, trying to fight the shadows, "that something like this must happen before great world-forces come into being. First, the two happy ones learn that love is giving. Their love goes on and on into a bigger thing than love for each other, and becomes love for the race. That's the greater glory. Avatars have that. The children of real lovers have such a chance for that vaster spirit! Indeed, you can almost always trace a great man's lineage back to some lustrous point of this kind."

Beth regarded him deeply for a moment. She could not adjust him to commonness. She was suffering. Bedient saw only the mystic light of that suffering. He had never loved her as at this moment.

"I always wish I could paint you, as you look when you are thinking about such things!" she said. "Just as you looked when you spoke about two people who have illumined each other, so that they turn their great anguish of loving upon the race.... Yes, I see it: prophets might indeed come from that kind of love."

Beth worked with uncommon energy for many minutes. All-forgetting—time, place, tension and the man near. Her spirit was strangely sustained under his eyes. The work flew, and left little traces of its processes in her mind—her concentration was deeper than memory.

*   *   *   *   *

"I'd like to ride with you," he said, rising to leave.

Beth had often spoken of her saddle-horse, which of late had been kept at her mother's country place. Bedient rented a very good mount in New York, but Beth remarked that her own had spoiled her for all others, adding that he would say so, too, if he could see Clarendon, the famous black she rode.

"I can't afford to keep him in the city long at a time," she explained. "Oh, it's not what he costs, but he's a devourer of daylight.... It breaks up half a day to get to the stables and change and all, and I haven't tried to ride after dark. We poor paint creatures are so dependent upon light for our work.... And yet riding adds to good health—just the right sparkle in my case."

"And that's royalty," Bedient declared.

Beth was thinking. He had spoken of riding with her before. He had been singularly appealing this day. Trouble had filled his eyes at the first sight of her, and she had felt his struggle with it.... Her mother had asked to see him, but there wasn't a good mate for Clarendon in or about Dunstan, where her home was.... She was so worn, mind and nerve and spirit, that the thought of a long ride lured strongly. She knew he would be different. Perhaps he might show, beyond the shadow of a doubt, that he was not identified with commonness.... He might bring the talk to the point of—Beth thrilled at this. She was far from ready, and yet with him before her, Wordling and the sea were remote and soundless.

"Could you get the good mare you ride—across to Jersey?"

"Yes," he said eagerly. "I could send a man over with her—a day ahead."

This was Thursday.

"I'll ride with you Saturday," she said finally. "You get your horse over to Dunstan Friday—to-morrow—and we'll start from here early Saturday morning. A day in the hills—and supper at night in my real home!"

She had never seen him so pleased, but Beth was a little startled at herself when she considered yesterday.... He was always so different when he came, from the creation of her mind when alone, and the doubts flew in and out. Then the little sacred book he had brought—so powerfully fathomed and marked—it was like bringing his youth to her, with all its thoughts and wanderings. He was particularly attractive to her in these little things, and she missed not a phase of such impulses. He delighted to see them in *her* house, he said, and she knew they had been his riches in the years of loneliness and wandering.... Far back in her faculties, however, the battle was furious and constant. Every faltering advance of faith was met and assailed.

"I thank you," he said. "In fact, I can't thank you.... What a day it will be for me to live over.... There's a little thing that needs doing. It will take me away for three or four days next week."

Beth almost laughed. She caught the laugh of mockery in time. The ride just arranged seized and held her attention, like some baleful creature. There was abomination about it, to her thoughts—the ease with which he had managed, her abject softness.... She was trembling within, all her resistance settling, straining, like a tree before the final stroke of the axe. Her hands trembled crazily and were cold.... She had given her word; yes, they would ride together. She could not evade his eyes, his question, if she refused now.... He must not see that she was whipped.... But she would not see him after that. He could not come back to her from the Wordling arms. She would not see him to-morrow. But the picture—

She had turned from the easel to her desk, and was fumbling

Will Levington Comfort

with papers there, her back turned to him. A half minute had passed since his last word... One word came from her:

"Yes?"

She had meant it to sound as if spoken absently, as if she were preoccupied in search for a certain paper. Instead it was an eldritch note in the room, like the croak of an evil bird... He was standing near the outer door. Something of her tumult must have come to him, she thought, for his voice was strangely altered when he asked:

"Will three or four days make any difference about the picture?"

... She would not see him again. He could not come back here to-morrow nor afterward. He must go away now... She thought of her wail to the Grey One that he would not go to the ocean with Wordling... It meant nothing to him; she could not punish *him* by keeping him away... But the picture—that final inner lustre. It had come to her this morning—what havoc in the memory—and she had seen it that day in the great gallery before his *Race Mother*, but had been unable quite to hold it in mind until the working light of the following day... She must not add to her own punishment, after all her care and labor, by failing in the last touch. And yet he must not come again...

"The picture, did you say?"

He repeated his question.

"Why, the picture is practically done," she said. "I'll sign and deliver it to-morrow. I think it will get to you to-morrow. The long, ridiculously long, preliminary work gave me the modelling, as well as I could have it.... This weather makes one think of the ocean or the mountains—"

She had forgotten this gray day of winds. Her sentence, and the design of it, had been founded upon the recent run of superb spring days.

"There's a little thing that needs doing by the ocean—that's why I go." His words seemed to come from a distance.

"It would not do for you to look at the picture here. You'd feel expected to say something pretty—or most would. I want it out of its work-light, then you can judge and send it back if it's bad. I'll try to have it at the Club to-morrow.... You did not know this was the final sitting, did you?"

She was talking feverishly, in fear of his questions. She knew it must sound strange and unreasonable to his mind.

"No," he said gently. "You always surprise me. And the ride—Saturday?"

"Yes, the ride.... We must start—"

"Early?"

"Yes. We'll meet—at the Thirty-fourth Street boat—at seven."

"I thank you. And good-by."

There was something amazing to her in his capacity not to question. In her weakness she was grateful almost to tears. She would not show him her hurt, but crossed the room hastily, and extended her hand with a brave smile.... Listening, she heard him descend the stairs.... Then from the front window, she saw him reach the street, turn to the

Avenue and mingle with men.

It was not like yesterday in the little room. That agony had worn her too much for another such crisis.... The thought fascinated, that there must be some hidden meaning to the queer promise she had been impelled to make—to ride with him Saturday.... The parting, his instant comprehension of some mood of hers, in which words had no place; his sad smile, and the look of gratitude when she came forward; his seeming content with all her decisions; his inability to question or ask favors—all these retained a remarkable hold upon her imagination. And even though, to her eyes, he stood as one fallen, there was poise in his presence.... Something about him brought back her dreams, whether or no, with all their ecstasy and dread. Already she was thinking of him—as one gone; and yet the studio seemed mystic with his comings and goings and gifts.... It came to her how her lips had quivered under his eyes, as she went forward to say good-by.... It was not three or four days, but "good-by," indeed.

* * * * *

Though she would have put the black mark of misery upon it, this was one of the greatest of Beth Truba's days. She had come into the world with a great faith to bestow—and some dreadful punishment, it seemed, made her bear it alone. It had long ached within to be given. It shamed her that she could not. With all her intellect, all her world-habit of mind, she believed that Andrew Bedient had fallen greatly— greatly, because he had shown himself so clean and wise. She granted to herself nothing but a thrilling admiration for him in his higher moments, but still she was associated with this fall, because she had permitted him to come to her, almost at will. And she had not been *enough* for him—what poison in that thought!

Yet, the unseen Shadowy Sister endeavored to restore her faith again and again, and garland the Wanderer with it....

Every instant of passing daylight harried her with the thought of the work yet to do. It might prove much—and to-morrow—the thought came with heaviness and darkening—the portrait must go to him. And the day after—he would go.... She dreaded to look at the picture now. Many touches of love, she had put upon it. Her highest thinking it had called, as his words had done. It had even stimulated her to an old dream of really great work. Beth Truba had long put that away.

The rapt look in his eyes; the rapt smile upon his lips when he spoke of his great theme; just to paint that, would be greatness. Just to put it once upon the canvas, that would be enough. It would show that she had seen more than man—deeper than flesh. One song, one picture, one book, is enough for any artist. She had always said that....

These thoughts stilled and softened her spirit—held her moveless in the centre of the room; but again the world returned, with all its play upon her finished intelligence.... He had not found her sufficient to restrain him from this ocean episode; and pride uprose—a vindictive burning that scorched full-length.

"He is very brave and evolved," she whispered bitterly, "but the man within him was not to be denied.... Wordling has that.... God, it seems as if there is nothing of that—in red-haired Beth Truba!... No, he must run off to the ocean, quite as if he had been a poor, impatient boy, like the Other!"

Her face crimsoned. The shame and agony of the thought brought her to her knees before the picture she had painted.

"And perhaps it *is* my fault," she whispered desperately. "Perhaps I have asked too much, and waited too long. Perhaps they see—what I do not—and women lie—and I only think I feel! Perhaps I *am* weathered and inflexible, and hard and old and cold, and they know, and become afraid!"

But there was stern denial in the face before her—reproach in the eyes she had made of paint.... In her terror before these thoughts, which struck home in the hour of her weakness, the art of the thing suddenly prevailed—good work, the valiant rescuer.... She remembered how her presence had aroused the giant in the Other. Her spell had done that. She had felt the crush of his arms, and queer fires had laughed across her brain. Then she fell again with the thought, that even that had not sufficed. Her pride had sent him away even after that—his laugh, his Greek beauty, his passion and all.... And now it came to her with fierce reality, that should the Other ever return, it would only make these later hours and later memories burn the deeper.... A temptation came to hold Bedient—as a woman could—to keep him from going to another woman, but her eyes fell with swift shame from the picture.

"I have not made you common—how can I be common with you?" she cried. "Oh, why could you not always remember your best, you, who have helped others so?"

The light, though gray, was still strong. Fixed upon the canvas, as she had never seen it before, was a revelation of one of those high moments which had exalted Vina Nettleton, and changed David Cairns in the whole order of his being. She almost listened for him to speak of the natural greatness of women.

"But you are forgetting those higher moments," she whispered. "That's the way with men and boys—to forget—

to run away for the little things beside the ocean—"

But the face denied; the face was of purity. It regarded her steadily in her long watching—a fixture of poise, happiness assured.... Then the need of haste and work, left deep in her mind, arose to the surface with a strong and sudden urging—the delivery to-morrow. Her heart, her flesh, her soul, all were at war and weary unto death. It was hideous to attempt to touch it again that day; yet to-morrow an evil light ... and now came the full realization of a remarkable fact.

The final inner lustre was there. The thing she had long been afraid to do, save in the exact perfect moment, was done. That Something of his was before her, its lifting valor not to be denied....

It was just before he had asked her to ride, she recalled now. An elate concentration had held her while she painted. She had not spoken; she had hardly known the world about her. It had been too big to leave a memory.... It was done. It pleaded for him. It was like the Shadowy Sister pleading for him. Swiftly, she signed the work. It was his. That was hard.

...In the veil of dusk she was still kneeling, her face ghastly with waiting.... And not until pride intervened again, and prevailed upon her to see him no more, after the last ride together, did she find some old friendly tears, almost as remote from the days she now lived, as Florentine springtimes of student memory.

TWENTY-THIRD CHAPTER

THE LAST RIDE TOGETHER

Bedient arose at four on Saturday morning and looked out of his high window. June had come. The smell of rain was *not* in the air. He was grateful and drew up a chair, facing the East. The old mystery of morning unfolded over sea, and there was no blemish.... Bedient had not slept, nor during the two preceding nights. While the abundance of his strength was not abated, deep grooves (that came to abrupt blind endings) were worn in his mind from certain thoughts, and he was conscious of his body, which may be the beginning of weariness; conscious, too, of a tendency of his faculties to mark time over little things.

Yesterday the picture had come. He had hoped hard against this. Its coming had brought to him a sense of separateness from the studio, that he tried not to dwell upon in mind, but which recurred persistently.... He could not judge a portrait of himself; yet he knew this was wonderful. Beth had caught him in an animate moment, and fixed him there. Her fine ideal had put on permanence.... "Hold fast to a soul-ideal of your friend," he remembered telling her once, "and you help him to build himself true to it. If your ideal is rudely broken, you become one of the disintegrating forces at work upon him."

He keenly felt the disorder in his relation to Beth. The thought that held together, against all others, was that Beth loved some one, just now out of her world. He wished she could see into his mind about this; instantly, he would have helped her; his dearest labor, to restore her happiness.

He had never been confident of winning. He loved far too well, and held Beth too high, ever to become familiar in his thoughts of her as a life companion. Power lived in her presence for him; great struggles and conquerings. He loved every year she had lived; every hour of life that had brought her to this supremacy of womanhood before which he bowed, was precious to him. In this instance he was myopic. He did not see Beth Truba as other women, and failed to realize this. His penetration faltered before her, for she lived and moved in the brilliant light of his love, blended with it, so that her figure, and her frailties, lost all sharpness of contour.

He had suffered in the past three days and nights. He was proud and glad to suffer. There was no service nor suffering that he would have hesitated to accept for Beth Truba.... This day amazed him in prospect, one of her beautiful gifts to him. It was almost as if she had come to his house, lovely, unafraid, and sat laughing before his fire. One of the loftiest emotions, this sense of companionship with her. There was something of distinct loveliness in every hour they had passed together. Not one of their fragrances had he lost. These memories often held him, like mysterious gardens.

...Bedient paced the big area in front of the ferry entrance long before seven. He saw her the instant she stepped from the cross-town car. The day was momentarily brightening, yet something of the early morning red was about her. His throat tightened at sight of her radiant swiftness. Her eyes were deeper, her lips more than ever red.... On the deck of

Will Levington Comfort

the ferry, before the start, she said:

"I feel as if we were escaping from somewhere, and could not tolerate a moment's delay."

...At ten o'clock they were in the saddle, and Dunstan was far behind. The morning, as perfect as ever arose in Northern summer; the azure glorified with golden light, and off to the South, a few shining counterpanes of cloud lay still. The half had not been told about Beth's Clarendon, a huge rounded black, with a head slightly Roman, and every movement a pose. He was skimp of mane and tail; such fine grain does not run to hair. While there was sanity and breeding in his steady black eye, every look and motion suggested "too much horse" for a woman. Yet Beth handled him superbly, and from a side-saddle. Clarendon had in his temper, that gift of show aristocrats—excess of life, not at all to be confused with wickedness—which finds in plain outdoors and decent going, plentiful stimulus for top endeavor and hot excitement.

"I've had him long," Beth said, "and though he has sprung from a walk to a trot countless times without a word from me, he has yet to slow down of his own accord. He can do his twelve miles an hour, and turn around and do it back.... You see how he handles—for me."

She delighted in his show qualities, rarely combined with such excellent substance. She showed his gaits, but rode a trot by preference. Bedient, who had a good mare, laughed joyously when his mount was forced into a run to keep abreast. Clarendon, without the slightest show of strain, had settled to his trot.... All Bedient's thinking and imaging during the years alone, of the woman he should some time find, had never brought him anything so thrilling as this slightly flushed profile of Beth's now. What an anchorage of reality she was, after years of dream-stuff—a crown of discoveries, no less—and what an honor, her gift of companionship! He felt an expansion of power, and strength to count this day great with compensation, should the future know only the interminable dull aching of absence and distance.

Bedient had started to speak of the picture, but she bade him wait.... As they rode along a country road, they came to an old ruin of a farm-house, surrounded by huge barns, some new, and all in good repair. A little beyond was a calf tied to a post. It was lying down, its legs still being largely experimental—a pitifully new calf, shapeless and forlorn.

The mother was nowhere around. Sick in some far meadow, perhaps, sick of making milk for men.

"That's a veal calf," Beth said.

The note in her voice called his eyes. Something which the sight suggested was hateful to her. Bedient dismounted and led his chestnut mare up to the little thing, which stared, tranced in hope and fear. The mare dropped her muzzle benignantly. She understood and became self-conscious and uncomfortable. One of a group of children near the farmhouse behind them called:

"Show off! Show off!"

"They sell its rightful food," Beth said, "and feed the poor little thing on cheaper stuff until it hardens for the butcher. Men are so big with their business."

"There are veal calves tied to so many posts on the world's highway," Bedient said slowly.

"When I was younger," Beth went on, "and used to read about the men who had done great creative things, I often found that they had to keep away from men and crowds, lest they perish from much pitying, dissipate their forces in wide, aimless outpourings of pity, which men and the systems of men called from them. Then—this was long ago—I used to think this a silly affectation, but I have come to understand."

"Of course, you would come to understand," Bedient said.

"Men who do great things are much alone," she continued. "They become sensitive to sights and sounds and odors— they are so alive, even physically. The downtown man puts on an armor. He must, or could not stay. The world seethes with agony—for him who can see."

"That is what made the sacrifice of the Christ," Bedient declared. "Every day—he died from the sights on the world's highway—"

They looked back.

"It was not the Cross and the Spear, but the haggard agony of His Face that night on Gethsemane that brings to me the realization of the greatness of His suffering," he added.

"And the disciples were too sleepy to watch and pray with him—"

"How gladly would the women have answered His need for human companionship that night!" he exclaimed. "But it was not so ordained. It was His hour alone, the most pregnant hour in the world's history."

They reached the crest of a fine hill at noon, and dismounted in the shade of three big elms. They could see small towns in the valley distances, and the profile of hilltop groves against the sky. The slopes of the hill wore the fresh green of June pasture lands; and three colts trotted up to the fence, nickering as they came.... Beth was staring away Westward through the glorious light. Bedient came close to her; she felt his eyes upon her face, turned and looked steadily into them. She was the first to look down. Beth had never seen his eyes in such strong light, nor such power of control, such serenity, such a look of inflexible integrity.... She did not like that control. It was not designed in the least to take away the hate and burning which for three days had warred against the best resistance of her mind.

That cool lofty gaze was her portion. Another—on the shore—ignited the fires. A devil within—for days and nights—had goaded her: "Yes, Beth Truba, red haired and all that, but old and cold, just the same, and strange to men."

"I've wanted this day," he said. "It was some need deeper than impulse. I wanted it just this way: A hill like this, shade of great trees that whispered, distant towns and woods, horses neighing to ours. Something more ancient and authoritative than the thing we call Memory, demanded it this way. Why, I believe we have stood together before."

Beth smiled, for the goading devil had just whispered to her, "You were a vestal virgin doubtless—oh, severely chaste!"... She said, "You believe then we have come up through 'a cycle of Cathay'?"

"If I had heard your name, just your name, over there in India," he replied thoughtfully, "it would have had some deep meaning for me."

"The 'cycle of Cathay' wasn't enough to cure you?"

He turned quickly, but didn't smile. "I think there was always some distance between us, that we were never equal, a difference like that between Clarendon and the chestnut. Only you were always above me, and it was the better, the right way. Beth—"

She looked up.

"Is there any reason why I shouldn't tell you how great you are to me—just that—asking nothing?"

"We are both grown-ups," she answered readily. "You won't mind if I find it rather hard to believe—I mean, my greatness. You like my riding and the portrait—"

"I can judge your riding. As for the picture, it is an inspiration, though I cannot judge that so well. But it is not those—"

"And what then, pray?"

"Beth Truba."

"A tired old artist whom nobody knows—really."

"I wish you wouldn't say that," he declared earnestly. "There is nothing alive this moment, nothing in the great sun's light, that has put on such a glory of maturity. Why, you are concentrated sunlight—to me!"

"That's very pretty," she said, and turned a glance into his eyes.... The same cool deeps were there, though his face held a singular happiness. She wondered if it were because she had not forbade him to speak. Did he think she was ready, and that her heart was free?

There was no one on the sloping hill-road, either to the right or left, and only the colts in the meadows. A good free thing—this elimination of human beings—though at this height, they stood in the very eye of the country-side. The chestnut mare was cropping the young grass by the edge of the highway, but there were matters for Clarendon to understand—far distances and movements not for human eyes. The colts racing up and down the hill-fence were beneath his notice. The great arched neck was lifted for far gazing and listening, and that which came to his foreign senses, caused him to snort softly from time to time....

Beth rode without hat. Her arms were bare to the elbows; her gray silk waist open at the throat. She stretched out her arms, and the sunlight, cut by the high elm boughs, fell upon her like a robe, woven of shimmerings. She seemed to want her full portion of vitality from the great upbuilding day.

"It's strong medicine—this high noon of June," she said. "One feels like unfolding as flowers do."

And then came over him—over all his senses—something flower-like in scent, yet having to do with no particular flower. It dilated his nostrils, but more than that, all his senses awoke to the strange charm of it.... The distance between them was gone that instant. Though it may have endured for ages and ages, it was gone. He had overtaken her.... A haunting influence; and yet of magic authority! Was it the perfume of the lotos and the bees? It was more than that. It was the sublimate of all his bewitchings—chaste mountains, dawns, the morning glow upon great heights, the flock of flying swans red with daybreak; more still, all the petals of the Adelaide passion restored in one drop of fragrance, and lifted, a different fragrance, the essence of a miracle! This was the perfume that came from her life, from her arms and throat and red mouth....

It was new out of the years. All his strangely guarded strength arose suddenly animate. A forgotten self had come back to him, all fresh and princely out of long enchantment.... And there she stood with face averted awaiting this Return!... This was the mysterious prince who had wrought in darkness so long, the source of his dreams of woman's greatness, the energy that had driven and held him true to his ideals, the structure into which his spiritual life had been builded (was this the world's mighty illusion possessing him?), and now the prince had come, asking for his own.... And she was there, stretching out her arms.

Mighty forces awoke from sleep. They were not of his mind, but deep resolutions of all his life, forces of her own inspiring which she must gladly, gloriously obey. Was it not her love token, this electric power, as truly as his mind's ardor and his spiritual reverence?... The miracle of her life's fragrance held him.... Even desire was beautiful in a love like this. All nature trembles for the issue, when love such as his perceives the ripe red fruit of a woman's lips.... But better far not to know it at all, than to know the half.

*　　*　　*　　*　　*

And Beth was thinking of the cool depths in his eyes a moment before, and of his words, "asking nothing."... "Why asks he nothing of me?... Because I am old and cold."... Some terrific magnetism filled her suddenly, as if she had drawn vitality from great spaces of sunlight, and some flaming thing from the huge hot strength of Clarendon.... And now the goading devil whispered:

"With another he would not ask, he would take! Only you— you do not attract great passions. The source of such attraction is gone from you. Mental interests and spiritual ideals are your sphere!... Second-rate women whistle and the giants come! They know the lovers in men. *You* know the sedate mental gardeners and the tepid priests. How you worship that still, cool gazing in the eyes of men! Books and pictures are quite enough—for your adventures in passion. In them, you meet your great lovers—of other women. You are Beth Truba of street and studio. You can send lovers away. You can make them afraid of your tongue, strip them of all ardor with your nineteenth century bigotry.... You have so many years to waste. Empty arms are so light and cool, *their* veins are never scorched; they never dry with age!... Oh, red-haired Beth Truba, all the spaces of sky are laughing at you! To-morrow or next day, by the ocean, another woman will start the flames in those cool eyes of his, and feel them singing around her!... Why do you let him go? Only a nineteenth century mind with the ideas of a slave woman would let him go!... Keep him with you. Show your power. Create the giant. By no means is that the least of woman's work!"

She shuddered at such a descent.

"Would you go back and be the waiting spider forever in the yellow-brown studio, breaking your heart in the little room when some woman chooses to bring you news of men and the world? You would not descend to woman's purest prerogative?... Greater women than you shall come, and they shall avail themselves of that, and their children shall be great in the land...."

"Oh, what a world, and what a fool!" Beth said aloud.

"Why?"

She turned at his quick, imperious tone.

"I don't—I don't know. It just came!"

Beth bit her lip, and shut her eyes. There was a booming in her brain, as from cataracts and rapids. His face had made her suddenly weak, but there was something glorious in being carried along in this wild current. She had battled so long. She was no longer herself, but part of him. The face she had seen was white; the eyes dark and piercing, terrible in their concentration of power, but not terrible to her. All the magic from the sunlight had come to them. They were the eyes which command brute matter.... The Other had become a giant; this man a god.

"What a day!" she whispered.

"Let's ride on!" he said swiftly.

The horses whirled about at his word. As his hand touched hers, she felt the thrill of it, in her limbs and scalp. He lifted her to the saddle. There was something invincible in his arms. The strength he used was nothing compared to that which was reserved....

She seemed the plaything of some furious, reckless happiness.... "Asking nothing! Asking nothing!" repeated again and again in her brain. And what should he ask—and why?... Her thoughts flew by and upward—intent, but swift to vanish, like bees in high noon. Atoms of concentrated sunlight, sun-gold upon their wings.... The good hot sun, all the earth stretched out for it, and giving forth green tributes. The newest leaf and the oldest tree alike expanded with praise.... What a splendor to be out of the city and the paint and the tragedy; to have in her veins the warm brown earth and the good hot sun—and this mighty dynamo beneath! She was mad with it all, and glad it was so.

Beth raised her eyes to the dazzling vault. One cannot sit a horse so—well. She lost the rhythm of her posting, but loved the roughness of it. The heights thralled her. Up, up, into the blue and gold, she trembled with the ecstasy of the thought, like the bee princess in nuptial flight—a June day like this— up, up, until the followers had fallen back—all but two—all but one—which one?... There was a slight pull at her skirt. She turned.

He was laughing. His hand held a fold of her dress against the cantle of the saddle. She could not have fallen on the far side, and he was on this.... A sudden plunge of a mount would unseat any rider, staring straight up.... Yes, he was there!... How different the world looked—with him there. She had ridden alone so long. She dared to look at him again.

His eyes were fastened ahead. Could it be illusion—their fiery intentness? She followed his glance.... The big woods—she knew them, had ridden by them many times— how deep and green they looked!... But what was the meaning of that set, inexorable line of his profile? What was he battling? That was her word, her portion. For hours, days, years she had been battling, but not now! No longer would she be one of the veal calves tied to a post on the world's highway, to consume the pity of poor avatars!... Avatars— the word changed the whole order of her thoughts; and those which came were not like hers, but reckless ventures on forbidden ground; and, too, there was zest in the very foreignness of the thoughts: Avatars—did they not spring into being from such instants as this—high noon, vitality rising to the sun, all earth in the stillness of creation; and above, blue and gold, millions and millions of leagues of sheer happiness; and behind—put far behind for the hour— all crawling and contending creatures....

And now the yellow-brown studio would not remain behind, but swept clearly into her thinking. Something was queer about it. Yes, the havoc of loneliness and suffering was gone.... And there seemed a rustling in the far shadows of the little room. Could it be the Shadowy Sister returning? And that instant, with a realism that haunted her for years, there came—to her human or psychic sense, she could never tell— *a tiny cry!*... Beth almost swooned. His hand sustained ... and then she saw again his laughing face; all the intensity gone. It was carved of sunlight. Everything was sunlight.

Beth spoke to Clarendon. She would ride—show him, she needed no hand in riding. The great beast settled down to his famous trot, pulling the chestnut mare to a run. Clarendon was steady as a car; the faster his trot, the easier to ride.... She turned and watched this magician beside her; his bridle-arm lifted, the leather held lightly as a pencil; laughing, asking nothing, needing not to ask. And she was unafraid, rejoicing in his power. All fear and slavishness and rebellion, all that was bleak and nineteenth century, far behind. This was the Rousing Modern Hour—her high day.

Nearer and nearer—the big woods.... She was thinking of a wonderful little path ahead. She had never ventured in alone, a deep, leafy footpath, soft with moss and fern-embroidered.... There was no one on the road ahead, nor behind; only young corn in the sloping field on the left, and now the big woods closed in on the right, and Beth reined a little.

There was no shade upon the highway, even with the wood at hand. The horses were trampling their own shadows in this zenith hour.... She watched his eye quicken as he noted the little path.

"Ah—let's go in!" he called, pulling up.

It was her thought. "I've always wanted to, but never dared, alone," she panted, bringing Clarendon down.

Bedient dismounted, pulled the reins over the mare's head and through his arm; then held up both hands to her.... Something made her hesitate a second. He did not seem to consider her faltering.

"Oh, Beth, why should *we* rush in there, as if we were afraid of the light?... Come!"

She knew by his eyes what would happen; and yet she leaned forward, until his hands fitted under her arms, and her eyelids dropped against the blinding light....

"It had to be in the great sunlight—*that!*.... How glorious you are!"

"Please ... put me down!"

But again, he kissed her mouth, and the shut eyelids. And when her feet at last touched the earth, he caught her up again, because her figure swayed a little,—and laughed and kissed her—until the fainting passed....

* * * * *

"... And—these—were—the—great—things—you asked permission to tell me?" she said slowly, without raising her eyes.

The strange smile on her scarlet lips, and the lustrous pallor of her face, so wonderfully prevailed, that he caught her in his arms again. And they were quite alone in that mighty light, as if they had penetrated dragons-deep in an enchanted forest.

"I cannot help it. You are stronger!" she said in the same trailing, faery tone.... "And that distance—between us—that you always felt—in 'the cycle of Cathay'—you seem to have overcome that—"

"It was another century—"

"Oh—"

"And now to explore the wood!"

"But the horses, sir—"

"They will stand."

... She would not let him help, but loosened Clarendon's bridle, and slipping out the bit, put the head-straps back. Bedient shook his head.

"It may slide askew that way, and worry him more than if the bit were in," he said.

"If you command, I shall put it back."

"Let me."

"No."

Smiling, he watched her. The frail left hand parted the huge foamy jaws, and held them apart—thumb and little finger— while the other hand, behind Clarendon's ears, drew the bit home. The big fellow decently bowed his head to take the steel from her. Then she patted the mouse-colored muzzle, and gave the reins to the man, who, much marvelling, tethered the two horses together.

Then they set forth into the wood.

TWENTY-FOURTH CHAPTER

A PARABLE OF TWO HORSES

They were nearing Dunstan on the way back. The light had flattened out, and the little town was stretching its shadows. They were silent.... Beth was trying to fit this day to days that had gone, but it was hard. This had a brightness apart from them, but it seemed to her now that the brightness was gone with the sun. She was tired—and *alone*. The thoughts in her mind had brought the sense of separateness.

She must soon know from him, if the day had served her end. She thought of her temptation in the studio—to hold him from the ocean, as a woman might, as a Wordling might. She had not needed quite to do that, merely to let herself go. The glorious lover in him had done more than she dreamed, in making her Beth of the bestowals, this day.

In the sunlight, she had been one with him. Rather startlingly it came to her now, that she could have asked anything *then*. But in those incomparable moments of the high day, there had been nothing to ask. How strange this was to her! How utterly had they put all commonness behind.

She trembled at the thought of another woman rousing that lover in him, looking upon the miracle she had evoked. She could not bear it, nor could she suffer him to know this thought of hers.

They were riding down into the town. Brightenings from the West were still upon the upper foliage of the trees, but vague dusk had fallen between their faces. His features were white and haggard.... She was afraid to ask him now. She would wait for the darkness. Had he heard a tremble in her voice, Bedient would have caught her bridle-rein and searched her face.

She clucked. Clarendon, with stables just ahead, was only too eager.... Bedient rejoined her after turning over his horse, and making the change of clothes. Beth met him at the gate of her mother's house and there was a smile in the evening light.

They did not sit opposite at supper. Bedient studied the little mother at the head of the table, but with a fear in his heart. A sense of disaster had come to him at the end of the ride. He knew nothing of what had formed about the short sea journey in Beth's mind; he could not have believed from her own lips that she had been tempted to hold him with passion. He would have expected faith from her, had some destroying tale come to her ears. He did not realize the effect upon others, of his aptness to ignore all explanation. Especially in this seagoing affair, he had nothing to say. It was not his way to discuss his adventures into the happiness of others.... Beth felt his reserve instinctively, a reason why it had been impossible for her to show him the document of disorder.

The talk at the supper table had to do with the portrait she had painted. Beth never forgot some of Bedient's sentences.... Then she told him about the new life of the Grey One; of the latter's call on Wednesday, with the great news about Torvin, and of the telephone message yesterday.

"More buyers have been to her studio," Beth said. "You see, Torvin can do anything. A whisper from him and they buy. The Grey One has disposed of several of her little things at her vogue prices—"

"I'm glad," said Bedient.

"It came in the nick of time. It means more than money or pictures. Margie Grey has won her race."

"I understand," he added.

After supper, they walked together outside. With her whole heart Beth prayed that the day had changed him from going. She had put off until the last moment any talk that would bring his answer. And now walking with him in the darkness, she thought strangely of her parting with the Other. All was forgotten save that moment of parting; all the old intimacies had dropped from mind, banished by the sunlit god she had met this day.... Bedient's defect would be quite as intrinsic as the Other's—if he went to Wordling now. She could have forgiven a boyish carelessness in either, but Beth could not forgive in any man that unfinished humanity which has a love-token for the obviously common and sensuous.... She was ill with terror and tension. And how pitifully human she was! A greater faith or a lesser strength would have saved her. Beth failed in the first. It was her madness; her mortal enemy—this pride.

"I doubt if there could be such another day of June," she observed at last, wondering if he caught the hard note in her voice.... This would bring his word. She would cry aloud with happiness—if the day had changed him.

"To-morrow—" he answered. "Beth, is there anything to prevent to-morrow—?"

"Riding together?"

"Yes."

"Not to-morrow. The horses had better rest a day. We must have done twenty-five miles to-day.... But early next week—"

She had turned away, as one averts the face from disaster. Even had she not turned from him, it was too dark to see his queer troubled smile, as he said:

"Monday, I go away. It's that ocean matter. Three days will finish it, I'm sure."

So this was her answer. Beth of the bestowals had not prevailed. This was the inner uprooting. Love-lady she had been—love-lady of thrilling arts this day—and yet his determination to go to the other was not altered.... She would not show him tears of rage and jealousy. She would not see him again. She meant to show him that the day had not stormed her heart of hearts. Her spirit was torn, and she was not above hurting him.... "Three days will finish it, I'm sure." To her the sentence had the clang of a prison door.... It was through the Other that she proceeded now.... How he had struck her through another!....

They had walked for some time through the evergreens. His listening had become like a furious draught, her brain burning intensely beneath it. It had been hard for her to begin, but that was over.... "It was not until to-day that there was any need to tell you," she was saying. "You were inspiring in other ways. I would have been stupid, indeed, not to have seen that, but somehow you seemed remote from everyday habiliments and workday New York—somehow inseparable from silences—until to-day—when you came singing *Invictus*. You did not let me tell you—out there—in the sunlight. You didn't let me think of telling you.... You mustn't judge me always so susceptible—"

She halted, lost for an instant in the emptiness.

"Please tell me about him," Bedient said.

"Why, he was only a working boy when he first came to our house—here," she went on. "I was just back from Paris—after years. I remember with what a shock of surprise I noted the perfection of his face. The angle was absolutely correct as the old Hellenic marbles, and to every curve was that final warmth which stone can only distantly suggest. Then he was tall, but so light and lithe—"

She knew he would not fail to see the flaw here—the artistic taint. She had heard him deplore the worship of empty line, saying that nature almost invariably travesties it.

"I was hasty, then, in my conclusion to-day," he said, questioning, "when I asked if there was any reason why I should not tell you how great you are to me?"

"It did not seem the time to tell you," she answered quickly. "I was wrong, but—it was not wrong to him! Please don't think that! I sent him away."

"Oh, I see better—thank you. And now go on, Beth, please—"

"You see, he was my work—"

Beth's mother now called from the front door. She was going upstairs and would say good-night to Mr. Bedient.

"Go to her," Beth whispered. "I shall see her later."

... And now she stood alone by the gate, her mind seething. Forces within falteringly implored her to go no further. She found in his few brief questions that old fidelity to truth that had been one of his first charms. This helped to unsteady her. Was she not wrong to judge this man by the standards the world had made her accept for others?... The day came back. Why had Wordling been so far from her mind out there in the sunlight? Radiant with health, thrilling with mysteries, in the summit of her womanhood, she had been above fear, and he above evil. The Shadowy Sister, too, had gone forth to meet him, majestic and unashamed. What spell was that which had come over her, a perfect vein-dilation in the brilliant light? Why, it had seemed to her that she could feel the pulse of flower-stems, and paint the nervous systems of the bees. Painting—what a pitiful transaction was art (in the divine stimulus at that hour) compared to the supernal happiness of evolved motherhood! And what exquisite homage had he shown her! And the long talk, his mind crowded with pictures like memories of a world-voyage! Again and again, there had come over her, some inner uplift, as if she were rising upon a wave.... She heard his tones now, as he spoke to her mother on the porch, and his gentleness throughout recurred.

The Other had gone from her world, and now he was going. Her mind shrank from the new and utter desolation.... The night seemed closing about her, as she stood beside the gate. Like some great foreign elemental, it was, until she was near to screaming, and perceived herself captive to madness—a broken-nerved creature in a strange place, stifling among aliens, undone in the torment of strange stars.... And, another, the ancient terror to strong women, now fell upon her, to show Beth Truba how mighty she was to suffer. The sense of her own fruitlessness drove home to her breast, of living without solution, realizing that all her fluent emotions, lovely ideals, all her sympathies, dreams and labors, should end with her own tired hands; that she must know the emptiness of every aspiration, while half-finished women everywhere were girdled with children.... He was coming toward her.

That instant, a merciful blankness fell upon her mind. Out of the fury and maiming, her consciousness seemed lifted to some cool blackness. There was just one vague, almost primal, instinct, such as a babe must feel—the need to be taken in his arms. The wall between them would have fallen had Bedient done that, but nothing was further from his thoughts. He, too, was groping in terrible darkness. Her spirit was lost to him.... There was no moonlight, so he could not discern the anguish of her face, and the sense of her suffering blended with his own.... A very wise woman has said that it isn't a woman's mysteries which dismay and mislead a man, but her contradictions.

"And now tell me the rest, Beth," he said quickly, looking down into the pale blur which was her face. "I must know."

She shivered slightly. She was dazed. Hatred for the moment, hatred for self and the world, for him, imperiously pinning her to the old sorrow; his failure to make a child of her, as a lover of less integrity might have done—it was all a sickening botch, about Wordling's pretty taunting face. She had not the strength of faculty to tear down and build again the better way.

"You were telling me that he was your work—of his face and all," Bedient whispered.

"Oh, yes.... Oh, yes, and you went away—"

"Yes," he said strangely.

"I must have been dreaming.... It hurt me so—he hurt me so. I remember—"

And now a cold gray light dawned in her brain, and the old story cleared—the old worn grooves were easily followed.

"Yes."

"But I—perhaps—I was inexorable." There was something eerie in that touch which held her for an instant.

"But you started to tell me more about him, I'm sure, at first," Bedient said. The idea in his brain needed this.

"I helped him in his studies," she answered angrily. There was something morbid to her in Bedient's intensity. "I helped him in the world, or friends of mine did. Yes, I made his way among men until he could stand alone. And he did, quickly. He was bright. Even his refinements of dress and manner and English—I undertook at the beginning."

Half-dead she had fallen into the old current, not compre- hending a tithe of his suffering.

"Oh, I put love into it!" she said dully. "I thought it the most glorious work I ever did."

"You tell me wonderfully about yourself, Beth, with these few sentences.... There is nothing finer in my comprehension than the mother-spirit in the maid which makes her love the boy or the man whom she lifts and inspires."

The cool idealist had returned. Beth did not welcome him.

"I believe that every achievement which lifts a man above his fellows is energized by some woman's outpouring heart.

She bestows brave and beautiful things of her own, working in the dark, until the hour of his test, as those fine straws of the Tropics are woven under water—"

"And what mockery to find," she finished coldly, "after you have woven and woven, that the fabric finally brought to light is streaky and imperfect."

Bedient's business of the moment was to learn if she were right in being as she said, "inexorable"; if she did not sometimes think that a finely-human heart might have come since to that flashing exterior, which had filled the girlish eyes. He could only draw from the whole savage darkness that the Other still lived in her heart.

"But he will not stay forgotten—is that it, Beth?"

Into the cold gray light of her mind, came a curious parable that had occurred to her, as they started out to ride this morning, before the great moments of high noon. And thus she related it to Bedient in the hatred which filled her, last of all from his imperturbable coolness:

"I saddled a great deal, even as a girl. In New York, years ago, the desire came to possess a horse of my own. I bought a beautiful bay colt, pure saddle-bred, rare to look upon; but something always went wrong with him. He galled, threw a shoe and went lame, stumbled, invariably did the unexpected, and often the dangerous, thing. Truly he was brand new every morning. I worried as if he were a child, but I wasn't the handler for him; he spoiled in my care; yet how I loved that colt—the first. He might have killed me, had I kept him.... It was over a year before I had the heart to buy again— Clarendon—big, courageous, swifter than the other, splendid in strength, yet absolutely reliable in temper. Day after day, in all roads and weathers, he never failed nor fell—until—"

Beth halted. The parable faltered here. She foresaw a dangerous question, and finished it true to Clarendon.

"Until—" Bedient repeated.

"Until now—and you have seen him to-day," she said hastily. "Always he seems to be aiming at improvement with eager, unabated energy. In many ways, it was hard for me to realize that a horse could be so noble.... And yet I gave to the first something that I didn't have for the second. Something that belonged to the second, was gone from me—"

A moment passed. Beth glanced into Bedient's face, but the darkness was too deep for her to see. When he spoke, it was as steadily as ever:

"I understand clearly, Beth. I should say, don't do the first an injustice. It was those very uncertainties of his, those coltish frights and tempers, that made you so perfect a mistress of the second, for you invariably bring forth the *best* from the second."

Something big came to her from the utterance. But nothing of the truth—that his heart had just received a death-thrust to its love-giving.... He had left his gloves in the house. He asked for a cup of water.... It was strange—his asking for anything. She could remember only, besides this, his wish expressed that she might ride with him. He had asked nothing this day. And it was a *cup* of water now.... They were in the lamplight, and he had drunk.... She was standing by the table, and he at the door waiting for her to lift her eyes.... Suddenly she felt, through the silence, his great strength pouring over her.

She looked up at last. There was a dazzling light in his eyes, as if some wonderful good to do had formed in his mind.

"Beth, was he the Other Man—who rested for one day on the mantel in the studio?"

"Yes."... The question shocked her. She could not have believed that it was harder for him to ask, than for her to answer....

He came nearer. Like a spirit he came.... He seemed very tall and tired and white.... Her hand was lifted to his lips, but when she turned, he was gone.

Beth did not shut the door.... The sound of a shut door must not be the last so strange a guest should hear. Beth was cold. She could hardly realize....

Bedient turned and saw the light streaming out upon the porch. She was not visible, but her shadow stood forth upon the boards, arms strangely uplifted. The mortal within him was outraged, because he did not turn back—into that open door.

III. EQUATORIA

Allegro Scherzo

TWENTY-FIFTH CHAPTER

BEDIENT FOR *THE PLEIAD*

Bedient dreamed:

He was sitting in the dark, in a high, still place; and at last (through a rift in the far mountains), a faint ghost appeared, waveringly white. Just a shimmering mist, at first, but it steadied and brightened, until the snowy breast of old *God-Mother* was configured in the midst of her lowly brethren on the borders of Kashmir.... And just as he was about to enter into the great peace, his consciousness beginning to wing with cosmic sweep, the rock upon which he sat started to creak and stir, and presently he was rolled about like a haversack in a heaving palanquin.

Thus he awoke, tossed in his berth aboard the *Hatteras*—and a gale was on. The ship, Southward bound, was far off the cape for which she was named, asking only wide sea-room, to take the big rollers with easy grace.

Bedient had not slept long. He had not slept for two consecutive hours during the past ten days. From the open door of *her* mother's house in Dunstan his whole life had felt the urge to India. But that could not be. It had the look of running away.

The little ocean matter had been happily ended.... The exact impulse to tell David Cairns of his intention to return to Equatoria, and the moment for it, had not offered, so Bedient had parted from his friend, as one going to a different room for the night. Nor had he seen Mrs. Wordling, the Grey One, Kate Wilkes or Vina Nettleton since the last ride; though for the latter, he left a page of writing she had asked.

Beth he had tried to see, four days after their parting in Dunstan, but she was not at her studio, nor with her mother. He did not seek further.

Bedient felt that he was needed in Equatoria, but there was another reason for his sudden return, than attention to the large financial interests. Though his home was there, Equatoria had no imperious call for him that his inner nature answered.... Only India had that. The very name was like water to a fevered throat. They would know in India. Old Gobind had always known:

"You will learn to look within for the woman. You would not find favor in finding her without. It is not for you—the red desire of love."

How he had rebelled against the authority of those sentences, but his respect for the deep vision of Gobind was complete. Moreover, the old *Sannyasin* had said he was not to return to India until he was ready to give up the body. No sense of the physical end had come to him, even in his darkest hour. There was much for him to do, and in New York, but the pith was gone from him. His desolation made the idea of returning to New York one of the hardest things he had ever faced. He had thought of Beth Truba in his every conception of service. She inspired a love which held him true to every ideal of woman, and kept the ideals flaming higher. And what form she had brought to his concepts! In expressing himself to her, direct world-values had attached to his thoughts. Through her he had seen the ways of work. Every hour, he blessed her in his heart—again and again; and every hour, the anguish deepened.

But work had a different look. Darkness covered his dreams of service. He was torn down; some great vitality was disintegrating. His projects would be carried out; he would continue to give, and continue to produce the things to give —but the heart, the love of giving, the spirit of outpouring to men—these were gone from him. There was a certain emptiness in following the old laws of his fuller nature. To give and serve now, was like obeying the commands of the dead. He had never turned to the past before. He would have been the first to tell another—that one who looks to his past for the sanction of some act of the present, has reached the end of growth.

Bedient could not lie to himself. He wanted to run away. He wanted to sit at the knees of some old Gobind. Never since the night his mother had taken him in her arms, had he so needed *to lean*.... Yes. he had failed to find favor—in finding the woman.

And now came to him the inevitable thought, and not without savagery to one of his nature: Was his high theme of uplift for women stimulated from the beginning by his need of a human mate? Was it a mere man-passion, which had charmed all his thoughts of women, from a boy? Was this the glow which had illuminated his work in the world, during the maturing silences of the Punjab? Was it physical, and not spiritual—this love of all women, until he had come into his love of one? And must he lose the broader love—in missing the love of one?

The answer lay dark in his consciousness. Ways to bring

happiness to women had come to him, but to carry them out now was mere obedience to the old galvanism. He faced this realization with deadly shame....

"You will learn to look within for the woman." And what was left within? In a kind of desperation, Bedient turned to this inventory. The old faith of the soul in God, in the Son, and in the Blessed Mother-Spirit still stood, apart and above the wreckage, unassailed. This was Light.

In these furious days of disintegration Bedient's soul-faith was not brought to test. A woman's might have fallen with her love.... But the mighty passionate being, that was roused to commanding actions in that high sunlit hour, died slowly and with agonies untellable.

The *Hatteras* steamed out of the gale, as she had done out of many another, in the same riotous stretch of sea-water. Bedient had become known aboard from his association with Captain Carreras. It was during the first dinner of the voyage that certain interesting information transpired from the conversation of Captain Bloom.

"Insurrection was smoking down there when we left ten days ago. We expected to hear in New York that the shooting had begun. Celestino Rey very nearly got a body-blow over, while we were hung up in port before the last trip up. Jaffier, the old Dictator, had just stepped out of his dingy little capitol, when a rifle-ball tore through his sleeve, between his arm and ribs. His sentries clubbed the rifle-man to death in the street—"

"It's rather a peculiar situation as I understand it," Bedient said. "The death of either leader—"

"Would mean an end to his party. That's it exactly," said

Captain Bloom.

A lively listener to this talk at the Captain's table was a dark-haired young woman with dancing brown eyes—Miss Adith Mallory. She was slender, and not tall, but spirited in manner; exhibited a fine freedom with her new acquaintances at the table, mostly gentlemen, but with an elegance which repelled familiarity. Miss Mallory seemed to find great fun in these revolutionary affairs, and a deep interest in Andrew Bedient, and his vast holdings on the Island. Her eyes quickly recalled to Bedient's mind a line of Tennyson's—"*Sunset and evening star, and after that the dark.*"

He saw very little of her until the *Hatteras* emerged into the warm, blue Caribbean, and he no longer had the excuse of rough weather to keep away from the dining-saloon. Miss Mallory favored every chance for a talk with Bedient, and once or twice he caught her regarding him with a strange, half-humorous depth of glance. One evening, as the ship was passing the northern coast of Porto Rico, they met on the promenade. The Island was a heavy shadow, off in the moon-bright South.

"... They say, Mr. Bedient, that if the revolution succeeds, it will make a great difference to you."

"Perhaps it may," he replied.

Miss Mallory had heard from the ship's officers, something of his relations with Captain Carreras. He laughingly deprecated his adequacy as a money-master.

"That's quite extraordinary," she said thoughtfully. "New York has not taught me to expect such from a man. Then the American dollar is not the sign of the Holy of Holies—to you?"

... Her talk was blithe. Presently she chaffed him for absences from the saloon during the rough weather.

"And you are such an old sailor, too," she finished.

"But my sailing was largely—sailing," he said. "It's different under steam."

"But we have been nearly three days in a turquoise calm, and I have watched you. A goldfinch would pine away on the nourishment you have taken! How do you manage to live?"

"You see how well I am," he said.

"You're not nearly—" Miss Mallory checked herself, and swallowed several times, before venturing again: "Do you know what I thought?"

"No."

"That you were in the clutch of mortal fear, lest you lose your fortune in the fighting."

"That *was* a bit wide, Miss Mallory—"

"In reparation for that injustice, I am going to tell you—what takes me to Coral City. I haven't told anyone else.... It's the prospect of a war. I've always wanted a revolution. You can never know how much.... You see, I'm an every-day working woman, a newspaper woman, but out of routine work. Some big things have fallen to me, but never war. Equatoria, the name and everything about it, has enchanted me for years—"

Bedient liked her enthusiasm. He explained much about the Island, Jaffier, Celestino Rey, *The Pleiad*, and the manner of men who frequented this remarkable palace. He advised

Miss Mallory not to be known as a newspaper woman, if she expected a welcome at *The Pleiad.*

The *Hatteras* finally made the coral passage, and was steaming into the inner harbor. Miss Mallory left Captain Bloom, who was pointing out the line of reefs, to join Bedient on the promenade-deck.

"I'm surprised and disappointed," she said. "I expected to hear shooting long before this."

"It may not be started," he suggested. "And now, Miss Mallory, we'd better not go ashore together. I'm known as a follower of Jaffier; and since you go to *The Pleiad,* the only really suitable place to live, you'd only complicate your standing in the community by being seen with me. If *The Pleiad* should happen to be invested in a siege, I'll see you comfortably quartered elsewhere. In any case, I am at your service."

Bedient was entirely unexpected at the *hacienda,* but a small caravan had come down to meet the steamer and carry back supplies. Coral City was feverish with excitement, although the revolutionists had not yet taken to gunning. Bedient dispatched a letter to Jaffier with greeting, a congratulation on his escape from death (regarded in the letter as a good omen), and among other matters, an inquiry in regard to the American Jim Framtree, whom he had met in Coral City, just before he embarked for New York. This done, Bedient procured a saddle-pony, and started alone up the trails to the *hacienda.*

He reached the great house in the early dusk. Such was the welcome Bedient met, that for a moment, he was unable to speak. It was spontaneous, too, for he was an hour ahead of the caravan. All was as he had left. Dozens of natives trooped in with flowers and fruits, and when he was alone upstairs, their singing came to him from the cabins.... Bedient did not realize how worn and near to breaking he was, until the outer door of his apartment was shut; and standing in the centre of the room, with a laugh on his lips, he had to wait two or three minutes, for the upheaval to subside in his breast.... A little later, he crossed to the Captain's quarters, opened the door, and stood in the dark for several moments, his head bowed. And a breath of that faint sweet perfume, which never wearied nor obtruded, came to his nostrils, as if one of the old silk handkerchiefs were softly waved in the darkness.

*   *   *   *   *

A convoy, in the charge of Dictator Jaffier's oldest and most trusted servant, reached the *hacienda* at noon the next day. Thus the reply to his letter was borne to Bedient. The cumbersome efficiency clothed an imperative need for money first of all. Bedient expected this and was prepared to assist.... A revolution was inevitable, the communication further divulged. The point in Dictator Jaffier's mind was just the hour to strike. He recognized the importance of striking first; but, he observed sententiously, there was an exact moment between preparedness and precipitation. Jaffier believed that Celestino Rey was looking for a shipload of rifles and ammunition; but the entire coast was guarded by the Defenders, especially *The Pleiad* inlet, where the Spaniard's rare yacht lay. A seizure of the contraband, it was naively stated, would be a most desirable stroke by the government.... The letter closed with the information Bedient had especially requested. The young American Jim Framtree, whose movements in part had been followed by Jaffier's agents, was at *The Pleiad* with his chief, Celestino Rey, and was doubtless an important member of the rebel staff....

Bedient read the letter carefully and glanced through it again. Jaffier's reliable held out his hand for it.

"If the Senor has carefully digested the contents—" he began.

"Yes, I have it all—"

The other took the letter and touched a match to it, stepping upon the crisp, blackened shell of fibre that fell to the floor. He carried back a New York draft for a large amount.

Bedient slept; that is, his body lay moveless from mid-evening to broad daylight, that first night at the *hacienda*. His consciousness had taken long journeys to Beth, remarkable pilgrimages to India (and found Beth there in the tonic altitudes). Always she regarded him with some strange terror that would not let her speak. Home from these far flights, he would see his body lying still in the splendid, silent room, fanned by soft night-winds, and quickly depart again.... It must have been the beautiful welcome from Falk and the natives. He had broken down quite absurdly, all his furious sustaining force had relaxed. Perhaps it had been necessary for him to break down before he could sleep.... Many times before, he had seen his body lying asleep.

He was more than ever tired and torn this day. Every vista of the hills held poignant hurt, because Beth Truba could not see this beauty. He dared not touch the orchestrelle. Falk brought coffee and fruit after Jaffier's servant had departed. Coffee at the *hacienda* was a perfect achievement. Eight years of training under Captain Carreras, who had an ideal in the making, and who claimed the finest coffee in the world as the product of his own hills, had brought the beverage to a high point. Bedient drank with a relish almost forgotten, but instantly followed that crippling pang—that it was not for

Beth; that she could not breathe the warm fragrant winds....
Bedient sprang up. Some hard, brain-filling, body-straining
task was the cry of his mind. This was its first defensive
activity against the tearing down of bitter loneliness. Until
this moment, he had endured passively.

Bedient determined to go to *The Pleiad*. He had thought of
various ways to get in contact with Jim Framtree, but there
were obstacles in every path, from the point of view of one
conceded by the whole Island to be Dictator Jaffier's right
hand, as Captain Carreras had been. The idea appealed more
every second. It would startle all concerned, Jaffier and
Celestino Rey especially. But the former had just received a
large financial assurance of his loyalty, and there was value
in giving the ex-pirate something formidable to cope with.
Moreover, to meet Jim Framtree again was Bedient's first
reason for sudden return to Equatoria.... He called for a pony,
and followed by a servant with a case of fresh clothing, rode
down the trail to Coral City.

TWENTY-SIXTH CHAPTER

HOW STARTLING IS TRUTH

Bedient entered *The Pleiad*, and with relief breathed the coolness of the vast shadowed halls. One does not ride for pleasure on a June afternoon in Equatoria, and Bedient was far from fit.... There were no guests about. A pale, slender, sad-eyed gentleman appeared in a sort of throne of marble and mahogany, and perceiving the arrival, his look became fixed and glassy.

"Just give me your name, please, if you wish," the pale one said, clearing as dry a throat as ever gave passage to words. Indeed, Bedient could only think of some one stepping upon nut-shells to compare with that voice. The sentence was spoken in answer to his glance about for a register or something of the sort.... No questions were asked regarding price, baggage, nor the nature of the quarters desired. A Chinese servant appeared, and took the case from Bedient's man, who was sent down to quarter in the city. The guest followed the Oriental. The stillness and vast proportions of the structure; the endless darkened halls robed in tapestries and animate with oils; the heavy fragrance from the gardens, crushed out of blossoms by the fierce heat; rugs of all the world's weaving, from the golden fleeces of Persia to fire-lit Navajos; a glimpse to the left, of a room walled with books, and sunk into an Egypt of silence; an acreage of covered billiard-tables through a vast door to the right—a composite of such impressions made the moment memorable. Bedient could only think of a king's winter palace—in summer.... He left the servant to return a moment to the desk.

"Have you a list of the men-guests?" he asked.

The pale one looked disturbed; or possibly it was disappointment that his colorless features expressed, as if such affairs were for the lesser servants of the establishment, and not in the province of gentlemanly dealings.

"No, we have no such list," he said. "Later in the day, when it is cooler, however, most of our guests are abroad, and you will doubtless have little difficulty in finding him whom you seek. You will become familiar in a few hours with our little peculiarities of management. There is little to complain of in the way of service, I believe—"

Rejoining the Chinese, Bedient was led to an apartment, the elegance of detail and effect of which was imperial, no less. With relief he stepped out of his riding clothes, bathed in a deliciously tempered shower, and sat down to think. The chair folded about him like a cool soft arm. The whole atmosphere was to him embarrassingly sensuous. The city was below, shadowed in the swift-falling night; the harbor lay in purple silence, the sun had sunk in a blood-orange sky.

A smile came to his lips at the heavy seriousness of life all about him; vice clinging tenaciously to world-forms, and leaning upon the purchasable beauty of marble and figured walls, its hollowness sustained with the perfections of service. Then he looked across the dark harbor to the sweep of deep red which alone remained of the sunset, thinking of Beth and the dividing sea and the dividing world, and why it

Will Levington Comfort

had happened so. He was ashamed because he could not think of the great work he had dreamed of doing for women, because Beth meant *Women* to him now, and he was not for her.... Would the visions of service ever come back?

This brought his mind to the thing he had come to *The Pleiad* to do, and the revolution all around it, in the very air. What a queer post—in the very fortress of insurrection. It was all boyish stuff. Many adventures might accrue. Would they be enough to keep his mind from realities?... He feared not. For an hour he sat there, regarding the lights of the city and harbor, until his thoughts grew too heavy, and the manacled lover within him was spent and blood-drawn from straining against his chains—the captive that would not die.... He arose wearily to find that a letter had been thrust beneath his door, and so silently that he had not been aroused from his thoughts. The paper was of palest blue and heavy-laid. His name was written with a blunt pen in an angular, eccentric hand, and the contents proved unique:

MR. ANDREW BEDIENT,

SIR: Many of my guests have caught the spirit of *The Pleiad* more readily and pleasurably, after making the acquaintance of one elsewhere designated, I believe, the proprietor. We do not use the word here, as we are friends together. The fact that my manager showed you apartments is enough to make me glad to welcome you. He makes few mistakes. Will you not dine with me at eight this evening in the Shield Room. If you have a previous engagement, pray do not permit me to disturb it, as I shall be ready at your good time.

With unwonted regard,

CELESTINO REY.

Bedient sat down again. The systems of the house moved him to amusement and marvelling. To think that the pale creature at the desk had weighed him from all angles of desirability; and like some more or less infallible Peter had allowed him to enter into the abiding peace of *The Pleiad*. It was rather a morsel, that he had not been turned away. Then to be invited to dine the first evening with the establishment's presiding individuality, who did not approve of the term, "proprietor." There was a tropic, an orient, delight about the affair.

"To think a stranger must lose or win caste in Equatoria, on the glance of that Tired-eyed," he mused. "I really must master this atmosphere."

Bedient thought of *Treasure Island Inn*, in the lower city, where a stranger would probably go, if denied entrance at *The Pleiad*. "Infested" was the word Captain Carreras had once used to depict its denizens.... A few minutes before eight Bedient left the room and descended. From the staircase, he perceived that the guests had, indeed, gathered at this hour. The company was not large, but rather distinguished at first glance. So various were the nationalities represented that Bedient thought the picture not unlike a court-ball with attaches present. The hum of voices was quickened with half the tongues of Europe, and now and then an intonation of Asia. There were more men than women, but this only accentuated the attractions of the latter, of which there were two or three sense-stirring blooms.

For just an instant on the staircase, Bedient stood among the punkah-blown palms to scan the faces below. Framtree was not there, but Miss Mallory appeared in a discussion with an elderly gentleman, and her usual animation was apparent. Bedient was struck with the fact that he had been singularly remiss. In the thirty hours which had passed since their parting, her likeness had not once entered his mind, and he had offered to see that she was comfortably ensconced. Her eyes turned to him now, but as quickly turned away. He had tried to bow.... And at this moment, Bedient perceived the languid eye of the man at the desk, cooling itself upon him. Crossing the tiles from the stairs toward this gentleman, moreover, he was covered with glances from the guests, eyes of swift, searching intensity. "How interested they are in a stranger," he thought. There was a sharpness of needles and acid in the air.

Low chimes from an indefinite source now struck the hour of eight. A Chinese stepped up to the desk beside Bedient.

"You are dining with Senor Rey?" the manager inquired lazily.

Bedient nodded, and turned to greet Miss Mallory. She caught his eye and intent, and promptly turned her back. For the first time, Bedient felt himself a little inadequate to cope with the psychological activities of this establishment. Reverting to the desk, the manager appeared dazed and absent-minded as usual.

"The boy," he said, indicating the Chinese, "will show you to the Shield Room."

Bedient trailed the soft-footed oriental through the bewildering hall, until he saw Senor Rey standing in a doorway—and behind him a low-lit arcanum of leather and metal.... The face of the Spaniard was startling, like the discovery of a crime. It was lean and livid as a cadaver. The pallor of the entire left cheek, including the corner of the lips, had the shine of an old burn, the pores run together in a sort of changeless glaze. In the haggard, bloodless face, eyes shone with black brilliance. The teeth were whole and prominent, as was the entire bony structure of the face and skull. Senor Rey had a tall, attenuated figure, with military shoulders. He moved with great difficulty, as if lacking control of his lower limbs, but in his hands was the contrast—long, white, swift and perfectly preserved. The scarred face and ruffled throat united to form in Bedient's mind the hideous suggestion that the Spaniard had once been tortured *full-length*—his flesh once thrawned in machinery of the devil.... Bedient's hand was grasped in a cold bony grip, and his eyes held for an instant in the bright unquiet gaze of the Spaniard.

"I welcome you, Mr. Bedient.... Do you plan to be with us some little time?" The Senor spoke in a low, monotonous way. His English was but little colored by native speech.

"I cannot tell yet," said Bedient. "I have long wanted to see your wonderful house, but this particular moment, I came to find a certain man—"

Bedient noted the yellow eyelids of the other droop a little. He understood perfectly that there were many men now at *The Pleiad* who were badly wanted.

"Don't mistake me, Senor Rey," he added. "The man I wish to talk with can only prosper for my coming."

"Frequently it happens that the one searched for in Equatoria—is the last found," the Spaniard observed.

Linen, silver, crystal and candle-radiance were superbly blended upon the small round table between them. Rey, as a talker, was artful and inspiriting. His disordered body seemed an ancient classic volume, done in scarred vellum—a book of perils, named Celestino Rey—and all things about, the spears, guns, skins, shields, even the grim shadows, were but references to the text. The dinner was perfect. A tray of wines and a sheaf of cheroots were placed upon the balcony, at length, with two chairs covered with puma skins. The Chinese assisted Rey thither, and when they were alone, he said:

"Do you feel at all like discussing the affair which really brings you to *The Pleiad*?... You neither eat nor drink nor smoke—perhaps you talk."

Bedient laughed. "Wouldn't it be the simplest way to believe me?" he asked. "I want to see Jim Framtree, and I heard he was here. The matter has nothing to do with Equatoria, the present unrest, nor with any relation of his or mine to the Island or to *The Pleiad*. You can make it possible for me to see him at once."

"Unfortunately, I cannot. My province in *The Pleiad* is to cut down tension to a minimum. So many gentlemen present are of a highly nervous temperament. My best procedure many times is to act negatively.... Doubtless Dictator Jaffier was very glad of your return to the dreamiest of climates—"

"Yes," said Bedient.

"I noted this morning that he dispatched a convoy to your *hacienda*, bearing doubtless the official welcome—"

"Yes, I met the party."

Bedient perceived that the Spaniard missed little that was going on in the city and Island; also that he believed Jaffier's convoy had something to do with his own presence at *The Pleiad*; and finally that Celestino Rey was not trained to truth. In fact, Bedient had done more to disconcert the master of the establishment by stating the exact facts, than by any strategy he might have evolved.... Bedient arose at length and took the cold hand. He could not forbear a laugh.

"I am flexible enough to appreciate your position," he said. "As an acknowledged resource of the government, I suppose it is rather hard to see me—at this particular moment in the history of Equatoria—as carrying anything so simple as a friendly token."

"You are very absorbing to me, Mr. Bedient," the Senor said delicately. "An old man may express his fondness.... I am glad *The Pleiad* pleases you. I have built it out of the clods that the world has hurled at me, and have preserved enough vitality to laugh at it all. I find it best to keep down the tension—"

The younger man assisted the Spaniard to his feet.

"Ah, thank you," said the Senor, bowing. "I am dead below the knees."

Bedient strolled a bit in the gardens. Framtree, if anywhere in the establishment, did not show himself outside, nor in the buffet, library, billiard-hall, nor lobby. The extent and grandeur of the house was astonishing, as well as the extreme efficiency of the service. A Chinese was within hand-clap momentarily. There seemed scores of them, fleet, silent, immaculate, full of understanding. Their presence did not bore one, as a plethora of white servants might have done. Bedient reflected that the Chinese have not auras of the obtruding sort.... In his room finally, he drew a chair up to the window, and sat down without turning on light.

He had never felt wider awake than now, and midnight struck. He could not keep his thoughts upon the different facets of the present adventure, but back they carried him through the studio-days, one after another, steadily, relentlessly toward the end. It was like the beating of the bass in one of those remorseless Russian symphonies.... The ride—the halt upon the highway at high noon—the kiss in that glorious light—her wonderful feminine spirit ... and then the blank until they were at her mother's house. He never could drive his thoughts into that woodland path. From the first kiss to the tragedy and the open door, only glimpses returned, and they had nothing to do with his will ... He felt his heart in an empty rapid activity, and his scalp prickled. The captive that would not die was full of insane energy that night....

Once Bedient went to the door, following an inexplicable impulse. At the far end of the hall, fully seventy yards away, stood Jim Framtree talking with a woman. A Chinese servant hurried forward to Bedient, as if risen from the floor.... Framtree and the woman separated. Bedient took a gold coin from his pocket, and thrust it hastily into the hand of the servant, saying: "Ask that gentleman to come here for a moment." The Chinese did not return, nor did Framtree call that night.

But even this slight development could not hold his thoughts.... Bedient wondered if the captive would ever die; and if he should die, would he not rise again at the memory of that first kiss in the June sunlight?... And so he sat, until the day. Then he noted another letter had been slipped under his door. It was of course from Senor Rey:

May I trouble you, my really delightful friend (it read), not to bestow any favors larger than a *peso* upon my servants? They are really very well paid, and do not expect it. Ten dollar gold-pieces for any slight service are disorganizing and increase the tension. I beg to be considered,

In a really mellowing friendship,

CELESTINO REY.

TWENTY-SEVENTH CHAPTER

THE ART OF MISS MALLORY

Bedient was not a student of disease. Perhaps he would have granted that destructive principles are pregnant with human interest in the abstract, but his intelligence certainly was not challenged by these dark systems of activity. He saw that even if his mind were not held in anguish, he lacked the equipment to cope with *Pleiad* affairs. As it was, his attention positively would not concentrate upon the rapid undercurrents, where the real energy of the habitues seemed to operate. It was all like a game of evil children, or rather of queer unfinished beings, a whirring everywhere of the topsy-turvy and the perverse—sick and insane to his weary brain.

It was clear that the Chinese had not carried the message to Framtree, but had consulted the Spaniard instead. Had Bedient told Rey that he had come to *The Pleiad* to find Jenkins, or Jones, or Judd, he would doubtless have been permitted to see Framtree at once.

None of the matters made the impression upon his mind as that one glimpse of Jim Framtree at the far-end of the hall. It was not that he was in the building, though this was of course important; but the magnificent figure of the man in evening wear was the formidable impression *The Pleiad* furnished. This concerned his real life; the rest was without vitality.

By this time, however, Bedient was willing to grant that *The Pleiad*, and even Coral City, formed a nervous system of which Celestino Rey was the brain.... He had given up hope of writing a note to Jim Framtree, realizing it would have no more chance of getting past the Spaniard than a clicking infernal-box.

Framtree was nowhere abroad when Bedient went below. The former moved apparently in a forbidden penetralia of this house of mystery. But surely he could not continue miraculously to disappear.... Bedient strolled down into the city. He sadly faced the fact that the *hacienda* had no call for him; little more than *The Pleiad*. He turned in *Calle Real* to look back at the great dome of the Spaniard's establishment. It was a gorgeous attraction of morning light.... A Chinese slipped into a fruit-shop—one of the house-servants. Bedient made his way to the water-front. The *Hatteras* was out there in the harbor, surrounded by lighters, preparing for the return voyage to New York. This was the lure. It came with a pang that disordered all other mental matters for a space.

Presently he found himself wandering along the water-front. With an exoteric eye (for the deeps of the man were in communion) he regarded the faces of all nations. Coral City held as complete a record of crime, cruelty, and debauchery as one could find in the human indices of any port. Many were closing their annals of error in decrepitude and beggary; others were well-knit studies of evil, with health still hanging on, more or less, and much deviltry to do. A blue blouse, or a bit of khaki; British puttees and a flare of crimson; Russian boots and a glimpse of sodden gray; or an American campaign-hat crowning a motley of many services,—explained that the soldiers of the world found

Equatoria desirable in not a few cases for finishing enlistments. It was quite as evident, too, that the criminal riff-raff of this world and hour found lodging in the lower city, as did its aristocracy in *The Pleiad*.

"A couple of hundred such as these," Bedient reflected, "led by some cool devil of a humorist, could loot the Antilles and get away before the intervention of the States. What an army of incorrigibles—an industrious adventurer could recruit here!"

Then the truth came to his mind. These belonged to Senor Rey's army. Only the Spaniard could command this part of the city to desperate endeavor. His *pesos* and influence, like alcohol, penetrated and dominated the mass.... Signs vehemently proclaimed that American beer was important among the imports of Equatoria; and in a certain street he encountered pitiful smiles and furtive gestures from the upper balconies.

"Strange," he thought, "wherever lawless men gather, their mates fly after them from court and slum. It is not men alone who love to venture—and venture to love!"

Bedient was ascending *Calle Real* once more, when his cheek was flicked by a tiny wad of paper which fell at his feet. A *carometa* was toiling up the slope from the water-front. He observed Miss Mallory's profile in the seat. She had not deigned to look, but with the dexterity of a school-boy the pellet had been snapped from her direction. He pocketed the message and laughed at her innocent and unconcerned expression. A little later he managed to read at a glance:

Meet the old military man you saw me with last evening. Perhaps he'll introduce us.

How quick she had been to sense the profundities of the Spaniard's establishment! Bedient was glad that she held nothing against him, and a bit surprised again that he had forgotten all about her reversal of form at his approach the night before.... He had little difficulty in making the acquaintance of Colonel Rizzio during the day, and was formally presented to Miss Mallory at dinner that evening.

"I have heard it's quite the mode here to have names as well as costumes for the climate," she said. "My wardrobe is limited, and I am Miss Mallory—as in New York."

It was an hour before they were alone together.

"My friend," she said, "you are looking ill—more than ever ill.... Isn't there anything I can do? Isn't there something you might tell *me*?"

Bedient felt her real kindness. "You are good," he answered. "I'm all right, hardly know what it means not to be fit.... And now tell me how you find things."

They stood in the centre of the coffee-room, so no one could listen without being observed. Yet their voices were inaudible five feet away.

"It was clear to me at once," she said, "that I had better not meet you as a friend. They probably knew we both came down on the *Hatteras*, but that's no reason for our being acquainted."

"And now we must be casual acquaintances—if your work would prosper," Bedient said.

"I suppose so."

"The more I think of it, the plainer it becomes that I've sort of disorganized Rey and his intimates. It really is odd for me to be here—"

Miss Mallory searched his face in her keen, swift way.

"When I came to understand at all," she said, "I didn't expect to see you here.... It isn't about the war, is it?"

"No," he replied. Then it occurred to him that she might meet the man he wished to see, and he added: "I have a message for a man named Framtree. Senor Rey apparently thinks this man would not be safe in my hands. At least, I'm not allowed to see him alone—"

"And he's here?"

"Yes, I'm sure of that."

"I haven't met anyone of that name."

"You couldn't mistake. In my opinion, Miss Mallory, he's easily the best-looking man on the Island."

"I'm sure I haven't met him."... She hesitated, smiling-queerly. "But if I should, is there any way I can help you?"

"Not by speaking to him about me. That would yoke you with my fortunes."

"How, then?"

Her eagerness appealed to him. "If you could tell me at any time just where I might find this Framtree—yes, that would help," he said, with a laugh.

"I'd be proud to help you in any way.... It's the most fascinating place I've ever been in," she added with an effort. "I haven't heard a thing about war, but the whole establishment is buzzing with conspiracies and mystery. There isn't any rest. Everyone is afraid of his neighbor; no one trusts himself to fall asleep in peace, for fear someone will pry his secret away—a terrible atmosphere—but what an adventure if it breaks into war before my eyes.... And I've met the Glow-worm—"

Her whole manner changed for an instant. Miss Mallory was now an emancipated creature, living to the very rim of her being. She belonged to the tropics, and was playing a game all spiced with enchantments.... Bedient remembered what Captain Carreras had said about the Glow-worm, on the day of his first coming to Equatoria. The story attached was that Celestino Rey had found this woman among the red lights of Buenos Aires, and had forced her to come with him. Bedient was not particularly interested, but Miss Mallory's study of the hidden-flamed creature, Senora Rey, and what she told him, adjusted easily to what he had already heard of the woman from South America.

"She's pure mother-earth and nothing besides," Miss Mallory went on. "Olive skin, yellow eyes with languid lids, lazy gestures, and a regal head of yellow hair. Something about her suggests that she might turn into an explosive at certain contacts, but she's horribly afraid. It really gives one a thrill to hear her speak of South America. She fondles the syllables and points strangely over her shoulder, at every mention of her land. She's dying the slow terrible death of nostalgia—"

"But of what is she 'horribly afraid'?" Bedient asked.

"Of the Spaniard—her husband. Somehow he has managed to madden her with fear. She trembles at his name or approach like a horse that has been cruelly beaten."

Only for a moment had Miss Mallory revealed the depth of her interest in the affairs of *The Pleiad*. An observer would have taken the pair for the merest acquaintances. The coffee-room murmured with many undertones. They arranged to meet at luncheon the following day and quickly separated. Miss Mallory was now aware that her avenues of action would be closed, if it were noted that she had more than a casual interest in Andrew Bedient.

The latter saw nothing further of Senor Rey for two days, and did not catch even a second glimpse of Jim Framtree. His hours of darkness and daylight were given over to the old destructive monotony—the dark drifting of his mind, all the constellations of love and labor and life shut off by the black mass of nimbus. His identity became lost to all order; the forces of his being seemed in some process of fermentation. His hours alone were animate with psychic experiences, but he attached no significance to them, because he believed them the direct result of physical weakness. Again and again he turned upon himself fiercely, discovering that an hour had passed, while he had been tranced in strange attention for the recurrence of some voice in his brain. Angrily, he would brush the whole phantasmagoria away, force himself back into the world of Equatoria, stride out of his rooms, if it were day, and down into the city; but the pressure of the deeper activities of his mind would steal back and command him. His physical nature was sunk into a great ennui, and the other forces were the mightier.

Bedient comprehended this descent; even wondered how far down a man could go—and live. It was the first thing that ever mastered him. The temptation to leave Framtree and to take even a flying trip to India—since New York was not for him—this was tangible, and he whipped it, though the conflict used up all his power. He had nothing left to combat the vague psychic thrall that appeared to be destroying his life. An understanding friend, as David Cairns had come to be, would have perceived startling changes in Andrew Bedient, and forthwith would have contended with the enemy for every inch of advance. Bedient was a bit awed by his great weakness. His physical deterioration did not trouble him, but his anchorage in the great work of his time had given way. He had to stop and think hard, to recall the least and simplest of his conceptions of service. His sense of shame was consuming in that all the good within him was gone, because he was destined to be denied a human mate.

As to his exterior fortunes, there was substance in the matters pertaining to the Glow-worm, which Miss Mallory brought, but they hardly held him past the moments of their telling. They had met for luncheon. She was unable to speak for a moment. Bedient wondered if he looked so badly as that. The woman summoned all her powers to compel his mind with what was so absorbing to her. He was not a little impressed by her exceeding kindness. They were seated opposite at a small table in the very centre of the luncheon-room.

"It's all right," she said lightly. "Senor Rey knows I am to have luncheon with you. We had a long talk this morning, and I think I left him in excellent spirits.... Oh, yes, he's an artist with the probe. I didn't give him a chance to talk about you, because I asked the first questions."

Her resourcefulness was delightful. "A friend's fortunes are truly safe in your hands," he said. "And now please tell me all about it."

TWENTY-EIGHTH CHAPTER

A FURTHER NOTE FROM REY

"I had a long mental work-out this morning in the room before breakfast," she began. "I even thought about what brings you here, and about my long talk with the Glow-worm last night, which I'll get to—if you are a very interested listener. After breakfast, I walked for an hour in the grounds. Have you been over to the Inlet, where Senor Rey's beautiful sailing-yacht lies—the *Savonarola*?"

"I've seen it from the road," Bedient answered.

"A stairway goes down from the bluff under the road, a hundred steps or more to the water of the cove. In fact, the tall spars of the *Savonarola* aren't nearly so high as the level of the bluff. I love a sailing-ship, and on the way back I met Senor Rey in his wheel-chair, and told him how the wonderful little harbor and his thorough-bred, lying there, had appealed to me. He inclined his head benignly. His yacht, I said, had the effective lines of her namesake's profile—and that pleased him. Followed, a technical discussion of different sailing-ships that once swept the waters of the world, I furnishing enthusiasm and a text-book inquiry now and then. This brought not only an invitation to sail within a few days, but also an invitation to a private dinner this evening in the Flamingo Room, 'with Senora Rey and a few most cherished guests.' And—I must not forget—the Senor informed me that his wife was very fond of me....

"I observed that the 'Flamingo Room' had a most enticing sound. He hoped I would find it so; said the idea was his own, and that, to him, the tint of a flamingo feather was the fairest of all tints—save one, to be found in the cheeks of an American girl. I answered that it was very clear to me now whose sense of beauty had made *The Pleiad* and its gardens the rarest delight of my travels."

Miss Mallory regarded Bedient's amusement appreciatively for a moment, and went on swiftly:

"Then I walked beside his wheel-chair through the shadowy, scented paths, and presently I mentioned you and Colonel Rizzio among the interesting people I had met. He declared you were a true gentleman—spoke feelingly—a stranger at *The Pleiad*, though not to the Island. I explained how you had kept aloof on the ship coming down, how you seemed to be the prey of some devouring grief.... All that I said, he regarded with that terribly bright attention of his. It made me think of a pack of hounds tossing and tearing at a morsel, the way his faculties caught my sentences, hounds playing a hare at the end of a run. Oh, devious and winding are the ways of the Spaniard—and past finding out! But I frankly confessed my interest in you, and that you were absolutely self-contained; indeed, it was because of that I appealed to him. I am sure he found that my sayings balanced in the most sensitive scales of his mind; and decided I was too young to be artistic with the fine tools of untruth.

"Finally, I asked about war, told him the New York papers predicted another war in Equatoria, and that I had never seen one. The Senor declared he was very sorry if my trip to

Equatoria proved a disappointment in any way, but he didn't see what there was to fight about; that no one deplored so much as he the recent attempt upon the life of Dictator Jaffier; and as for himself, he was identified with all the interests of Equatoria, which were moving forward exceedingly well.... Altogether it was an absorbing half-hour."

* * * * *

"And now I must tell you about Senora Key," Miss Mallory continued hurriedly, since they could not be seen talking together long.... "She asked me to come to her rooms, and I followed a servant. I couldn't find the place now alone. A small room in orange lamplight! The Glow-worm was lying upon a tiger-rug; very tall and silken she looked, and her great yellow eyes settled upon me. It seemed to me that her emotions had no outlet, but turned back to rend and devour each other. I couldn't help thinking that first moment, that some one must pay a big price for making her suffer. Queer, wasn't it? And pitiful—how she seemed to need me. It is true, she trusted me from the beginning, seemed dying to leap into some one's heart. And she told me her story in whispered fragments—heart-hunger, hatred, and mystery—these fragments. I've really been challenged to build a character out of her, and since I thought about her half the night, I ought to be able to make you see and feel her story. I wonder if I can? It came to me something like this:

"There had been a night—ah, long ago—in which Senor Rey summoned her from her companions. It was in a house in Buenos Aires. The Senor had come to that house before. The Senor was always feared. He was always obeyed. She, nor any of her companions, could *taste* the wine he bought for them. It did not make them laugh like other wine. Oh, yes, they drank it, but they could not taste the flavor—with him in the room!... On this night the Senor had bade her come

Will Levington Comfort

with him. She could not answer, but obey only. She remembered how hushed her companions became when she went away with the Senor; how strangely they had looked at her—what helpless sorrow was in their eyes.... Even now she could see the faces of her companions gathered about; the Senor smiling at the door; his carriage with black, restless ponies and shining lights; the driver upon his seat, like to whom she quickly became—never answering the Senor, and always obeying!... Ah, yes, there had been a hush in her house as she left it, laughter in all the other houses about; and away they had driven, past the last of the lights—

"Such was the tale, whispered, overlapped with repetitions, a succession of touches like that, done lightly but with a passion—oh, you should have been there to understand! The meaning of a wild, sad life was in them. And her big yellow eyes were hungry upon me. I seemed to see the vast South American town, as old as Europe in sin and as new as Wyoming in heart."

"You make me see it all," Bedient said.

"Can you understand that the Glow-worm is expiring to get back to that old mad life?" Miss Mallory asked.

"Yes, from what you tell me of her."

"It is true, only it must be so *he* cannot follow.... It must be as it was before he came—when she could taste and feel and see—as it was before the chill settled down upon her senses, before the shuddering began. That's how she expresses it.... She overpowered me a little at first. I was slow to realize how one's intents and sensations could be absolutely physical. I could pity, but there was something actually creepy about her. I was inane enough to ask if she could not return for a visit. She sank back and shut her eyes and clenched her hands, saying:

"'When he is dead or when he is tired of me, I shall go back—not for a visit, but to *stay*! He would not let me go for a visit, and I could not—oh, I wouldn't dare to run from him! Always I'd think him after me. There would be no sleep for me. I'd think him after me—you know how it is in a dream, when you are like a ghost—all limp in the limbs, but trying to run! It would be like that, if I fled from him—always expecting him to clutch me from behind!... My God, if he would only make me mad! But he won't—he won't!'

"'What do you mean?' I asked."

"'I mean,' the Glow-worm whispered, drawing my head down to hers, 'I mean I would kill him. Oh, he's all but dead! I could kill him with my hands, if he would fill me with rage, so I could forget his eyes. He is all alive in his eyes!... But it shall never be. He will say—do this and come and go and rest and rise, and do that—and I shall obey like the Chinese.... Oh, tell me what you would do, if the Senor said to you, looking right into your skull, 'Come with me to-night!'"

"I told her I should laugh at the Senor, and suggest possibly that he had drunk too much wine. She seemed unable to comprehend, and repeated, 'If he should look right into your skull, could you say that?' I assured her I could, and she tried to believe, but she concluded that I only *thought* I could be that strong.

"Then she told me it had been months since she talked to anyone without being afraid; that she felt at once it would be safe to talk with me; that so much she wanted to tell had been shut up like a swelling in her throat—'ah, God, so long!'... 'And then you would say with a laugh—as you tell me,' the Senora went on, as if memorizing my method. Her lips mumbled and trailed the words, so deep was the effort of her mind. 'You would say, "Senor Rey, you have drunk too much wine!" and he would answer with a laugh, too, "It is true, no doubt, as you say. I am an old and a very foolish man, my dear Senorita Mallory!" and you would smile and think of it no more.' The Glow-worm laughed in a lost, mirthless way, and held me tightly as she finished, 'But that very night, just the same, you would find yourself with him! And he would laugh at you then and say, coming closer, "Forgive an old and foolish man."'

"I was startled at the way she said it," Miss Mallory concluded. "'You mean he would have me anyway?' I said.... 'Yes,' the Glow-worm replied wearily. 'My lord gets what he desires—all but his youth—he cannot get that—and his fear of hell—he cannot get rid of that! And he is afraid to die!' She spoke the last triumphantly, as if it were the only happy thing she could think of.... That was last night—and that is all.... To-morrow evening join me in the lobby a little before eight.... Here comes the servant and we must talk about orchids—until I finish this sherbet—"

The following evening Bedient met Miss Mallory in the main hall, and exceeding cleverness was required to impart her information, as they moved together among the crowd.

"The handsome man is here. I saw him last night," she said, without the faintest trace of excitement. "I am beginning to share some of the Glow-worm's fear of Senor Rey. It's all tremendously thrilling. The place is a mine of terrors—all the worse for this beautiful setting and the gardens.... The Sorensons are the horrible Russian pair. I met them at dinner in the Flamingo Room, and after listening to the Senora, the courtesies of the Spaniard were like so many cold shuddery waves of dread. Again last night, after the dinner, the

Glow-worm drew me into her boudoir and poured into my ears months of accumulated toxins of hate and fear—"

"I'm sorry they have frightened you," Bedient said. "Your kindness to me—"

"Oh, I'm not really afraid," she said hastily. "It's all very wonderful. The Senora repays me with a most devoted attention—services of her own hand, and not a little sweet and endearing in their way.... Presently she asked me if I had met the imposing Senor Framtree. Of course I had not. She said he had been here for many weeks, but she had only met him a few times—always with the Senor.... 'He is the sort of man I am not allowed to meet alone,' she said languidly, her eyelids drawn against the yellow light. 'But I have no choice—no choice here,' she went on, 'though I feel sorry for him.'

"I asked why, and she said he was alone in a strange country, and that it was dreadful to be young—and alone in a strange country. Plainly she had something more to say, so I told her to speak what was in her mind. The substance was that Mr. Framtree had lasted much longer than most, therefore he must be a very great artist with the cards. Many men had come with fortunes to *The Pleiad,* and most of them were ready to gamble with her lord, who invariably got their money in the end. It was not only the money, but he had a vast pride in his mastery, and in the house he had built. It was not possible for him to continue to lose any length of time. Then Senora Rey informed me that the two were together now, and if she dared, she could show me some things about her lord's house.

"I begged her to, though fearfully, you may believe. She said it was risking murder if we were caught, but I saw she wanted to show me. Also, I thought of many things, and it looked important—for one in my capacity not to miss. So I asked again.... 'You see, I can refuse you nothing,' she said. 'I love you for coming to me. I am a woman again—even young and glad. Before you came, I was a snake crushed at midday—that could not die until the dark.'

"I think the adventure really fascinated her, because she hates the Senor so. Anyway, I followed through several inner rooms of oppressive magnificence which the Spaniard reserves for his own use. Then we entered a corridor. No lock could be seen, but the Senora touched the panel in a certain way. It closed of itself as we entered, with the sound of a lock indeed—a heavy, oiled, smooth-running click, but very soft. I hated to hear it behind. The corridor was narrow and dim. It was high, but the thickly shaded lamps were far apart and close to the rugs, so that one's shoes were lit, but faces hardly recognizable. Low voices mingled in a bewildering complication throughout the corridor. There was a sliding ladder with carpeted steps, which could be pushed noiselessly along one wall. An arrangement like it is used in libraries to reach the upper shelves. The Glow-worm was trembling, and squeezed my hand repeatedly to insure silence, and slid the ladder along nearly to the end. I could hear her quick, frightened breathing. The thing was locked by some unseen turn of the Senora's finger, and I was directed to climb. Up three steps, and I saw light through the wall on the level of my eyes. Closer, it appeared that only a dark gauze almost transparent hung between me and another room. The gauze covered a slit plenty large enough to look through.

"Senor Rey and the handsome man were facing each other in a dull green room. The latter's back was toward me, and a table was between them, but they were not at cards. The young man's profile was half-turned so I could see, and he moved restlessly in his chair. He lit a cigarette as I stood there, and the Senor observed that it was sad to be old. You could hear their words, as clearly as you hear mine. The

Framtree gentleman laughed softly. He has a manner, I confess. He declared that he didn't believe there was ever a time when the Senor could have solved the problem at hand.

"The Glow-worm was pulling at my skirts to come down, but I listened a moment longer. The Senor said he must have done Dictator Jaffier an injustice all these years in considering him the stupidest of men. The other replied that 'four nights more' would tell the story; that it was irksome to wait even that long. I had to leave, for the Senora was becoming frenzied, but I caught one more remark from Senor Rey, as mysterious as the rest. '*But he'll be gone before that*,' he said."

"What an astonishing bit of work!" Bedient exclaimed.

"We reached the quarters from which we came—the orange lamplight room—in safety, but the Glow-worm's face was livid with fear. I suppose mine was, too. She said the whole house was so arranged.... I told her they were not playing cards, and something of what I had heard. The Glow-worm was sure they were talking about 'a young man, known to be one of the mainstays of the government,' who had come to stay at *The Pleiad*—for some incomprehensible reason. Evidently, she has not seen you.... What do you suppose Rey meant by, 'He'll be gone before that,'—within four days?"

"I don't appear able to learn anything by myself," Bedient said. "It would seem the best way—to wait and see."

"Oh, but I wouldn't—please!... Is it worth that to see this Framtree, whom the Spaniard has probably commanded to keep in hiding? I am afraid—for you!... And the whole house, even the sleeping-rooms, are under that devilish eye. I dared not turn on the light last night—"

They parted after less than twenty minutes. Bedient did not go in to dinner.... To him, the night was but a sorry repetition. Miss Mallory's disclosures could not long hold his thoughts. He had no intention of telling Jaffier that something big was to happen within four days. What was strangest was the fate which made it so hard for him to come into contact with Framtree. He could not give up this thing—this last link to reality. He felt himself better off here—than alone at the *hacienda*.

This time, between two and three in the morning, he was so tense and animate that he heard the soft, swift tread of a Chinese in the hall and the faintest possible rustle of a paper thrust under his door. He waited a moment before turning on the light.... It was another missive from the Spaniard, and read:

MY ESTEEMED BEDIENT:

The request herein to be set forth may appear to you as a reflection upon the quality of my friendship, as it certainly is an indication of the force of your personality. You are felt in this establishment, my valued friend, like some tarrying Nemesis. Permit me to observe, and I am smiling as I write, that you have a wearing effect upon many of my guests. Personally, I should ask nothing finer of the Fates than the privilege to devote myself exclusively to you—but that is impossible now. To-morrow at noon my servants will assist you to any quarters elsewhere, that you may have chosen by that time—if, indeed, you are staying longer in Coral City. Believe me, when a certain tension is lifted, my house will be open to you again, as is always the heart of

CELESTINO REY.

TWENTY-NINTH CHAPTER

AT TREASURE ISLAND INN

The morning rode in grandly upon the sea. Bedient was early below, and overtook Miss Mallory in the gardens. She seemed particularly virile. A pair of Senora Rey's toy-spaniels were frisking about.

"These are not my favorite kind, but I like dogs," she said.... "How men reveal their earth-binding! A laugh is enough—or a fear, a word, a convention—and you have a complete discovery of limitations."

Bedient fell into her mood. "And what manner of man would he be who could keep hidden from such very old and very wise eyes his covering of clay?"

"First, he would be without vanity," she said readily. "Then, he would do noble things thoughtlessly and unwatched. He wouldn't be dollar-poisoned, nor could he fail to help all who are poor and whipped, whether wicked or not. And he would have enough intelligence to enfold mine, so I wouldn't be constantly banging against his walls.... In a word, he would be great without knowing it. Do you think I ask a great deal?"

"Yes, but I should like him," Bedient answered.

"And now what is it?" she asked quickly. They had turned upon the main-drive, away from the trees. "I can see you have something to say."

"I shall take up lodgings for the next few days in the city below—at *Treasure Island Inn*. Senor Rey has ordered me out of *The Pleiad*."

Her face colored instantly, and yet she said, "I'm very glad to hear it. At least, you will be safe in *Treasure Island Inn*."

"I had not considered that, Miss Mallory, though I've a great respect for all that you think important.... I still intend to see Jim Framtree—and before the end of 'the four days' spoken of night before last. The fact is, I have nothing else to do. Celestino Rey may mean to start his rebellion then, so there is only to-morrow and next day. It would be next to impossible for me to meet this man with hostilities begun."

She was quite astonished at this stir of action.

"Can't you tell me anything more?" Her appeal was penetrating.

"Only that I've got to see him. It's not to do him harm," he said. "The story isn't altogether mine.... I can't help laughing at this move of Senor Rey's—and yet—"

"It hurts, doesn't it?" she urged.

"Not exactly that, but it makes me all the more determined to get to Framtree."

"I'm glad if it does hurt," she said hastily. "You look like death, but the apathy is gone. Even red rage is better than that. I think you are better. It was about your illness—that I wanted you to tell me.... Good-by."

"I hope," Bedient said suddenly, "that Rey isn't afraid of *you*—that you are clear from the impulse that made him send me downtown."

"I've been careful.... I'll help, if I can. Good-by.... Aren't 'good-bys' hideous?... But we can't be too careful.... At *Treasure Island Inn*?"

"Yes, and where—*you* couldn't call!"

"But I shall know where you are."

Bedient returned to his rooms, and Miss Mallory resumed her walk.... An hour and a half later, Bedient walked out of the big gate of *The Pleiad*, and down to the city.... For the first time in several days, Celestino Rey breathed long. Assassination was only one of the things he had feared....

Forty-eight unavailing hours passed in *Treasure Island Inn*. This night would bring an end to the mysterious four days. Bedient was at bay before the remnant of what had been and hoped. To his own eyes, he was an abject failure now, even in these physical affairs—he who had dared to arraign New York workers in almost every aspect of their life! The last beacon of his spirit was blown out in the storm; his mind had long since preyed upon itself, the pith gone from it, through drifting in dark dream-tides; and now he who had been trained from a boy to physical actions weakly succumbed before the old Spaniard's will and strategy. Yet he could not find it within him greatly to care.

Treasure Island Inn had interested him at first, not so much through its exterior contrast to *The Pleiad* (which was complete enough for any city to furnish), but because its wretchedness in the sense of money-lack was less than in its moral poverty. Its evils were so open and self-reviling; its passages so angular, so suggestive of blood-drip and brooding horror; its rooms so peeled, meagre and creaking— depravity so sincere. Crime certainly had not been spared around the world to furnish its living actors for *Treasure Island Inn*. All the ragtag was there—not a lust nor a mannerism missing.

And now that life had cast him into this place, Bedient found himself utterly unable to contend with the squalor of fact and mind; indeed, he was quite as ineffectual as he had been in the midst of the glittering deviltry of *The Pleiad*.... Abased before realities; lost to the meaning of every excellence of his life-training; shattered by psychic revolts; his brain reflecting the strange mirages and singing the vague nothings of starvation—but enumeration only dulls the picture! In every plane of his nature, he was close to the end, forty-eight hours after his arrival at the Inn of the lower city.

Certain things had become mature, irrevocable: That he was a superfluous type in this Western world of his birth; that Beth Truba had left the highway, where pass the women of earth, to enter his most intimate environs and possess him entirely; that passing on, she had left but the stuff of death. The time had been when he would have depreciated in another man the utter weakness into which he had fallen.

Bedient unearthed a companion at *Treasure Island Inn*, one whom he did not doubt for an instant to be the chief of Rey's agents assigned to watch his every movement. But even as a spy, old Monkhouse had helped him to sit tight, during that forty-eight hours. For Monkhouse talked alluringly, incessantly,—and asked only to be with the stranger—and many a time, all unknowing, he banished for the moment some devouring anguish with a tale of disruption told to a turn. The Island did not hold more loyal devotion than his for Dictator Jaffier, to hear Monkhouse tell it; and how Celestino Rey had reached his ripe years, with such hatred in the world, was by no means the least of Equatorian novelties.... Here was a desperado in the sere, shaking for the need of drink, when he first appeared to Bedient. On the final forenoon of the latter's stay at the Inn, he sat with Monkhouse in the big carriage doorway on the street-level. The old man was elaborating a winsome plan to capture the Spaniard at sea; and though Bedient mildly interposed that he wouldn't know what to do with Celestino if he had him,— the conspiracy was unfolded nevertheless:

"You're a good lad," Monkhouse communed. "I belave in you to the seeds. C'lestin'—an' may Heaven deefin' the walls as I speak his name—has nine an' seventy ways of makin' off with you. Boy, I've known the day in these seas when he'd do it for practice. But he's old now an' tender of hear-rt. He laves it to your good sense to lave him alone. 'Tis well, you trusted no one save old Monkhouse. Adhere to it, lad, or I'll be mournin', one of these gay mornin's, with you gone—an' your name on no passenger list save—what's the name of that divil of a pilot—Charybdus?"

"Charon?"

"True for you, lad. Charon it is. What with drink an' the sinful climate, I've forgot much that many niver knew."

Monkhouse winked his red lashless lids, and meditated the while, as he pressed the juice of an orange into the third of a cup of white rum, and stirred in a handful of soggy brown sugar.

"Hark to you, boy—come closer," he whispered presently. "Nothin' that sails in these par-rts can scrape the paint of the *Savonarola*. At the same time, you can do nothin' by stayin' ashore. What's the puzzle? 'Tis this, lad: you must get one of thim gasolin' launches that move like the divil and smell like the sleepin' sickness! You can get one at the Leeward Isles betchune here an' sun-down.... Listen now, come back in good time, standin' on your own deck, with old Monkhouse for a mate, and three or four clane-eyed American boys lookin' for adventures—an' hang out at sea waitin' for the *Savonarola*. God save the day whin he comes! We'll meet him on the honest seaboard in the natural way, where he can't spring the tricks of *The Pleiad*, nor use the slather of yellow naygurs that live off the cold sweat of him—"

Hereupon Monkhouse drained his already empty cup, the sign that another sirocco was sweeping his throat. His mind wandered until it was brought: "Many a man's soul has filtered up through salt-water off these shores, lad, because he talked less of his memories than his troubles—but you won't betray me, boy!... My Gawd, lad, to have C'lestin' in the hold under 'me feet—as he wanst had me—but let that pass—or lyin' deeper still under the *Savonarola* with the fishes tuggin' at his carcass. Ah, 'tis deep fathims under the *Savonarola*, me lad—"

Bedient had not been listening for a moment. A *carometa* was moving slowly toward him, down the *Calle Real,* and he fancied the flutter of a handkerchief from its side window. It was nearly noon. The dazzle of sunlight upon the glass of the *carometa* was in his eyes, so he could not see the face within, but a slim hand signaled again. The vehicle approached with torturing slowness until the dazzle nickered out and he hurried forward to greet Miss Mallory, whose face blanched at the sight of him.

"You look as if you would fall!" she whispered. "But I'm so glad to see you again—"

"I was just going to say it.... It's been dull—and I haven't done—" He opened the door of the *carometa*.

"Quickly, they're watching from your house," she managed to say between commonplaces, "*pick up that crumpled letter at my foot*!... But it won't do for you to follow the suggestion in it—you're not able!"

"If there's anything to do, I'm able," he declared, tucking the paper into the hollow of his hand.

"We miss you at *The Pleiad*," she said with her usual animation. "I wish I had time for a good talk now, but I'm actually rushed to-day. I'll see you again, though—"

Bedient sauntered back smiling, and sat down with Monkhouse for a little space. The eyes he saw were large, red-rimmed and troubled; tales and conspiracies flagged miserably. Bedient chaffed him for having become incoherent, and left shortly for his own room, where he pressed out two of the thinnest possible sheets of paper, closely written on both sides, and made them his own to the least detail:

DEAR MR. BEDIENT:

I hardly know how to begin, I am so excited and have so much to say. (The letter was dated less than two hours before.) Senor Rey, the Glow-worm, the couple known as "the Sorensons," Mr. Framtree and myself are sailing to-night on the *Savonarola*. There will also be Chinese, probably three, two to manage the yacht and one for the cabin. I'm not quite sure, but I think we are to have supper

aboard. I have been aboard the yacht. The cabin takes up a large part of the hold. There are two doors forward. The one to the left opens into the galley, and the one to the right opens into the forecastle, where there are three berths for the crew, a few ship's stores, piles of cordage, tackle, chains, etc. The berths, of course, will not be occupied this trip, as we plan to be out only a few hours, and the sailors will be on deck.

There is a fine place for concealment in this forecastle. (Possibly under the lower bunk; numerous bedding-rolls lying about might be pulled in after one.) The difficulty will be in getting aboard. There is but a single companion-way to the cabin. It will not be locked this afternoon early, but doubtless there will be a servant or two making ready for the sail. Provisions will be boarded this afternoon, as Senor Rey is a bountiful entertainer. It may happen that the Chinese, in loading the provisions, will be a considerable distance off, or even up the steps to the cliff, for moments at a time. This is the random chance I think of.

The undergrowth is dense on the steep slopes which jut down to the water of the Inlet. One might conceal oneself there, and await the offered chance, not more than twenty or thirty feet from the cabin door. This is the really discouraging part of the whole preliminary, but I may be able to assist you further at the proper time. There seems absolutely no other way to arrange an interview for you with Mr. Framtree.

As for me, I have learned much at *The Pleiad*. The Spaniard's systems are infamous—a fact that has been terribly impressed upon me. I shall lose my home in *The Pleiad*, but this is the last of the mysterious "four days." It will be better and safer for me to follow the fortunes of the war after this, from the side of the Defenders.

A dangerous step, but I shall take the chance of the sail, even if you decide that your part is too uncertain. In any case be very sure to destroy this letter. If it should fall into the hands of Rey's innumerable agents,—I'm afraid I shouldn't come back from the party. There is operating in the city as well as in *The Pleiad* as perfect a system of espionage as one would encounter in the secret service of a formidable nation.

Safely secreted in the forecastle during the early afternoon, you could not fail to hear, some hours later, a signal tapped on the deck forward. This signal would come after supper, when it was dark, and everything propitious as possible. The sailing party would be divided at this time, say half on deck and half below. The signal— three double taps—"tap-tap ... tap-tap ... tap-tap"—given sharply, unmistakably, with a heavy cane or something of the kind.

Emerging from the forecastle (with a look and a command behind, as if to your hidden compatriots), it would seem that you would have the occupants of the cabin rather neatly at your mercy. If the affair there were attended by luck, and managed quietly enough, you might continue and surprise the deck party, but let us not rely too far upon fair chances. There is a strong flavor of danger about the *coup* at best. I do not consider here any aid which I *may* render; so that you are one against eight—three white men, three (?) Chinese, and two women.

I have reasons for helping you.

You seem to want this meeting, and I believe war is imminent. Let me impress upon you: Take every precaution; think out every possible step before joining action. Senor Rey is a cultivated criminal. Sorenson may prove dangerous. Framtree looks big enough to laugh—if he is cornered. The Chinese are Chinese.

I am writing at crazy speed. You should have this by noon, and lose no time after that. Oh, yes, the *Savonarola* carries two small boats. If the surprise is successful, these boats may be useful to eliminate the Chinese and the Sorensons. You will be armed, of course. I am just adding thoughts at random. A little red chalk-mark on the white frame of the companion-way will tell me that you are aboard, if I should miss seeing you.

Yours in excitement, but not without hope,

ADITH MALLORY.

I *know* what you can do.

THIRTIETH CHAPTER

MISS MALLORY'S MASTERY

Bedient felt the blood warming in his veins. This was the last of "the four" nights. Miss Mallory's determination to sail with the Spaniard was enough to spur him to attempt joining her; if, indeed, his absolute need to break the deadly ennui had not banished hesitation. He glanced through the letter again, and burned it.

"Monkhouse," he said below, "I've had about enough of Coral City this time, and I'm riding back toward the *hacienda* this afternoon. I'm leaving a little present for you with the management of the Inn. Some time I'll send a pony trap down for you, when I'm hungry for more tales—"

The old man was more mystified than ever, but the business of the Spaniard had to wait until he hunted up the management, with whom his relations had worn thin. Bedient found his servant, ordered the ponies, and the two rode up *Calle Real*, before one in the afternoon. They passed *The Pleiad* bluffs, overlooking the Inlet, where the *Savonarola* lay, and on for a mile or more into the solitude. Here Bedient sent forward his servant with both ponies and let himself down the bluff to follow the shore back.

The sand was white as paper and hot as fresh ashes. The muscles of his face grew lame from squinting in the vivid light. There was not a human being in sight on either length of curving shore, nor a movement in the thickly covered cliffs. The world was silent, except for the languorous wash of the little waves and the breathing of a soft wind in the foliage. For an hour he made his way mostly under cover around the shore to the mouth of the Inlet, from where he could see Jaffier's gunboat on the watch.

The distance was about a thousand yards back to where the yacht lay. The cut was a natural stronghold, opening sidewise on the face of the shore, so as to be invisible from the open water. It was deep enough for an ocean-liner, but too narrow for a big steamer to enter with her own power. Bedient turned into the thick, thorny undergrowth, which lined the eastern wall of the Inlet, and made his way around its devious curvings, silently and slowly. The growth on the cliffs was so dense in places that he had to crawl. The heat pressed down upon the heavy moist foliage, and drained him like a steam-room. He had wobbled from weakness and the heat in the saddle, even on the breezy highway. Again and again, he halted with shut eyes until his reeling senses righted. The thousand yards from the mouth of the cove to the moorings of the *Savonarola* wound like a Malay *creese* with an interrogation point for a handle. The distance consumed an hour, and much of the vitality he had summoned by sheer force of will. He lay panting at last in the smothering thicket, thirty feet from the rear-deck of the *Savonarola*. Yet there was a laugh in his mind. It was altogether outlandish, when he considered his small personal interest in such an affair.... He thought of the listening eyes of Beth Truba—had he told her of such an adventure of his boyhood.... And he thought of the clever and intrepid Adith Mallory, and what she had meant by the last added line of her letter, "I know what you can do."

Someone was already aboard, for the cabin-door was open. The sliding hatch connected with the thick upright door, so that a single lock sufficed for the cabin, which opened from the aft-deck. The still, deep water of the cove drew Bedient's eyes constantly, and kept alive the thought of his terrible thirst. The words of old Monkhouse repeated often in his brain, "Ah, 'tis deep fathims under the *Savonarola*." He slipped a little steel key from the ring, smiling because it was the key to one of the Carreras cabinets at the *hacienda*, and placed it in his mouth. He had done the same with a nail when in the small boat with Carreras, the only boat that reached shore from the *Truxton*. It started the saliva.

There was but one man in the cabin so far, as Bedient ascertained through the ports,—a Chinese, and he was sweeping industriously. Miss Mallory's idea that he steal in, while the boat was being provisioned, seemed a far chance. He might have boarded the craft now, and surprised the oriental in the cabin, but he had no grudge against him, and Rey's Chinese were not purchasable. He thought of the forlorn last chance—to creep back to the mouth of the Inlet where it was narrowest, and wait on a sheltered ledge there for the *Savonarola* to be ejected with pikes from the crooked mouth. He might leap on the deck as she swung around, but he would then have to face the whole party.

After an interminable period—it was past three in the afternoon—the Chinese appeared from a cabin, and sat down on the low rail aft, mopping his shaven head. "I don't wish you any harm, little yellow man," Bedient thought, "but you'd be most accommodating if you would fall into a faint for a minute or two—"

At this juncture, Bedient was startled by the clapping of hands from somewhere up the winding steps toward *The Pleiad*. The Chinese leaped up to listen for a repetition of the signal, which his kind answers the world over. The hands were clapped again, and then the voice:

"Oh, Boy, won't you come up here for a moment? I'm afraid to climb down all these steps alone with this big package. It must be put aboard for to-night."

"The unparalleled genius—" Bedient breathed.

The Chinese understood, and stepped ashore quickly. Bedient began to roll forward with the first movement of the boy. The red chalk mark would hardly be needed. He had just torn his finger upon a thorn. Seeing the blood rise, it occurred that one is never without a bit of red. At the base of the bank he turned his eyes upward. The Chinese was plodding up the stairs, the woman holding his mind occupied with words.

Bedient leaped across to the deck, and sank into the cabin of the *Savonarola*. From the shaded roomy quarter then, he ventured a last look. John Chinaman's broad back was still toward him, and Miss Mallory was laughing. "How good of you!" she said to the boy. "The steps looked so many and so rickety, and I was all alone. Here's a *peso* for you. We'll be aboard about six." She laughed again.

"What a bright light to shine upon a man!" Bedient thought, as he covered his bleeding finger with a handkerchief, to avoid leaving a trail in the spotless cabin. He moved forward toward the right compartment, unsteadily; then entered and closed the door.

* * * * *

This was Adith Mallory's especial afternoon and evening. She was emphatically alive. One of her dearest desires, and one which had long seemed farthest from her, was to do some big thing for Andrew Bedient. The plan was hers, every thought of it, and now she saw him safely stored in the forecastle.

She tried to put away all thoughts of fear. The party, of which she was the blithest,—ah, how she loved sailing!— stepped on board at six. Framtree was brought to the meeting. Celestino Rey was beguiled from his *Pleiad* throne, and helped to a seat in this floating Elba. Here, too, came the Sorensons and the Chinese—mob-stuff. There is a mob in every drama—poor mob that always loses, of untimely arousings, mere bewildered strength in the wiles of strategy. Poor undone mob—its head always in the lap of Wit, to be shorn like Samson.... And the Glow-worm—that incomparable female facing the South, her great yellow smoldering eyes, filled with the dusky Southern Sea, and who knows what lights and lovers of Buenos Aires, flitting across her dreams?... Had there been absolute need for an ally, Miss Mallory could almost have trusted the Senora.

"We didn't care to heat up the cabin from the galley," Senor Rey declared as they descended for supper, "so I have had our repast prepared at *The Pleiad*, save, of course, the coffee. You will not miss for once the *entree*, if the cold roast fowl is prime, I am sure. There are compensations."

"Miss an *entree*!" Miss Mallory exclaimed. "I could live a week on pickles and lettuce-leaves, to stay at sea in such weather!"

"Astonishingly fine sailor is Miss Mallory," the Spaniard enthused. "She talked ship with me like a pirate, and knew my *Savonarola* from boom to steering gear at a glance. You all must thank Miss Mallory for our little excursion to-night."

The lady in question wondered if the forecastle-door were proof against the voices in the cabin. She did not turn her eyes to it, but happened to note that the Spaniard caught a glance from Jim Framtree, as he spoke his last words; also that Framtree arose, looked aft from the cabin doorway, and turned back with a smile. Miss Mallory followed his eyes a moment later and discovered that Dictator Jaffier's gunboat had moved. Steam was up; her nose was pointed their way; more still, she was leisurely trailing! Senor Rey did not miss the American woman's interest.

"The Dictator is always so good about giving the *Savonarola* armed convoy," he said.

Miss Mallory became deeply thoughtful, but roused herself, realizing it did not become her in this company. She imagined that the great yellow eyes of the Glow-worm were regarding her with queer contemplative scrutiny. Sorenson felt the call to remark something, and the *Savonarola* was obvious.

"Fine little craft for a honeymoon," he observed, "that is, of course, if the lady in question enjoyed sailing. It's amusing to picture some women on a sailing-trip—"

"And some men on a honeymoon," added Miss Mallory.

This delighted Framtree.... Sorenson was rather a ponderous Slav with languages. He was not accustomed to conserve his thirst until dinner-time. Indeed, he had brought aboard on this occasion an appreciation for sparkling refreshments, that had been assiduously cultivated during the long day. Already Sorenson had endangered his domestic peace, through attentions, delicate as you would expect from a bear that walked like a man. These were directed toward the American woman. She broke every shaft with unfailing humor, and girded her repugnance as added strength for the End. There were moments she did not relish. Strain settled with the darkening day. She thought of the face she had seen at her carriage at noon—a tortured face—and what he had passed through since, cramped in the forecastle! Perhaps he was unconscious from the heat and the suffocating place—and from the illness she could never understand.... But in Miss Mallory all these thoughts and conditions drew upon as perfect a nervous organization as could be found anywhere in these complicated days—and it was over at last.

Sorenson and his wife followed her on deck after supper, the other three tarrying below. There was no moon. The breeze abaft the beam was a warm, steady pressure that coaxed a whispering of secrets from the sails, and sent the willing craft forward with her bow down to work, and a business-like list. One Chinese was serving below. The remaining two were squatted aft by the wheel. Madame Sorenson took a chair on the cabin-deck, amidship. Miss Mallory moved past her and forward. The thought in her brain was: If Sorenson follows me now, anything that should happen to him is his own fault. She carried playfully a heavy cane, found in the cabin. Sorenson embraced his own disaster in joining her.

"How enticing the water looks!" she observed.

"It does 'pon my word," said the Russian.

Each noted that the foresail hid the face of Madame Sorenson, although her shoulders were expressive.... The look upon Sorenson's flushed features held Miss Mallory true to her latest inspiration.

"You are a good swimmer?" she asked in a lowered tone, but carelessly.

"Ah, yes, there are many grand swimmers in my country among the coast men."

"You must have been on shipboard a great deal, Mr. Sorenson.... One can always tell by the way one acts on a small craft. Many are afraid at first of the low gunwales on a yacht like this."

Miss Mallory felt the disgust of Madame Sorenson for them both; felt it was deserved. "Ah, yes, Miss Mallory," he declared, delighted with her and himself and the world.

He raised one foot to the railing, and his manner became all the more at home, as he lifted his cigar with a flourish. "Like our host, I have sailed many seas and not a few with him," he added.

He was standing close to the rail, directly over the forecastle. Miss Mallory drew a step or two nearer, and announced, as if such a remark had never been thought of:

"What a perfect little thing of her kind the *Savonarola* is!... I believe she is staunch enough to go anywhere.... Just listen how tight and solid her planking is!"

She would have signaled that instant, but her approach had been Sorenson's cue for a certain fond attention and endearment, which ended in a briny obfuscation....

It had been such a little push, too. She tossed a lifering after him, saw him come up and catch his stroke—as she tapped the deck with her stick—the three doubles sharply....

And now a sunburst of small but striking events. Madame Sorenson had not seen, but she launched a scream with the splash. The Chinese, squatted aft, had not seen, but like good servants, with well-ordered minds, they rushed from the wheel to the davits, and proceeded to get a small boat into the water, a temperate thing to do with a man overboard. Miss Mallory did not scream, so as to disturb anybody, but hurried aft, urging the Chinese. "Both go!" she called. "He's such a big man!"

The boat was launched. Sorenson was swimming—his oaths proved that—but rapidly receding. The Glow-worm rushed out of the cabin, Framtree following. The latter halted, however, at a sharp command of the Spaniard. Then Miss Mallory heard Bedient's voice. It was not lifted above the normal tone, and hoarse with thirst.

She craned her head forward from the wheel to peer into the cabin. Bedient's face was like death. He did not even have a pistol in his hand, but there was a look in his eyes she had never seen in any eyes before, and he was smiling. The disturbance on deck, Bedient's face and command, had held Rey and Framtree, but the former's hand now reached toward his hip. Bedient caught it with an incredibly quick movement, and took the gun from the Senor's pocket.

"Just to reduce tension to a minimum, Senor," he said.

The third Chinese opened the door from the galley, but a look and gesture from Bedient sent him back, and the lock was turned upon him. Bedient now placed the gun upon the table, and directed his attention to Framtree.

"You made it rather hard for me to have a talk with you, my friend," he said.

The place was terrible with strain....

There had been a moment, as the Spaniard's hand crept to his pocket, in which Miss Mallory was powerless with fear, but she could not scream. It was as if Bedient's eyes had held her, too. She watched the pistol now. It was out of Key's reach, and he could not rise from a chair without great difficulty. Framtree did not seem to be armed, for which she was greatly attracted to him.... He had started to speak two or three times, but found no words. The appearance of Bedient seemed to have fascinated him for a moment, but now he managed to declare:

"It must have been the Chinese who turned, Senor.... Somebody went overboard—I think Sorenson."

And not until now did Miss Mallory venture to take her eyes from the cabin interior.... Madame Sorenson was fighting windmills of hysteria. Far back there was a blotch in the darkness, and a curious blend of sea-water, Russian and Chinese, as Sorenson was dragged into the boat; back farther still the lights of Jaffier's gunboat.... And now she found the Glow-worm staring at her, the big face drawing closer, and a rising flame of hope in the strange eyes.

"What have you done, dearest?" she questioned softly.

"He could swim. He told me he could swim," Miss Mallory heard herself repeating vaguely.

THIRTY-FIRST CHAPTER

THE GLOW-WORM'S ONE HOUR

Sorenson and the two Chinese were now eliminated. Senor Rey, disarmed, was not a physical menace; third Chinese was locked in the galley; in a sense Bedient and Framtree equalized; Madame Sorenson was having trouble to overcome her own hysteria; and Adith Mallory uncovered no hostility in the Glow-worm—quite the opposite. Framtree answered Bedient:

"I suggested to the Senor that he let me see you, but he thought to the contrary. He is my commanding officer.... As for you, Bedient, all I have to say is that you carry—a maniac's luck. I think—I think if you hadn't looked so like a dead man, Senor Rey would have done the natural thing, as you came forth from the forecastle."... The big chap glanced at the pistol on the table. "What is it you want with me?"

Again and again, in the stifling forecastle, Bedient had swooned from the heat, the vile air and his utter weakness. Only he had nailed to his brain surfaces, through terrific concentration, an expectancy for Miss Mallory's signals; otherwise they would have failed to rouse him. He had come forth more dead than alive, with only a glimmering of what he was to do, until he saw the hand of Celestino Rey move toward his pocket. Then a strange jolt of strength shook him, and he had the pistol. It was like that day on the *Truxton*. Afterward he heard the words of Miss Mallory insisting that Sorenson could swim, and amusement helped to clear his consciousness. A queer sense that he was not to lose in these lesser affairs possessed him; that enough strength, enough intelligence would be given, a peculiar inner sustaining which he was odd enough to accept as authoritative.... And now he heard Framtree's words, and a water-bottle on the table beside the pistol magnetized his eye. He poured out a glassful and drank, and the thought came—apart from his listening to Framtree—if only other agonies could be eased with the swift directness of his thirst-torture that moment.

"I wanted you to go back on the *Hatteras*, Mr. Framtree," he said. "The *Henlopen* won't sail for a week. We won't lose sight of each other, so there is time. As for our talk, we must be alone."

The words crippled Framtree's hostility, but he did not forget Rey. It was a hard moment for him.

"One wouldn't think you had a week—to judge by the chances you took in turning this trick to-day," he said.

The Spaniard's bony shoulders sank a little in his lids dropped for an instant.

"You proved so hard to reach in these days of preparation," Bedient replied, "that I feared I might fail altogether in case of eventualities. And we had reason to think that to-night marked the end of Equatorian peace."

Rey moistened his lips, watching Framtree, but did not speak.

"It must be damned important," Framtree said.

"It is," Bedient answered, and the American woman listening intently at the wheel did not miss the change in his voice.

Meanwhile the yellow-brown face of the Spaniard had scarcely altered, except perhaps that the pallid scar had a bit more shine about it. His eyes moved around the cabin, darting often at the pistol, halting upon the knob of the forecastle-door in the fear that others might be concealed there; inscrutable black brilliants, these eyes, and to the woman at the wheel the cabin was evil from their purgatorial restlessness.... Suddenly he started, and commanded Framtree:

"See to the ship's course!"

"It's all right, Senor Rey," Miss Mallory called. "I can hold her. We're scudding along beautifully, and our convoy is keeping pace—"

The Spaniard's bony shoulders sank a little in his chair. He interpreted this, as did Framtree, as an order. It was his first positive assurance that the American woman was against him.

"But the Chinese, Miss Mallory—" he said, with rare control.

"Oh, they have picked up Mr. Sorenson.... They can see the light at the point of the Inlet. Mr. Sorenson will need a change of clothing—"

There was a laugh from Framtree, rich, ripping, infectious. It released accumulations of fever and strain from all but the Spaniard, who joined nevertheless.... Bedient stood somewhat rigidly by the table. Waves of mist alternated with intervals of clear perception in his mind.

Miss Mallory had entered into reaction. The laugh of Jim Framtree was the only good omen to her. She wasn't quite so afraid of him after that.... As for the wheel, the situation was not nearly so blithe as she had represented to Rey. The *Savonarola* had changed course, while the Chinese were getting the small boat overside. The Inlet had been astern and a little to star-board then. She had wondered, at the time, at the course, because Captain Bloom of the *Hatteras* had shown her how the reefs stretched out, forming a great breakwater for Coral City harbor, and the *Savonarola* had seemed to be making for trouble.... She jumped with a thought now. Perhaps Rey had intended to run over the coral with his lighter craft, or perhaps he knew a lesser passage; and thus elude Jaffier's gunboat, or strand the latter upon the reefs....

The Inlet light was now straight to port, but the breeze was brisker, and she hated the thought of losing it. She had handled the tiller of small craft, but would not have dared to bring around the *Savonarola* with her vast sweep of sail, even had she cared to regain the original course.... Bedient could not hold these two men at bay all night. He looked as if he might fall any moment. And now he had postponed his talk with Framtree. This was beyond her. She had counted upon him for a message that would make Framtree *his*. She did not realize the meaning of the few words already spoken. There might be pistols secreted, where Framtree could find them. One shot and she was *alone*.... Bedient did not even adequately care for the pistol he had. There was a large stain of red upon the breast pocket of his coat,—a coat that had been white in the morning, but now grimed from the forecastle. The stain terrified her.... Where was the voyage to end? Certainly they could not go back to *The Pleiad* Inlet, nor over the reefs to the main harbor; and this strain could not last. These were bits of her furious thinking during the last few moments, while Bedient stood beside the table like a freshly risen Lazarus.... The Glow-worm moved past her, as a sleep-walker might have done, murmuring that she must have a glass of wine or die. Madame Sorenson moaned at being left alone, and followed the Senora into the cabin. And now Senor Rey asked blandly:

"Why don't you send the two ladies ashore also, Miss Mallory? There is an extra boat—also an extra Chinese—"

"*You won't do that, dear*?" The Glow-worm turned back to her with a horrified look. Her tone was not to be forgotten.

"No, Senora," Miss Mallory answered. "It is well to have at least one small boat."

"Excellent wisdom, I am sure," said Rey, as his eyes settled upon the Glow-worm.

She drained a glass of wine, and sank into a chair in a still huddled fashion. There was something unnatural in the fixed inclination of her head. She had betrayed herself, and watched Rey now out of the corners of her eyes—and in dissolving fear—quivering under his stare and voice. Madame Sorenson was sitting near, dazed from sensational expenditure, her lips moving without sound. There was something hideous in the tension, and in the whole cabin arrangement. Framtree had taken a seat across the aft doorway. He could turn from the woman at the wheel to the light with a movement of his head. He appeared to be much mixed in mind and resigned to await developments. Bedient stood silently watching these changes of position. Miss Mallory felt she must scream before many minutes. She wanted Bedient to know all the fears that distressed her, but dared not speak lest she betray the weakness of their position as she saw it. Once she thought Framtree was laughing at her.

"What a pleasant little party!" Rey remarked at length. "Too bad you can't join us, Miss Mallory." And now he turned to Bedient with a scornful laugh: "Why don't you use your men in the forecastle to man the ship, and relieve the lady at the wheel?"

"They are off watch, Senor," Bedient said, smiling.

"How tired they are! How silently they rest!" the Spaniard replied softly, and his long hands caressed each other.

Framtree glanced from Bedient to Miss Mallory, who realized with added dread that the forecastle bubble was pricked. She wondered how he had conveyed the impression that others were behind.

"Better let me help you with the wheel, Miss Mallory," Framtree said, decently enough.

"No."

"Shall I get you a glass of wine?"

"No."

Rey seemed to have caught a sudden hope. At least, Miss Mallory imagined so; and that he tried to cover it with words.

"Mr. Bedient," he said pleasantly, "I do not wish to under-rate your genius in the least, but I should like to pay a compliment to your remarkable fellow-worker."

"I have several to pay, as well, Senor."

"I should be glad for her to hear," Rey added.

"If you mean me," Miss Mallory called, "I am listening intently."

The Spaniard leaned forward, appearing to cover his eyes with his fingers. Miss Mallory could hardly restrain a scream for Bedient to look out for the pistol, but nothing happened. Senor Rey sat back and began reminiscently:

"I was sailing and garnering in these waters before either of you men, and certainly before any of the women present, were alive. I made Equatoria interesting, and a delightful place to live. I have met in the old days, sometimes in strategy, sometimes in open warfare, the most crafty and daring seamen the world could send to the Caribbean. All, to the last man, I have overmatched in strength and cleverness. A ship has at last changed hands beneath my feet. It is well. I have lived long and am content. Only, I wish to say that it is a bright pleasure to think that no man, however brilliant or daring, outgeneraled me—but a delightful American girl."

"It's a tribute that I shall always remember, Senor," Miss Mallory responded, "and one that comes from a master of his profession."

Out of this pleasantry brewed a change. The Spaniard stared from face to face for several seconds. What came over him cannot be told—a break in his fine control; a sudden realization that he was whipped; a resurgence of all the shattered strategies in his brain, many of which certain others of the party did not yet understand; his doubt of Framtree, or his inability to reach the weapon,—the exact point which goaded him to black disorder was never known, but the fury of it concentrated upon the Glow-worm. Her mortal fear attracted it.

The look he turned upon her was demoniacal, harrowing as a

dream of hell. All else stopped—words, thoughts, even hearts. Miss Mallory craned down to see. The Sorenson woman panted as one dying of thirst. The Senora shrank back. Her face seemed dim, fallen, but she could not lose his eyes. Rey was speaking, leaning forward in his chair, and heaping words upon her like clods upon a corpse:

"... But to-night, things were spoken which could only have come to them—through you! Celestino Rey has been outgeneraled by a clever American girl, but he has also been betrayed by a South American cat—the tortoise-shell of a bagnio-litter—"

Both white men commanded him to stop. The Spaniard turned a glance from Framtree to Bedient.... The woman at the wheel, straining downward, saw the Glow-worm rise with an appalling shudder, as the eyes of her lord left her; saw her body huddle forward toward him, her hands fumbling in her hair.

"My dear Bedient," the Spaniard was saying, "I regret this domestic scene. You must excuse a man who has so recently discovered his Glow-worm to be a scorpion—"

The crouching figure of the woman—in the rage she had prayed for, and as she had prayed for it, *with his eyes turned away*—hurled forward as one diving into the sea. The flying body seemed huge in the little cabin. The concentration of her weight struck him in the throat. His head whipped back like a flaunted arm. The chair had been screwed to the floor, but the weight of impact ripped the fastenings out of the heavy planking. Backward Rey was borne, beneath a stabbing creature whose cries were as some bestial mystery of the dark.

It was Framtree who tore her loose, and tightened upon her

wrist until the fingers opened and the little knife—concealed how long in her hair?—dropped like a feather to the carpet. Swiftly it had let out the life of the Spaniard.... Bedient opened the galley-door at a gesture from the woman. The Chinese came forth.

"It was I—your mistress, Boy—who killed the Senor. You may look. Then fix him quickly, so he will sink. I want him to sink!" she panted.

Bedient waited for Framtree to look up. The eyes of the two men met.

"The first and last chance of war in Equatoria is eliminated," Bedient said.

Presently he moved out of the cabin, and sat down beside Miss Mallory. Each had held out a hand to the other, but they had not words.

The place was being made clean within.... The Glow-worm could not be silent, muttered constantly to the Chinese. "... You shall go back to South America with me. I shall be very good to you.... Oh, do open some wine, Boy! I am so very thirsty!" and on, until she saw the face of Framtree, moodily watching. She sank into a chair shuddering, and covered her face. "Don't look at me so horribly!" she cried. "Ask Senorita Mallory about it—ask her about me."

He jerked up, but did not answer at once. The Glow-worm screamed at him to speak.

Framtree crossed the cabin, and dropped his huge hand upon her shaking shoulder.

"I have nothing to say, Senora.... It was a matter between you and him.... But I'm glad to help you. It bowled me over a little, that's all."

His voice was big in the hush that had fallen upon the cabin.... Framtree helped the Chinese carry forth the weighted body.... As it paused for an instant on the gunwale, the searchlight from Jaffier's gunboat flicked athwart the *Savonarola*—sinister tableaux in its ghostly light.... Without a sound the Glow-worm fell backward to the cabin floor, as if touched by the finger of the Destroying Angel. Bedient worked upon her until consciousness was restored.

"What next in this terrible night?" Miss Mallory asked in an awed voice, when Bedient rejoined her.

"Such an end has hung over him for more years than we have lived," he said. "I call it rather wonderful—as it came about. Hundreds of men will continue to live because of this death. It means an end of war-making, the release of this turbulent spirit."

Bedient turned to the light. She saw the red stain upon the breast of his coat.

He glanced down, and felt in the inner pocket. "It's the red chalk," he said with a laugh. "It got crushed somehow, and it was oily. The forecastle melted it."

...Plainly at this moment they both heard the sound of a steamer's screw—ahead. But there were no lights. Bedient took the wheel and brought the *Savonarola* sheering away to the south of the sound, which had stopped abruptly.

Nothing was seen, not even a denser shadow in the moonless dark. Framtree joined them, and they waited expectantly for Jaffier's index of light to pick up the mystery. Ten minutes passed before the gunboat, following doggedly, and whipping her light over sea, suddenly uncovered the dark from a big tramp steamer, aimed at the Inlet. For an instant it was lost again, but the searchlight swept back, groped until the tramp was caught, and this time held—in all her unlit wickedness.

"Framtree," said Bedient, "I believe we are about to lose our convoy—"

"Looks that way," Framtree replied. "Miss Mallory has steered—"

"Miss Mallory has steered—Equatoria off a revolutionary shoal," Bedient finished.

"You mean the Senora—?" Miss Mallory intervened.

"No."

"I'm very tired and stupid; please tell me in little words," she pleaded.

"You changed the ship's course?"

"I didn't. It changed itself. I didn't dare to change back, because of the reefs," she added hastily. "Didn't the Senor mean to run the convoy aground if they didn't give up the chase?"

"I hadn't thought of that," Bedient said. "Mr. Framtree, hadn't you better explain to Miss Mallory?"

"No, that's for you."

"Perhaps you will correct me if I am wrong.... The black

tramp yonder was making for *The Pleiad* Inlet, with a cargo of guns and ammunition for the rebellion. The little sailing-trip of Senor Rey was designed to pull the gunboat afar off in the Southwest, the original course, as you say, to permit the tramp to make the Inlet unmolested. Jaffier won't need the guns, but they're a moral force—"

"As a war correspondent," Miss Mallory remarked, "I am rather a spectacular failure."

"It's a boy's game," said Bedient.

THIRTY-SECOND CHAPTER

IN THE LITTLE ROOM NEXT

They sailed around open water until daybreak, when Bedient brought the *Savonarola* into a river-mouth on Carreras land, and forcing her in out of the current, dropped anchor. The small boat was launched and pulled ashore. Six, a silent and weary six, they were. The *hacienda* was five miles inland. Bedient sent natives there for saddle-ponies, and made the party comfortable until these were brought. The roads would not permit vehicle of any sort, and though saddling was an ordeal for the Glow-worm and Madame Sorenson, the distance was not great, and from every eminence there were flashes of morning glory upon the endless company of hills.

Falk and Leadley stood upon the great porch as the cavalcade drew up. They steadied and leaned upon each other in this climacteric moment of their service.... There was breakfast with Carreras coffee, and the party separated for rest. The still torrid day became more vivid, and the native women and children hushed one another under the large open windows.... Miss Mallory was last in the breakfast room. Bedient saw that she wanted to speak with him, and they walked out on the porch together.

"You say it will be six days before the *Henlopen* leaves for

Will Levington Comfort

New York?" she asked.

"Yes, and no *Pleiad* for you, Miss Mallory. There will be changes and disorder down in the city.... I'll make you comfortable as I can."

"Oh, I'll like that! It's so still and restful—and—from here—last night seems ages behind.... It would have been unbearable, but for what you said about the other men's lives saved. Then the Glow-worm had told me so much! He was unspeakable.... As for Sorenson, I just couldn't have done that had I thought of sharks first!... I wonder what Rey meant to do—just before ... yes, yes, let's forget him!... When you are rested, there is something I have to tell you."

"And there is something for me to say—but now?" he questioned.

"I want you to let me take care of you—during the six days—"

The old feminine magnetism thrilled him again. It was so strange and unexpected from Miss Mallory—a breath from the old Dream Ranges. It quickened him to the race of women, even to the great work, as he had not been quickened since the night he looked back at the empty open door.... He did not speak, but held out both hands to her.

"I think you are living and moving at this moment," she went on fervently, "upon some strange force that other people do not have. Since we left New York, I have watched you—seen you almost every day. You are like a traveler who has crossed some terrible and forbidden land. You do not eat nor sleep. I must help you. Please let me.... Oh, it isn't as if I were a girl! I've worked with men—done a man's work among the newspapers. I'd call it bigger than all that has happened for the good fortune of Equatoria—if I could make you look as—"

She checked the tumult of words. There was a misty look in her eyes—and his. He smiled and held himself hard, to say steadily:

"A man doesn't often win so dear a friend—"

"You have found about me so much of humor and scheming," she said pathetically, "but since I came to understand a little, I've wanted to show you other things—"

"I could not have relished your humor, nor used your plans, had I not felt so much besides." He pointed over the shining lands. "Great good can come from all this—perhaps you'll help me—where the suffering is blackest in New York. With that big tramp steamer in *The Pleiad*, and Celestino in command, it would have been hard to save this. You did it—"

"If I did, it's not *vital* to you. It does not bring you rest. How clearly I see that!"

Bedient turned aside from her tearful searching eyes. He was facing the old battle; and yet a certain uplift came from her brave spirit. It was one of the big intimate warmths of the world, one of the fine moments of life in the world. Her giving was true. He could think of no other who could have helped him in this way, save Vina Nettleton. These two had not entered his mind together before. And they were unlike in every way, except in their pure quality of giving.

"Please tell me that other matter now—why you were so good to me, even on the steamer?"

"But I want you to rest."

"I would rest better—"

Miss Mallory looked up at him for a moment, and embarrassment came to her face—different from any look of hers before.

"It was in New York.... I wore a white net waist and a big bunch of English violets," she said, watching him. "It seems very long ago, but it isn't—hardly ten weeks. There was darkness and *Hedda* was telling young *Loevborg* to drink wine and get vine-leaves in his hair—"

"And you were the one?" Bedient said.

"'So fleet the works of men, back to their earth again,
Ancient and holy things fade like a dream,'"

she repeated.

"I remember."

"And do you remember the first scream?... If I were a lost and freezing traveler in Siberia, the first cry of a gathering wolf-pack could not have more terror for me than that scream. And, I can hear the snapping of the chair-backs still, hideous secrets from human lips, and the scraping, panting, packing. I was hurt in the first crazy rush. I crushed the violets to my lips to keep out the smoke and gas.... Then your voice, 'Now's the time for vine-leaves, fellows,—there's a woman for everyone to help!' I heard you laugh and challenge the men to their best manhood.... And all the time, I thought I was dying.... Then your foot touched me, and I heard you say, 'Why, here's a little one left for me—'"

"Your hair had come undone," he said softly.

"And you never looked under the violets—"

"I went back to look for you. I wasn't gone a minute, but you had vanished."

"They took me away in the car—then I thought of the story and I didn't see you again, until you brushed by me in the Dryden ticket office in New York—the day before we sailed—"

"And you've been my good angel ever since—"

"I want to be—now.... Please get me a glass of warm milk."

He obeyed. From her bag she produced a powder and, at her word, Bedient held forth his tongue....

"And now I want you to drink the milk—all of it. You put down asterisks in the place of breakfast—quite as usual. I considered my self-control remarkable at the time."

He drank the milk slowly, as she had ordered.... The moments were sensational. Picture after picture passed through the light of his mind, as from other lives, and the loves of many women; and then the whole story that he had told Beth Truba rushed by—the mother's hand and the little boy—the city, the parks, the ships—the hours upon her arm, when she had made him over anew to face the long voyage alone—the questions he had asked—the last port with her, which he had never been able to find—the last ride with Beth—until he was shaken with the rush of visions. Everything that he was, and hoped to be, everything that he had thought of beauty and truth and giving, every aspiration and every inspiration—seemed gifts of women! His very life and all that had come to him—gifts of women. And all their loving, wistful, smiling faces were there—among the Dream

Ranges.... Now this one was speaking:

... "I want you to show me where I am to rest and where you are to rest."

Up they went together and softly.... He led her into his own room, but she saw his things and would not.

"This is where you belong," she whispered. "You will rest better here.... Please don't dispute.... But let me be near, if you will."

He showed her a little room that joined his own. Falk had made it ready.

"Just the place for me.... And after you have lain down, please whistle softly. I shall come in and read to you until you are asleep."

"It's like a fairy story already," he said.

* * * * *

He closed his eyes, and the pictures took up their swift passing again. It was not the drug, but the new thing in this life of his—a woman's ministering.... She came in presently, her hair loosened. She wore one of his silk night-coats, the sleeves rolled up; and very little, she looked, in the heelless straw sandals. She was pale. He saw the throbbing artery in her white throat. The polished ebon floor had a startling effect upon her black hair.

"You are like Rossetti's *Pomegranate* picture," he said, and added with a strange smile, "Do you know there is something true about you—arrow-true?"

She sat down in the chair near him and picked up the Book. "What shall I read?" she asked without looking up. "It must be something that will soothe, and not make you think, except happily."

"It's all there.... The stately prose of Isaiah—I love the ringing authority of it—"

She read. There were delicate shadings of volume, even in her lowered voice, which lent a fine natural quality to her expression. Bedient knew the words, but he loved the mystery of this giving of hers—her giving of peace to him.... He had obeyed her implicitly, and the morning had become very dear.... Ill and weary, all his nerves smarting with terrific fatigue, as the eyes smart before tears, and yet her ministering had made him a little boy again.... His eyelids were shut and he was happy. It was a bewildering sense, so long had he been, and so far, from a moment like this. His immortal heroine was close once more—she of the answered questions and the healing arms. So real was it, that he thought this must be death.... A sign from *her* made him know that it was not.... Queer, bright thoughts winged in and out of his mind. There was a drowsy sweep to the atmosphere—no, it was the nuances of the voice that read to him.... "When one comes to see in this life a clearer, brighter way for the conduct of the next, he has not failed." His mind went over this several times.... And presently he felt himself sailing through space toward one bright star. For eternities he had sailed—dominant, deathless—often wavering in the zones of attraction of other worlds, but never really losing that primal impetus for his own light of the universe.... And so while she read, Bedient drifted afar, sailing on and on toward his star....

She saw that he slept, and her head dropped forward until it touched the edge of his bed, but very softly.... And there, for a long time, she remained, until the woven cane left a white impress upon her forehead.

Late in the afternoon the others met below, but Bedient had not awakened. Miss Mallory joined them and told what she had done, and how ill he had been for need of rest.... When the day was ending she stole through the little room into his. Still he slept, so softly, that she bent close to hear his breathing.... All the furious moments of action in recent days passed in swift review, as she stood there in the dark. And from it all came this:

"It is a good thing for a woman to serve a man, with hand and brain,—as one man might serve another—and there's high joy in it; but a woman must not serve a man that way— if she'd rather have his love than hope of heaven."

... And when he awakened, she was still beside him.

THIRTY-THIRD CHAPTER

THE HILLS AND THE SKIES

Varied were the emotions of Dictator Jaffier and Coral City generally, while Bedient slept through that long day of surpassing fortune to the Island. He communicated certain facts to the Dictator next morning, and a day later, the government forces entered and took possession of *The Pleiad* without firing a shot.

It did not transpire at this time that the vast inflation of war-sentiment in Equatoria was pricked with a knife, so small that a woman could conceal it in her hair.

Bedient intervened between Jaffier and Senora Rey, and upon the latter a substantial settlement was made, as well as a generous annuity. Within three days, the Glow-worm had left Coral City for an Antillean port, to connect with a South American steamer. The Sorensons and one Chinese accompanied her. The Glow-worm shone as one lavishly rich, but trembled with fears which she dared not express, until Equatoria should sink from her horizon.

Jaffier's gunboat, which had followed the *Savonarola* on principle and deserted for the unlit tramp, drove this latter destiny-maker through the coral passage in daylight, and around to the harbor, amid the subdued rejoicing of the Defenders. Subdued, because the Defenders were jerky with fear of a trick, even with the guns and ammunition safely stored in the Capitol—until the message from Bedient to Jaffier made certain mysterious issues clear.

The Pleiad guests were not summarily routed, but the force of law, and the flood of light, suddenly turned upon every corner of this establishment, destroyed the atmosphere for crime and concupiscence. The paintings and various beautiful collections of the late art-lover-and-patron, were gathered together in one of the great wings of the establishment, and opened to the people. The magnificent grounds became a public park.

Bedient was regarded with something akin to awe for his activity at *The Pleiad*, and on board the *Savonarola*. Jaffier could readily perceive how large were the pecuniary interests of Carreras' heir in the complete demolition of the Spaniard's power, but such single-handed effectiveness had a supermasculine voltage about it, despite Bedient's laughing explanations. The Carreras interests became, in Jaffier's mind, second only to the interests of the government. A handsome present and a rich grant of land were privately conferred upon Miss Mallory, at Bedient's suggestion, for her brilliant services to the government.... But these are dry externals. A careful resume of happy adjustments from Jaffier down to Monkhouse following the last sail of the Spaniard, would weary.... Three days after the spent and silent six rode up to the *hacienda*, Bedient was left with but two guests, Miss Mallory and Jim Framtree, who were awaiting the New York steamer.... In effect, the parable of the horses had been retold to Framtree. Bedient took him for a night-walk over the hills for this.

"But Beth showed me very clearly—where I wouldn't do at

all," the big man said intensely. "And clearly, I saw it, too,—raw and unfinished beside her, I was."

"Did she ever show you that little picture of you she painted?" Bedient asked.

"No. All she had of me were a few kodak prints—"

"She probably painted the picture from them," Bedient said. "I saw it on her mantle one day, and instantly our little talk in Coral City recurred to me. I knew you. Beth Truba didn't mention your name.... The portrait is exquisitely done.... Why, Jim Framtree, that portrait meant more to her than my comings and goings in the flesh—"

"I can't quite understand that, Bedient!"

"I knew there was some power in her heart that I did not affect. I related it to the picture, and when she told me the parable, I asked her outright if the picture and her heart's knight were one. She answered 'Yes.'... And so, Jim, I stand in awe of you. You've won and held what is to me the greatest woman of our time. I don't know anything I wouldn't do for you—with that light upon you—"

"You've got me thinking faster than is safe, Bedient. Do men turn this sort of trick very often for each other?"

"It was glad tidings," Bedient said. "The fact is, I have no better thing to give, than services for such a woman. It's clear and simple, that my business is to make her as happy as I can from the outside.... And, Jim, she must not know I told you, nor that I hunted you up. It wouldn't be best.... Just go back to New York, ask to see her, and try again. She'll be glad—"

"You're sure of that?"

Will Levington Comfort

"Well, I shouldn't be sure. It's her province.... I want her to have the chance."

"...You ought to know how I feel about all this, Bedient," Framtree said unsteadily, "since you know her."

Bedient liked that.

"I made it a bit hard for you," he replied, "the way I told it—as if you didn't count at all with me—only as something she wanted—but you do, Jim—"

"...We'll come back, or I'll come back," Framtree said, and he turned away from the other's eyes.

Bedient had looked upon him that moment, as if he would add his own soul's strength to the strength of Framtree.... The hours that followed, to the moment of the *Henlopen's* sailing, were hours of building. Framtree found himself locked in the concentration of Bedient's ideals—matters of manhood fitted about him, that he had not aspired to. And it was not easy to fall from them, when Bedient believed in him so truly.

And Miss Mallory lured back Bedient's strength. He ate, drank and slept at her bidding.... So little she said, so instant to understand, so strange and different she was, waiting upon his words as upon a master's.... The last evening at the *hacienda* (the *Henlopen* had arrived in the harbor) he played for them upon the orchestrelle. Music came forth new and of big import to his consciousness.... He had tried the soul-rousing *heimweh* from the slow movement of Dvorak's *New World Symphony*, when Miss Mallory, looking over the rolls, discovered the *Andante* of Beethoven's Fifth.

"Don't you remember—the orchestra—that night?... It's wonderful and mysterious—won't you—?" But she saw the look that came into his face, and did not finish. Instead, she put the roll away quickly, knowing she had touched a more vital association than a theatre fright.

"Don't mind, and please forgive me—"

...That night they stood together at the door of the little room, for she had refused to change. Bedient said:

"Every time I think of you I feel better, Adith Mallory.... I shall think of you often, always as if you were in the little room next to mine."

They went aboard the following night, and sailed at dawn. Bedient rode back to the *hacienda* during the morning.... How strange it will be—alone, he thought; stranger still, he faced the prospect without dread.... A hush had fallen upon the hills, and upon his heart. Some mysterious movement was stirring at the centres of his life....

A box of pictures had come on the *Henlopen*; also a letter from Torvin. There were three canvases in the latest shipment, and seven had come to the *hacienda* while he was in New York. He hung them all in a room where there was good North light, and kept the key with him. And so there was a gallery for the Grey One in that house, as well as the little room next to his. He smiled at the thought that a man's life becomes a house of his friends.... Torvin reported that Miss Grey had disposed of several pictures direct from her studio; that he had marketed eight pictures beside the ones shipped to Equatoria, and that there was a sprightly demand for her work....

* * * * *

That night, as Bedient ascended the stairs, a long sigh

escaped him. So uncommon a thing was this, that he stopped to reflect. It was like one casting off a worn garment. Some old, ill, tired part of him passed away, and out of the great still house. He did not loathe it, but sped its passing, happily, gratefully.... Then the thought came, "Why do I attract all this beauty of friendship and loyalty?"... All the eager activity of others in his behalf recurred—the gracious image of that Mother of myriad services, before all—and the fragrant essence of a hundred deeds of love for him.... "I must hurry to keep pace, but I can't—with these infinite favors!" he whispered.

A passion for service surged through him—to pray, and serve, and love and do; to write and give and lift and smile; always to help; to fall asleep blessing the near and the far; to awake prodigal with strength.... Such a spirit of giving brimmed into his life, that his flesh thrilled with the ecstasy of illimitable service.

The material things about him—walls, staircase, even the lamp-globes—were shadowy and unreal in the midst of these mystically glowing conceptions.

The sense of perfect health came to him—a steady, rhythmic radiation; not a tired, weak fibre, but a singing vitality of every tissue, as if it were cushioned in some life-giving fluid—a pure perfumed bloom of health.

Bedient turned upon the stair. He wanted no man-made room, but the night and the hills and the skies.... Bare of head he went forth.

THIRTY-FOURTH CHAPTER

THE SUPREME ADVENTURE

The night was full of sounds, sights, odors, textures—that he had never sensed before. He smelled the wild oranges from the hillsides, and the raw coffee that lay drying on the great cane mats before the native cabins. His limbs seemed lifted over the rocky ways; he loved the dim contours in the starlight, and the breath of the sea that came with the night-wind. The stars said, "Welcome," and the hills, "All is well."

Mother Earth was lying out in more than starlight—but not asleep. She was laughing, wise, sweet in eternal youth. Always she had been dear to him, this Flesh Mother. Her storms and terrors she had shown, but never harmed him. He loved her, sea and mountain and plain—*God-Mother* and the Kashmir border—the highway ride with the lustrous lady and its sunshine—the path through the wood.... What a boy and girl they had been! How he had loved her—and the day—how he had suffered for it!

And now Bedient knelt upon the stones, uplifted his hands to the starlight, and cried in a low voice: "God bless Beth Truba, and help me to bless her at every turning of her life! God bless Beth Truba for the sensitizing sorrow she gave me, without which this hour could not have been revealed to me!"

... He seemed to be leaping from crest to crest in an ocean of happiness.... Some glorious magnetic Presence strode beside him. The night quivered with mighty energies—strange brightenings flashed before his eyes. He wanted nothing—but to give.... All was clear to him. Immortality was here and now: This life but a hut upon the headland of interminable continents, yet as much a part of immortality, as the life of the star-clothed Master who blinded Saul on the road to Damascus.

What a symphony—the flower, the star, the drop of rain, the rose, the child, the harvest, the voice of love, the soul of Woman,—all from the Luminary, God,—all His immortal symphony.

He was filled with light—as a still, clear harbor at high noon—gems and treasure-horns flashing in the depths. He *realized* God. This was a ray of God that penetrated him—the spiritual essence "all science transcending."

With joy, a sentence he had once heard returned, "Prayer is not catching God's attention, but permitting him to hold ours!"... Faith and truth are one; Faith is the scaffolding in which the structure of Truth is builded; that which is Faith to us, is Truth to the angels.... As never before, he realized that wisdom comes from the inner light of man, and not from the comprehension of externals.... He knew now the meaning of ecstasy on the faces of the dying, and remembered with confusion and alarm that men of this day were afraid of Death!... How much more should they fear birth—birth, the ordeal of the soul—the putting on of flesh. Great souls put on flesh to hasten the way of their younger brothers to the Shining Tablelands. That is pure Spirit—to lift the weak and show the way to those dim of sight.

Integration of spirit—that is power, that is progress. Compared to this, a mere education of the mind is vain and dull—a hoarding of facts, as coins are hoarded; a gathering of vanities, as clothes and adornments are gathered together. His soul cried out within him: Teach the Spirit of God. "The soul who ascendeth to worship God is plain and true."... Teach the Spirit, break daily new ground of giving and devotion. Growth of Spirit—*that* is blessedness! *That* is the exalted end of all suffering in the flesh. The world is good; all is good. There is no evil, but the ignorant uses of self-consciousness. Man has fallen into dark ways that belong to the awful ascent from the dim innocence of animals to the lustrous knowledge of God.

Treasure every loving impulse; the number of these is your day's achievement—thus the Voice went on. Love giving; let the throat tighten with emotion for others, and the hand go out to the stranger; love giving, but love more—him who receives. Preserve humility in your blessedness. There is nothing to fear, no darkness of destiny, nothing to fear for the growing and humble spirit. Death! It is but the breaking of a rusty scabbard to loose a flashing blade!

"Oh, that I were a hundred men—to die before all men—to die daily!" he cried out. "But I shall live. I shall live with the poor. I shall feed them the bread of the body; and, if I may, the bread of life. I shall be brother to the poor, and they shall hear of their kingdoms.... Oh, God, help me to utter the glory of life, the sublimity of the human soul!"

And now he saw the terrible need of pity for those who wrap themselves in the softest furs, who feed upon the breasts of doves and drink the spirit of purple and golden grapes— those whom the world serves, and who are so arrogant in their regality. He must not forecast the falling of such, but pity them—and speak, if they would listen—for their need is often greater than that of the menials who cringe before their empty greatness, blinded by their kingly trappings. The world so often betrays them at the end, strips them to nakedness and leaves them to die—for they are the cripples, the sick, the blind in spirit.... Delicately he must attend the brutal and arrogant; not hate them, even when he perceives their devastation among the poor. Everywhere to give tokens of his health and power.

His love came back—as in lightning, his love came back! Not the love of one that he had known—that was good, inevitable, even the restless agony of it. Through the love of one, comes the love of many.... But this was love of the world! It surged over, through him—like the fire of the burning bush—that did not devour.... He had abstained from evil before, but held the taste for certain evils. *Now the taste was gone*—for every fleshly thing. Wanting nothing, he could love, indeed.

*　*　*　*　*

How strange and wonderful! All that he had thought before, and expressed in New York, had seemed his very own—the realizations of Andrew Bedient—but this night his every thought, almost, had a parallel, from one or another of the great ones who had gone this high way before.... He perceived that he had been old in self-consciousness, so, that, in a way, his New York utterances were stamped with his own individuality. In this greater consciousness he was a child; its glory was beyond words. He could only echo the attempts of those whose lips had faltered with ecstasy.

If any man is in Christ, he is a new creature; the old things are passed away; behold, they are become new.

Such was Paul's clear saying.... The difference between Andrew Bedient at this hour and the self he had been was great as that between the simple consciousness of the ox and the self-consciousness of man.

This was the borderland of Gautama's Nirvana; this the Living Water, Jesus offered to the woman at the well; this the Holy Ghost that appeared unto the Hebrew saints and prophets—Moses, Gideon, Samuel, Isaiah, Stephen; this the genius of Paul, the ecstasy of Plotinus, the paradise of Behmen, the heavenly light of St. John of the Cross; this, the Beatrice of Dante, the Gabriel of Mahomet, the Master Peter of Roger Bacon, the Seraphita of Balzac, the radiant companion of Whitman, and the *I* of Edward Carpenter.

The light would have killed one who had not integrated spiritual light to reflect it. The light of the Illuminati is terrible to eyes filled with evil. This was the "smile of the Universe" that Dante saw.... He, Andrew Bedient, loved infinitely and was infinitely loved. The words of a hundred saints echoed in his consciousness—and out of them all came this command:

Make men to know that this which has come to you, will come to them. The few have gone before you, but the many have not ascended so far.

And now he saw the whole road of man, from the simple consciousness of animals, through human self-consciousness, to the cosmic consciousness of prophets—and beyond to Divinity. Always the refinement of matter, and the attraction of light—spiritual light. He saw the time when a self-conscious man was the best specimen of the human race. So for cosmic consciousness, the time would come; and as the centuries passed, the earlier would it appear in the life of the evolved.

A clear expression of what had taken place within him now appeared—his own expression to make it clear for men. In the summit of self-consciousness, his mind was like a campfire in the night—a few objects in a circle of red firelight and shadow. The crown of cosmic consciousness now come, was *the dawn of full day upon the plain.*

Full day upon the plain—distances, contours, the great blooms of space; a swarm of bees, a constellation of suns; the traffic of ants among the dropped twigs of the sand, the communion of angels beyond the veils of heaven; the budding of a primrose, the resurrection of a God—and all for men, when the daybreak and the shadows flee away.

He saw that this was the natal hour of the world's soul-life, and that it would come through the giving spirit of Woman. He saw great souls pressing close to every pure, strong, feminine spirit; the first fruits of the centuries hovering close to great women of the world, praying for bodies to toil with, eager to turn from their heaven to labor for men.... And this was the *shekinah* of Andrew Bedient—the spirit of his message.

*   *   *   *   *

His blood ceased to flow; he heard the flight of angels; he was bathed in Brahmic splendor—until he could bear no more....

He awoke in the "ambrosia of dawn"; in that strange hush which lies upon the world before fall the floods of rosy red.... He arose, his feet stumbling with ecstasy. Light winged over the hills—and afar off, he saw the roofs of the *hacienda* sharpen with day....

His face was like morning upon a cloud. The natives vanished before him; Falk and Leadley shrank back, wondering what manner of drink he had found in the night.

THIRTY-FIFTH CHAPTER

FATE KNOCKS AT THE DOOR

During the month that followed, Bedient wrote at length to all his friends in New York. Nightly he roamed the hills and rode his lands throughout the long forenoons. It was a season of sheer exaltation. The great house had become dear to him. His own fullness was enough. There was no loneliness— "loneliness, with our planet in the Milky Way?"... He felt a sense of authority in what he wrote, altogether new, a more finished simplicity—the very white wine of clarity.

Then he placed great energies of planting upon the lands Jaffier had conferred upon Miss Mallory; and carried out plans for the increase of his own harvests. In fact, he was more interested than ever in this base of his future operations in New York. He realized the need of help—an ordering executive mind. His brain and body quickly adjusted to the great good which had descended upon him—work and praise, and love for all things. With these, his hours breathed.

One midnight in July, as he lay awake, an impulse came to play Beethoven's symphony—in the dark.... He arranged the four rolls to hand, turned off the lights again, and sat down before the orchestrelle. The opening bars, which the Master designated, "*So pocht das Schicksal an die Pforte,*" lured his every power of concentration. He was one with it, and movements of the dark swung with the flow of harmony. The silence startled him. It was hard to re-assemble his faculties to change the rolls for the '*Andante*....

The three voices returned to his mind—man and woman and the luminous third Presence. That which had always been dim and formless before, now cleared—the place and the man. The room was large and had the character of a music studio, or one department of a large conservatory. A grand piano, a stand for violin, pictures of the masters, and famous musical scenes on the wall—more, there was music in the air—intervals when the three figures seemed to listen. A violin was across the man's knee, a bow in his right hand.

The man was down, whipped. The world had been too much for him. The face was not evil, nor was it mighty. A tall young man—a figure knit with beauty and precision. It was the figure of a small man enlarged, rather than one of natural bulk. Bedient's recognition of the man was not material; some inner correspondence made him know.... He was sitting upon a rocker, too small and low for him. The long, perfect limbs stretched out would have appeared lax and drunken but for their grace of line. The bow-hand dropped limp, almost to the floor. The other moved the violin about, handled it lightly, familiarly, as one would play with a scarf. Fugitive humor flashed across the face, relieving the deep disquiet, but the laugh was an effort of one who was confronted by demolished fortunes. His whole look was that of a man who has been shown some structural smallness of his own, shown beyond doubt—his ranges of personal limitation, made clear and irrefutable. He recognized his master in the woman opposite.... Yet powerful natural elements within him were bearing upon the hateful revelation. They sought to cover the puny nakedness, and make an hallucination of it all. He was not evolved enough to accept the truth with humility.

*   *   *   *   *

The woman was psychically torn. The agony of her face cannot be pictured, nor her martyrdom of sustaining courage. She could not see the third Presence, but it was there *for her*. It was above her, yet was called by her natural greatness. There was a line of luminous white under her eyes, that left the lower part of her face in shadow. The eyes were shining with that dissolving supernatural light, that comes with terrible spiritual hunger. Her dark hair had fallen in disarray.

In the first transcendent happiness she had conceived a child. The hideous disillusionment was now—months before the babe. And her struggle at this moment of her heart's death—was to keep the madness of sorrow from despoiling the child, that lay formative within—to preserve the child whole, and in her original greatness of ideal, in the midst of her own destroying, and against the defiling commonness that had just been revealed in the father....

She had crossed the last embankment of agony; her struggle was finished. She had conquered. The Presence had come to hold her mind true, in this passage through chaos.... Her own death she would have welcomed, save that the babe must live. It had come to her as a daybreak from heaven. It must not be crushed and weighted with this tragedy of pure earth.... She held the blight from the child!

She *knew* this. She arose and smiled. Into her soul had come a sense of the amplitude of time—a promise of adoration—a blessing upon her courage—a knowledge of her child's lustre. The Angel had whispered it. Blithe, lifting, loving, the message had come to her from the Presence.

The man perceived that he had hurt her mortally; that his meaning to her had vanished. He arose to approach her, but a gesture of her hand made him sink again into the low chair. He seemed trying to realize that she had passed beyond him, indeed,—trying to realize what it would mean to him.... Pitiful, boyish and unfinished, he struggled to adjust his own life to her going—and watched her bind her hair.

Every movement of the conflict held a globe of meaning for the son of this woman, a third of a century afterward. Her tragedy had marked it imperishably upon the tissue of his life, with Beethoven's *Andante* movement for the key. Strains of it may have come to that music-room with these towering emotions.... More than this Andrew Bedient saw the sources of his own heritage! From another aspect he viewed the deathlessness of time, the beauty of physical death, the radiance of the future, the immortality of love. It was revealed how all the agony of the world arises from the knitting together of soul and flesh, the evolving of soul through flesh. Spirit is given birth in flesh—and birth is pain. Death is the ecstasy of the grown spirit. Spirit prospers alone through giving, and greatly through the giving of love. Spirit shines star-like in the giving of woman—in the fineness and fullness which she *loves* into her children, binding glory upon them with her dreams. Thus is expressed her greatness; thus women are nearest the sources of spirit; thus they fulfill the first meaning of life on earth. And the woman who preserves the nobility of her conception of Motherhood— against the anguish of a broken heart and a destroyed love— God sends his Angels to sustain her!...

Bedient was aroused at last in the silence and in the dark.... He knelt in a passion of tribute to his immortal heroine, whose spirit had danced with him above the flesh and the world. He saw again that he was ordained to look within for the woman; that his heart was his mother's heart; his spirit, her spirit—this twain one in loving and giving.

Will Levington Comfort

IV. NEW YORK

Allegro Finale

THIRTY-SIXTH CHAPTER

THE GREAT PRINCE HOUSE

There were calms and conquests on the brow of Vina Nettleton. She had been in Nantucket one whole day alone, before David Cairns came. Such a day availeth much, but she shuddered a little at the joy she took in the prospect of his coming. Vina had learned what his absence meant a month before, when three entire days elapsed without a call from Cairns at the studio. He had been away on a certain happiness venture.... There had been no word yet, but here, Nantucket—Vina breathed deeply at the name. Almost every day their thoughts had turned a sentence upon this meeting.... He stepped forth from the little steamer late in the afternoon in a brisk proprietory fashion, but the treasures of boyhood were shining in his eyes; and he searched her face deeply, as if to detect if mortal illness had begun its work amid the terrible uncertainties of separation.

"Do you remember, at first, I was to find you down among the wharves with *Moby Dick*?" she said.

"To-morrow morning—for that," he replied.

She showed him the way to his hotel, and the house where she was a guest. But they supped together.

... They walked in Lily Lane in the dusk.

"It's too dark to see the Prince Gardens," she told him. "They're the finest on the Island, and the house is the finest in Lily Lane.... There doesn't seem to be a light. I wonder if the old sisters are gone?... The Princes were a great family here years and years ago, but gradually they died out and dwindled away, until last summer there were only two old maiden-aunts left—lovely, low-voiced old gentlewomen, whom it was so hard to *pay* for their flowers. But they lived from their gardens and now *they're* gone, it seems. I must ask to-morrow what has become of them. And yet, the gardens are kept up. Can you see the great house back in the shadows among the trees?"

Cairns believed he could make out something like the contour of a house in denser shadow.

"The fragrance of the gardens is lovelier than ever," Vina went on, "and listen to the great trees whispering back to the sea!"

They walked along the shore, and stared across toward Spain, and talked long of Beth and Bedient.... And once Vina stretched out her arms oversea, and said:

"Oh, I feel so strange and wonderful!"

Cairns started to speak, but forbore....

They met early in the morning, down upon the deserted water-front. An hour of drifting brought them back to Lily Lane. There was a virginal pallor in the sunlight, different from the ruddy summer of the Mainland, as the honey of April is paler and sweeter than the heartier essence of July flowerings. The wind breathed of a hundred years ago, and the sublime patience of the women who hurried down Lily Lane (faded but mystic eyes that lost themselves oversea through thousand-day voyages), to welcome their knight-errants, bearing home the marrow of leviathans....

"The gardens are kept up," Vina said, standing on the walk, before the Prince house. "Perhaps the old sisters are still there, and we may get some flowers from them—"

"I think, if you'll let me walk ahead and talk with the gardener," Cairns said, "we'll be allowed to go in—at least, for some flowers."

She laughed at the audacity of a stranger in Nantucket, but bade him try.

"If you fail, it's my turn," she added.

Cairns seemed to have little trouble in negotiating with the gardener, and presently beckoned.

"I've done very well for a stranger," he whispered. "We're to have the flowers. More than that, we are to look through the house. The sisters are away—"

"David—"

"But I told him who you were—about your friends and relatives in Nan—here.... I assure you, he believes we have never set foot out of New England."

There was a sweet seasoning in the house; decades of flowers and winds, spare living, gentle voices and infallible cleanliness—that perfumed texture which years of fineness alone can bring to a life or to a house.

"See, the table is set for two!" Vina whispered, "as if the sisters were to be back for dinner. Everything is just as they left it."

They moved about the front rooms, filled with trophies from the deep, a Nantucketer's treasures—bits of pottery from China, weavings from the Indies, lacquers from Japan—over all, spicy reminders of far archipelagoes, and the clean fragrance of cedar.

On the mantel in the parlor stood a full-rigged ship, a whaling-ship, with her trying-house and small-boats—a full ship, homeward bound....

The gardener had left them to their own ways.

"That's because he knows your *folks*," Cairns said softly. "Shall we look upstairs?"

"Oh, do you think we'd better?"

"Don't you want to?"

"Yes—"

"It isn't a liberty—when we have the proper spirit."

"Isn't it, David?" ... With hushed voices and light steps, they passed up and through the sunny rooms. Fresh flowers everywhere, and one bright room with two small white beds.

"The maiden-aunts," Cairns said hoarsely.

At length, he held open for her to enter, the door of the great front room, filled with Northern brightness from a skylight of modern proportions.

"Why, David," she whispered raptly, "it's like a studio! It *is* a studio!"

And then she saw the scaffoldings, the ladders and panels which do not belong to a painter.

She faced him....

The room was filled with adoration that enchanted the light. The branches of the trees about the lower windows, softly harped the sound of the sea ... Vina's hands were pressed strangely to her breast, as she crossed to an open window.... And there she stood, face averted, and not moving her hands, until she felt him near.

* * * * *

"But I must tell you that the thought was not mine first of all, Vina," Cairns was saying an hour afterward. "You used to talk to me a great deal about Nantucket—about the houses in Lily Lane, the little heads about the table, and how you walked by, watching hungrily like a night-bird—peering in at simple happiness. I couldn't forget that, and I told Bedient—how you loved Nantucket. One night at the club, he said: 'Buy one of those houses, David, and let her find out some summer morning slowly—that it is hers—and watch her face.' Then he suggested that we both come over here to see about it. That's what took us away a month ago."

There was a soft light about her face, not of the room. Cairns saw it as she regarded him steadily for a moment. "I love your telling me that, David," she said.

"I could hardly hold the happiness of it so long," he added. "Last night it was hard, too.... So Bedient and I came over and met the maiden-aunts. Such a rare time we had together—and yet, deep within, he was suffering."

"He went away almost immediately afterward, didn't he?"

"Yes.... Vina, do you think he couldn't make Beth forget the Other?"

"No, David."

Her unqualified answer aroused him. "I haven't seen Beth for weeks," he said. "She has been out of town mostly. I must see her now."

"Yes?"

"Vina, what a crude boy, I was—not to have known you—all these years. It seems as if I had to know Bedient first."

"Perhaps, I did too, David."

"And Vina, it was a word of Beth's that started me thinking about you—that made me realize you were in the world.... This moment I would give her my arms, my eyes—for that word of hers."

"She is the truest woman I have ever known," Vina said.

... "The Other is back in New York," Cairns told her a moment later. "I saw him an hour before leaving, but not to speak to.... How strange it would be—"

Vina shook her head.

"Come back to New York with me to-day!" he said suddenly. "Our friends are there. You wouldn't trust anyone to pack the panels you'll need for work here.... Then we'll come back together for the long summer's work—will you?"

"Yes."

There was a quick step below—not the step of the man of flowers. Vina glanced at Cairns, who was smiling.

"I've arranged for servants, of course," he said. "I think dinner is nearly ready.... The table wasn't set for maiden-aunts—"

"The long summer's work together—" she said, in an awed voice.

"But first, our dinner together—you and I—here—oh, Vina!"

"... But, David,... you said—dinner first!"

THIRTY-SEVENTH CHAPTER

BETH AND ADITH MALLORY

Beth Truba dreamed:

She had been traveling for days and years, over plains, through the rifts of high mountains, across rivers and through great lonely silences, with just a dog for a companion. A white dog with small black spots, very playful and enduring, and though not large, he was very brave to contend with all that was fearful. At night he curled up close to her and licked her hand, and in the morning before the weary hours, he played about and made her laugh.

They came at last to a great desert. There was no other way, but to cross, if she hoped ever to reach her journey's end.... On and on, through the burning brightness they went, forgetting their hunger in the greater thirst. The nights were dreadful with a drying, dust-laden wind, and the days with destroying brilliance. At length one mid-day, the dog could go no further.

He sat down upon his haunches and looked at her, his tail brushing the sand—eyes melting with love for her. She put her hand upon his head, and the dry tongue touched her fingers.... She must leave him. He seemed to understand that she must go on; his eyes told her his sufferings—in that he could not be with her. And so she went on alone.

When she turned he was watching, but he had sunk down upon the sand. Only his head was raised a little. Still she saw the softness of the eyes; and his ears, that had been so sharp in the happy days, had dropped close about his head.

On she went, looking back, until the spot on the sand where he lay was gone from her eyes. And she knew what it meant to be alone. The days were blazing, and the nights filled with anguish to die. At last her hour came.... So glad she was to sink down a last time and let the night cover her.... But the sound of running water—water splashing musically upon the stones, and the breath of flowers—awoke her after many hours. A cooling dawn was abroad, and in the lovely light she saw low trees ahead—green palms around a fountain— fruits and shade and flowers.... She arose, and from her limbs all weariness was gone. There was a quick bark, and her dog came bounding up—and Beth awoke, thinking it was her soul that had returned to her, restored.

*　*　*　*　*

Beth realized that she had half-expected Bedient to re-enter that open door.... Reflecting upon the days, she found that he had done none of the things she had half-expected. Only, while she had believed herself comparatively unresponsive, he had filled her with a deep, silent inrushing. One by one he had swept away the ramparts which the world had builded before her heart. So softly and perfectly had he fitted his nature to her inner conception that she had not been roused in time. But the Shadowy Sister had known him for her prince of playmates.... She wondered how she could have been so wilful and so blind with her painter's strong eyes. Even her pride had betrayed her. Wordling and the ocean could not continue to stand against all the good he had shown her.

Beth had run away for a few days. She could not bear her mother's eyes, nor the studio where he had been. Better the house of strangers, two hours from New York up the Hudson.... She heard he had gone back to his Island.... The June days drowsed. The mid-days were slow to come to as far hills; and endless to pass as hills that turn into ranges. The sloping afternoons were aeon-long; and centuries of toil were told in the hum of the bees about her window, toil to be done over and over again; and sometimes from the murmur of the bees, would appear to her like a swiftly-flung scroll, glimpses of her other lives, filled like this with endless waiting—for she was always a woman. And for what was she waiting?...

Often she thought of what Bedient had said about the women who refuse the bowl of porridge, and who therefore do not leave their children to brighten the race. These he had called the centres of new and radiant energy, the spiritual mothers of the race. And one night she cried aloud: "Would one be less a spiritual help, because she had a little of her own heart's desire? Because she held the highest office of woman, would her outer radiance be dimmed? To be a spiritual mother, why must she be just a passing influence or inspiration—a cheer for those who stop a moment to refresh themselves from her little cup, and hurry on about their own near and dear affairs, in which she has no share?... He stands in a big, bright garden and commands the spiritual mother to remain a waif out on the dusty highway. 'How much better off you are out there!' he says. 'You can show people the Gate, and keep them from going the wrong way, on the long empty road. Nothing can hurt you, but yourself. It is very foolish of *you* to want to come in!'"...

She remembered that some fine thing had lit his eyes like stars at the parting. Time came when she wished she had seen him at the studio, or at her mother's house, when he called before going away.... The sharp irony of her success brought tears—and Beth Truba was rather choice of her tears. The portrait had made a stir at the Club, and the papers were discussing it gravely.

It brought back the days in which he had come to the studio, and what it had meant to her for him to move in and out. How dependent she had become upon his giving! The imperishable memories of her life had arisen from those days, while she painted his portrait. Beth realized this now—days of strange achievement under his eyes—errant glimpses of life's inner beauty—moments in which she had felt the power to paint even that delicate and fleeting shimmer of sunlight about a humming-bird's wing, so intense was her vision—their talks, and the ride—well she knew that these would be the lights of her flagging eyes—treasures of the old Beth, whose pictures all were painted.

It was hard to have known the joy of communion with his warm heart, and deeply seeing mind—and now to accept the solitude again. She felt that his going marked the end of her growth; that now it was a steady downgrade, body and mind.... Some time, long hence, she would meet him again.... She would be "Beth-who-used-to-paint-so-well." They would talk together. The moment would come to speak of what they might have been to each other, save for the Wordlings of this world. She would weep—no, she would burst into laughing, and never be able to stop! It would be too late. A woman must not be drained by the years if she would please a man of flesh. She could not keep her freshness after this; she had not the heart to try.... Thus at times her brain kept up a hideous grinding.... She could feel the years!... Jim Framtree saw them.

She had found a note from him two days old under her studio-door. He had telephoned repeatedly, and taken the trip over to Dunstan to see her.... Would she not allow him to call? And now Beth discovered an amazing fact:

She had been unable to keep her mind upon him, even during the moment required to read his single page of writing. She wrote that he might come....

She heard his voice in the hall. The old janitor of the building had remembered him. Beth's hands, which had lain idle, began leaping strangely from the inner turmoil. She wished now she had met him somewhere apart from the studio. His tone brought back thoughts too fast to be tabulated, and his accent was slightly English. She divined from this he had been out of the country—possibly had returned to New York on a British ship. How well she knew his plastic intelligence! It was so characteristic and easy for him—this little affectation.... She was quite cold to him. Bedient had put him away upon the far-effacing surfaces of her mind.

The knocker fell. Rising, she learned her weakness. As she crossed the room the mirror showed her a woman who has met many deaths.

He greeted her with excited enthusiasm, but the tension which her change in appearance caused, was imperfectly concealed by his words and manner.... She knew his every movement, his every thought before it was half-uttered, as a mother without illusions knows her grown son, who has failed to become the man she hoped. They talked with effort about earlier days. He treated her with a consideration he had never shown before. The challenge of sex was missing. Duty, and an old and deep regard—these Beth felt from him. She attributed it to the havoc of a few weeks upon her face.

She wished he would not come again; but he did.

It was the next morning—and she was painting. Again the knocker and his cheery greeting. Beth sat down to work—and then thoughts of the two men came to her. She should not have tried to paint, with Framtree in the room.... Thoughts arose, until she could not have borne another. The colors of her canvas flicked out, leaving a sort of welted gray of flesh, from which life is beaten. She rubbed her eyes.

"Jim," she said at last, "why did you come back?"

He came forward, and stood over her. "I wanted to see if there was any change, Beth,—any chance."

She regarded him, noted how effective is humility with such magnificent proportions of strength.

"There isn't, Jim," she answered. "At least, not the change you look for. I'm sorry if you really wanted it, but I think in time you'll be glad—"

"Never, Beth."

She smiled.

Framtree hesitated, as if there were something further he would like to say. He refrained, however.... Beth gave her hand, which he kissed for old love's sake.

* * * * *

On the following Sunday morning, Adith Mallory's Equatorian news-feature appeared. The entire truth and all the names were not needed to make this as entertaining a Sunday newspaper story as ever drew forth her fanciful and flowing style. It was Equatoria that caught and held Beth's eye, and she saw Andrew Bedient in large movement behind the tale. The feature was dated in Coral City ten days before. Beth was so interested that she wanted to meet the correspondent, and wondered if Miss Mallory had returned to New York. She dropped a card with her telephone number, and the next morning Miss Mallory 'phoned. Her voice became bright with animation upon learning that Beth was upon the wire.

"There's no one in New York whom I'd rather talk with this moment, Miss Truba."

"And why?"

"That portrait at the *Smilax Club*—I saw it yesterday. I'm writing about it.... The face I know—and you have done it tremendously! I can't tell you how it affected me. Don't bother to come down here. Let me go to you."

"I shall be glad to see you, Miss Mallory,—this afternoon?"

"Yes, and thank you."

The call had brightened Beth's mood somewhat. A bundle of letters had been dropped through her door as she talked. Beth saw the quantity of them and remembered it was Monday's first mail. She busied about the studio for a moment.... Letters, she thought,—these were all she had to represent her great investments of faith. Letters—the sum of her longings and vivid expectations. No matter what she wanted or deserved—a voice, a touch or a presence—it had all come to this, the crackle of letter paper. What a strange thing to realize! A fold of paper instead of a hand—a special delivery instead of a step upon the stair—a telegram instead of a kiss!...

"I belong in a cabinet," she sighed. "I guess I'm a letter-file instead of a lady."...

There was a large square envelope from Equatoria.... With stinging cheeks, Beth resented the buoyant happiness of the first few lines. Until a clearer understanding came, it seemed that he was blessing her refusal of him. How unwarranted afterward this thought appeared! The letter lifted her above her own suffering. Her mind was held by the great vital experience of a soul, a soul faring forth on its supreme adventure. He did not say what had happened in words, but she saw his descent in the flesh and his upward flight of spirit—the low ebb and the flashing heights.... How well she knew the cool brightness of his eyes, as he wrote! The god she had liberated that sunlit day was dead—not dead to her alone, but to any woman of Shore or Mountain or Isle.... With a gasp, she recalled Vina Nettleton's first conception, that Bedient was past, or rapidly passing beyond the attraction of a single woman.

Beth saw that she had helped to bring him to this greater dimension. There was a thrill in the thought. There would have been a positive and enduring joy, had he not gone from her to another. Truly, that was an inauspicious beginning for Illumination—but miracles happened. This thought fascinated her now: Had she seen clearly and made the great sacrifice of withholding herself—that he might rise to prophecy—there would have been gladness in that! She felt she could have done that—the iron Beth—given him to the world and not retained him for her own heart. He said that other women had done so. What an instrument!

But strength did come from his letter; there was a certain magic in his praise and blessing. It gave her something like the natural virtues of mountain coolness and ocean air. Austerely pure, it was. Plainly, pleasure had not made him tarry long.

Beth and Miss Mallory had talked an hour before the name
of Jim Framtree was innocently mentioned by the
newspaperwoman. It was not Beth's way to betray her fresh
start of interest, even though she gained her first clue to the
meaning of the fine light she had seen in Bedient's eyes at
parting.... The blood seemed to harden in her heart. The
familiar sounds of the summer street came up through the
open windows with a sudden horror, as if she were a captive
on cannibal shores.

"No one knows why he wanted this talk with Mr. Framtree,"
Miss Mallory was saying. "He wanted it vitally—and you
see what came of it—a revolution averted—the fortunes of
the whole Island altered for the better—and yet, those were
only incidents. He was so ill—that another man would have
fallen—and yet he went to *The Pleiad*—and aboard the
Spaniard's yacht, as you read.... I knew his courage before—
from the *Hedda Gabler* night—but it was true, he didn't
know me! The only result I know was that Mr. Framtree
came to New York—"

It seemed to Beth that her humanity was lashed and flung
and desecrated.... "But he did not know," she thought. "He
did not know. He could not have hurt me this way. He
thought I could not change, that I should always worship the
beauty of exteriors. I told him the parable—and he went
away—to send me what he thought I wanted!..."

Miss Mallory had come with a tribute of praise to a great
artist. She found a woman who was suffering, as she had
suffered, in part. A great mystery, too, she found. It was
almost too sacred for her to try to penetrate, because it had to

396   Will Levington Comfort

do with him.... She wondered at Miss Truba's inability to speak, or to help herself in any way with the things that pressed her heart to aching fullness.... She had found it wonderfully restoring to talk of him—with a woman who knew him—and who granted his greatness from every point.

The long afternoon waned, but still the women were together. All that had taken place was very clear to Beth—even this woman's ministerings.

"And he is better—beyond words, better!" Miss Mallory added. "I received a note from him this morning. The *Hatteras* arrived yesterday. I came up on the *Henlopen* eight days ago. So it was my first word. Something great has happened. He is changed and lifted."

"Has Mr. Framtree finished his mission?" Beth asked.

"Yes. He intends to go back to-morrow afternoon. He finished sooner than he thought. He is going to help Mr. Bedient in the administration of the vast property.... It seems that no one ever touches Mr. Bedient, but that some great good comes to him. I am going back, too—"

"To live?"

"Yes." Miss Mallory explained what Dictator Jaffier had done for her, adding:

"It was all Mr. Bedient's doing.... You see what I mean, about the wonderful things that happen to others—where he is.... Yet I would rather have that picture of him you painted—than all Equatoria—but even that should not belong to one—"

"You love him then?" Beth asked softly.

"I dared that at first, but I didn't understand. He is too big to belong that way.... I would rather be a servant in his house—than the wife of any other man I ever knew. I am that—in thought—and I shall be near him!"

After a moment, Beth *heard* the silence—and drew her thoughts back to the hour. She seemed to have gone to the utmost pavilions of tragedy—far beyond the sources of tears—where only the world's strongest women may venture. The Shadowy Sister was there.... Beth had come back with humility, which she could not reveal.

The dusk was closing about them.

"You have been good to come—good to tell me these things," Beth said. "Some time I shall paint a little copy of the portrait for you. I'm sure he would be glad."

THIRTY-EIGHTH CHAPTER

A SELF-CONSCIOUS WOMAN

Two days later Beth answered a 'phone call from David Cairns.... He was just back from Nantucket ... for a few days.... Very grateful to find her in.... Yes, Vina had come over, too.

Beth was instantly animate. Vina had planned to be gone a month at least.

"I'd like to come over alone first—may I, Beth?" Cairns asked.

"Yes."

"Within a half-hour?"

"Yes.... I shall prepare to listen to great happiness."

... Beth reflected that she looked a belated forty; that she had lost her charm for the eye of Jim Framtree, who had treated her like a relative. She was ashamed to show her suffering to David Cairns—ashamed that she cared—but it was part of her. Happiness was in the air. She must listen. She marveled at her capacity to endure....

The dews of joy were upon David Cairns. Between Bedient and Vina, he had been born again. He looked at her—as all who knew her did now—and then again in silence. It always made her writhe—that second stare. It gave her the sense of some foreign evil in her body—like the discovery of a malady with its threat of death in every vein.

He told her that Vina and he were to be married at once. Beth gave to the story all that listening could add to the telling of happiness.

"And, David," she said. "I claim a little bit of credit for this glorious thing—"

"Credit, Beth!" he said rousingly. "I told Vina I could worship you for it!"

"Don't, please—David. I don't need it. I'm too happy over you both.... And then, it wasn't all mine, you know. I think Mr. Bedient saw you together in his mind. I think he meant me to startle you to your real empire—"

"Did he?" Cairns asked eagerly.

"Hasn't it turned out perfectly?"

Beth did not miss the gladness which this hint gave him. She knew that Bedient's thought of it would be like an authority to Vina as well.... She felt herself drawing farther and farther back from the lives of the elect, but joyously she urged David to tell about their house in Nantucket.

"And, Beth," he said intensely. "That was Bedient's doing, too. I have—all I have seems to be the happiness part."

"Poor dear boy—how hard!"

"...I was telling him how Vina loved Nantucket," Cairns went on, "some of the rare things she said about the Island and the houses in Lily Lane, and how I planned to go over and find her there this month. He knew we were coming on very well.... One night at the Club, he asked me why I didn't buy one of those houses in Lily Lane, fix up a studio in one of the upper rooms, and then show it to her some summer morning and let it seep in slowly that it was hers—and my heart, too—"

"Beautiful!" Beth exclaimed. A trace of color came to her face.

"I'm telling it badly. Vina will tell you better. Anyway, he wouldn't let me go over alone. You remember when we went away together—for three or four days early in June?"

"I didn't know you—were you with him?"

"Yes, we went together—found the house in Lily Lane—"

"And he went back to Equatoria—right after that?"

Her tone had risen, the words rapid.

"Yes—and without letting me know."

Cairns noted vaguely that Beth's face seemed farther away.

"David, you were with him—those three days, beginning Monday, the first week in June—you—were—with—with—him—?"

"Every minute, Beth—"

"David, how did Mrs. Wordling know—you were going?"

"Why, Beth, she didn't. No one knew—"

"Are you sure? Isn't there some way she could have heard—at the Club?"

He hesitated. He had caught her eyes. They horrified him.... He remembered.

"Why, yes. We were talking—it was the night he first spoke of going over to Nantucket with me. Mrs. Wordling was behind at a near table. I told him we'd better talk lower—"

No sound escaped her. Cairns sprang up at the sight of her uplifted face.... Her eyes turned vaguely toward the door of the little room. He was standing before it. She seemed only to know—like some half-killed creature—that she was hunted and must hide. She couldn't pass him into the little room, but turned behind the screen. He did not hear her step, but something like the rush of a skirt, or a sigh.

There was no sound from the kitchenette. Cairns could not think in this furious stress. After a moment he called.

No answer.

It did not occur to him to go to her. Scores of times he had been in the studio, but he had never passed that screen.

He called again.... Not a breath nor movement in answer. He did not think of her as dead, but stricken with some awful madness. She had stood transfixed.... Yet her old authority was about her. He feared her anger.

"Dear—Beth,—won't you let me come—or do something?... In God's name—what is it?"

He listened intently.

"Beth, I'll go and get Vina—shall I?"

Terrible seconds passed; then her voice came to him—trailed forth, high-pitched, slow—an eerie thing in his brain:

"*I thought I was a good queen, but I have been hard and wicked as hell. I'm Bloody Beth.... He asked for bread and I gave him a stone.... Bloody Beth of the Middle Ages.*"

"Beth—please!" he cried.

"Go away—oh, go away!"

Cairns' only thought was to bring Vina to her. Some awful hatred for himself came forth from the back room. He turned to the outer door, saying, aloud:

"Yes, Beth, I'll go."

The door shut and clicked after him—without his touch—it seemed very quickly. He descended the steps—a sort of slave to the routine of death—as one who finds death, must run to perform certain formalities. At the front door he stopped a second or two, as if his name had been called faintly. He thought it a delusion—and went out. Crossing the street, he heard it again:

"David!"

It was just enough for him to hear—a queer high quality.

He glanced up. Beth was leaning out of the lofty window.... More than ever it was like death to him—the old newspaper days when he was first at death—the mute face aloft, the gesture, the instant vanishing, when he was seen to comprehend.

Her door was ajar. She called for him to come in, as he halted in the hall. Beth came forth from the little room, after a moment, and stood before him, leaning against the piano. Her face was grayish-white, but she was controlled.

"Once you told me you loved me," she said. "A happy man should be ready to do something for a woman he once told that."

"Anything, Beth."

"It came forth from your happiness—so suddenly. You have found me out.... You made me see—that I believed the lie of a worthless woman—"

She halted. The last words had a familiar ring.

"I believed a despicable thing of Andrew Bedient—and sent him away.... He must never know. I could not live and have him know that I believed it. I am paying. I shall pay. I only ask you to keep it, forever—all that you saw—all that was said—to-day—"

"I will keep it, Beth."

"Even from Vina. Vina is pure. He would read it in her eyes—if she knew. I wonder that he loved me.... God!... You have enough of the world left—to bury this evil thing—for me. I am glad of your happiness."

"Vina will want to see you to-day."

"She may come.... You may say I have been ill. It is true.... I shall stay and be with you for your marriage. You want me—"

"We came back to New York for that."

"Yes.... And then I shall go away."

Cairns lingered. "But Beth, Bedient will always love you. He will come back—"

"It is not the same. You will see when he writes. I made him suffer—until a great light came—and he is the world's—not mine."

"Beth," he said humbly, "you are Absolute!"

"I shall come back—strong enough to meet him—as one of the world's women—or I shall stay away," she said.

THIRTY-NINTH CHAPTER

ANOTHER SMILAX AFFAIR

The *Hatteras* was warping into a New York slip the day before Christmas. Bedient was aboard. There was to be a little party for him, given by Cairns and Vina at the *Smilax Club* that night. The Cairns' had come over from Nantucket for the winter, and were living at the Club. This was Bedient's third trip to New York in the half-year preceding. He had not seen Beth, but there had been letters between them—of late, important letters, big with reality and understanding. She had been in Europe since July, but had promised to be home for the holidays. Vina's last letter told him that Beth would be at their affair of greeting to-night.

Adith Mallory saw Jim Framtree in New York, after her hours with Beth Truba. It was the day before he sailed for Equatoria. Framtree asked her not to tell Mr. Bedient that the name of Framtree was spoken in her conversation with Beth. This request gave her a clearer understanding.

Bedient may have guessed that the mystery of the return of Jim Framtree was penetrated by Beth, but he did not ask Miss Mallory, nor mention Framtree in his letters to the lustrous lady. He doubtless wondered at the hasty return of his young friend, but it was a privilege of Beth to return his gifts—one of the glowing mysteries of Beth.

Just now, Bedient caught the waving hand of David Cairns in the small crowd below. Fifteen minutes later they were in a cab together.... Beth had returned to New York. This was the answer to Bedient's first question.

"Are you going to stay with us this time, Andrew?" Cairns asked, raptly studying his friend.

"Yes. Several weeks at least."

"At the Club?"

"No. I shall go back to Broderick Street to-morrow."

This was a broken arrow of black sorrows near the East River, straight East from Gramercy. Bedient had found it in the summer, where it had lain rotting in its wound.

"So the New York office of the Carreras plantations is to be in Broderick Street," Cairns said thoughtfully.

"But I'll be with you often.... And, David, I've brought up a small manuscript which I want you to read. After that we'll advise together about its publishing—"

"That *is* important—if the stuff is anything like your letters to me.... Have you thought of attaching your name to this beginning?"

"Not more than *A.B.*"

*   *   *   *   *

"Is everything bright down yonder?" Cairns asked after

a moment.

"Bright past any idea you can have. Framtree is doing greatly—indispensable—and loves the life. Miss Mallory still unfolds. She's a Caribbean of buried treasure—"

"And *they*?" Cairns asked.

"Are friends."

...Vina met them in her studio. The three stood for a moment in silence among the panels. It was not yet four in the afternoon, but the dusk was thickening.... Vina put on her hat.

"I've just received word from Mary McCullom," she said. "She's in Union Hospital—I don't know—but I must hurry. The word said that Mary McCullom wanted me—nothing more. That was her maiden-name. I knew her so. Her husband died recently, but I didn't hear in time to find her. She must have left New York for a time. They were *so* happy.... I'm afraid—"

David went to her.

"No, you mustn't go with me, David. There are too many things to do—for to-night—"

"Let me go, Vina," Bedient said.

In the cab, she told him the story of Mary McCullom's failure as an artist and conquest as a woman—the same story she had told Beth Truba—and what meant the love of the nurseryman—to Mary McCullom.

Vina's voice had a strange sound in the shut cab. She felt

Bedient's presence, as some strength almost too great for her vitality to sustain. He did not speak.

"Sometimes it seems almost sacrilege," she said in a trembling tone, "to be so happy as we have been.... I should have persevered until I found her—after her ... oh, what that must have meant to her!... And she used to rely upon me so—"

* * * * *

"... Oh, Vina!" the woman whispered, holding out her arms. "I have wanted you!... I have waited for you to come.... I knew you would. I always loved you, because you made me take him!... We were so happy.... Draw the coverlet back—"

A new-born child was sleeping at her breast.

Vina had knelt. Her head bent forward in silent passion.

"Won't you, Vina—won't *you* take him?"

Vina covered her face, but made no sound.

* * * * *

"She will take the little one," said the voice above them.

Both women turned their eyes to Bedient. Mary McCullom smiled shyly.

"I remember—David—Cairns," she said, in an awed tone. "This is not—"

"No, dear, but it is enough. I will take your—baby."

The smile brightened.... "Oh, we were so happy," she

whispered.... "And Vina—tell him when he is older—how his father and I loved—the thought of him!"

"He will bless you," Bedient said.

A glow had fallen upon the weary face of the mother.... "Yes," she answered. "He will bless us ... and I shall be with my husband.... Oh, now, I can go to my husband!"

*　*　*　*　*

Hours afterward, when it was over, Vina looked into Bedient's face, saying:

"You may ask David—why I hesitated—that first moment."

"I know, Vina—God love you!"

Before they left the hospital, he said: "We won't speak of this to-night.... Everything is arranged.... To-morrow morning, we will come for the little boy.... It is time for us to be at the Club."

"I had forgotten," Vina answered vaguely.

*　*　*　*　*

Kate Wilkes and Marguerite Grey were waiting that evening in the Club library. David Cairns had left them a moment before, called to the telephone.

"Rather a contrast from that other night when we foregathered to meet *The Modern*—fresh from the sea," Kate Wilkes observed.

"Yes," said the Grey One.

"David no longer belongs to the coasting-trade in letters," Kate Wilkes went on whimsically. "He has emerged from a most stubborn case of boyhood. Now he's got Vina's big spirit, and she has her happiness and is doing her masterpiece—"

The women exchanged glances. "You mean the Stations?" the Grey One asked in her quiet way.

"Beth has done a great portrait—enough for any woman— just *one* like that," Kate Wilkes added, ignoring the other.

"For a time—I thought Beth and Mr. Bedient—" the Grey One ventured.

"No," the other said briefly. "Beth loves her work better than she could love any man. She's the virgin of pictures. Have you seen her since she came back?"

"Yes. As lovely as ever."

"And your 'rage' is on again.... I'm mighty glad about that, Margie. You were suicidal. Does the great fortune hold true?"

"Oh, yes," the Grey One said, "I'm doing right well. Some of my things are going over the water."

"Poor little Wordling.... I wonder what she has drawn of the great Driving Good—since that night?... I think it would puzzle even Andrew Bedient—to make her hark to any soul—but New York's—"

"And you, Kate—this Eve—what has the Year brought?"

"Nonsense, I'm glass; hold oil or acid with equal ease," Kate said, leaning back in the big chair. "I've got a bit of work to do, and a few friends whose fortunes have taken a stunning turn for the better. And I mustn't forget—letters from *The Modern* when he's away, and talks when he's in New York.... What astonishes me about Andrew Bedient is that he wears. He set a killing pace—for our admiration at first—at least, I thought so—but he hasn't let down an instant. He stands the light of the public square. I granted him a great spirit, but he has more, a great nature to hold it. He can mingle with men without going mad. There's many a prophet who couldn't do that—"

David Cairns joined them. "They will be here in a few minutes," he said. "Beth is due, too.... Talking about Bedient?"

"Yes—"

"I was just thinking," Cairns said, "that we were in a way concentrates of New York and the country, and he is talking to all the people through us."

"You are strong, aren't you, David—for him?" the Grey One asked.

"Yes, and I shall be stronger."

"I like that," said Kate Wilkes.

"He'll work through us—and directly," Cairns went on. "I'm glad to wait and serve and build for a man like that. Why, if a thief took his purse, he would only wish to give him a greater thing.... Moreover, he's one of the Voices that will break Woman's silence of the centuries."

"I believe much that he says—all that he says," Kate Wilkes

replied, "that Woman is the bread-giver, spiritual and material; that it is she who conserves the ideals and rewards man for fineness and power—when she has a chance. But I also believe that Woman must conquer in herself—the love of luxury, her vanity, her fierce competition for worldly position—if only for the disastrous effect of such evils upon men. They force him to lower his dreams of her, who should be high-priestess."

"He has not missed that," Cairns said, "but there have been multitudes to tell Woman her faults. Bedient restores the dreams of women.... It is Woman who has turned the brute mind of the world from War, and Woman will turn the furious current of the race to-day from the Pits of Trade, where abides the Twentieth Century Lie."

"David, you're steering straight through the Big Deep," Kate Wilkes told him.

"I should have been of untimely birth, if he had not come to me as the most rousing and inspiring of world-men. His face is turned away toward a Great Light. He has put on power wonderfully in the last few months.... He moves with men, but he sees beyond. I know that! And all makes for the most glowing optimism. He sees that our race is on the shadowy borders of cosmic consciousness, as the brightest of our domestic animals to-day are on the borders of self-consciousness. He sees that Woman will be the great teacher when humanity rises. Every thing is bright to him in this shocking modern hour, for it heralds the advent of the Risen Woman!... Yes, I am full of this. I have been getting his letters, and writing about the things he has made me think. The good that we do for the race—comes back—for we are the race always. I've already found so much that is good in the world, that I praise God every morning of my life!"

Beth had come. She was standing beside him.

"Glorious, David," she said.

And now Vina appeared, to lead them to the big round table in the room of the cabinets.

"He will be here in a minute," she said.

At each place of the table was an engraved card, which Vina explained: "When Mr. Bedient first came to my studio—to me it was a wonderful afternoon. I asked him to write for me some of the things he said, and I thought you would like to keep—what came of the request—his *Credo*:"

I BELIEVE

In the natural greatness of Woman; that through the spirit of Woman are born sons of strength; that only through the potential greatness of Woman comes the militant greatness of man.

I believe Mothering is the loveliest of the Arts; that great mothers are hand-maidens of the Spirit, to whom are intrusted God's avatars; that no prophet is greater than his mother.

I believe when humanity arises to Spiritual evolution (as it once evolved through Flesh, and is now evolving through Mind), Woman will assume the ethical guiding of the race.

I believe that the Holy Spirit of the Trinity is Mystic Motherhood, and the source of the divine principle in Woman; that Prophets are the union of this divine principle and higher manhood; that they are beyond the attractions of women of flesh, because unto their manhood has been added Mystic Motherhood.

I believe in the Godhood of the Christ; that unto the manhood of the Son and Mystic Motherhood was added, upon Resurrection, the Third Lustrous Dimension of the Father-God; that, thus Jesus became the first fruit of earth, and thus He is enhanced above St. Paul and the Forerunner, becoming Three in One—Man, risen to Prophecy through illumination of the Holy Spirit, and to Godhood, through his ineffable services to Men.

I believe that the way to Godhood is the Rising Road of Man.

I believe that, as the human mother brings a child to her husband, the father,—so Mystic Motherhood, the Holy Spirit, is bringing the world to God, the Father.

All had read, when Bedient entered. He went first to Beth....

"It's our own original gathering," he said, after a moment, "—but Mrs. Wordling—where is she?"

Cairns' eye turned to Beth. She fixed hers upon him, as if it helped to hold her strength.

Kate Wilkes answered: "We can find out in a moment—in the West somewhere with her company—"

"She's in Detroit this week," came slowly from Beth. "I saw it to-day in a dramatic paper—"

"Thank you.... We'll send a telegram of greeting. She must know she isn't forgotten."

He wrote it out.

Kate Wilkes glanced at the Grey One, as if to say: "Here's something to make her forget the soul of New York."

"I'm thankful to be here," Bedient said, in a moment. "It's like one's very own."

FORTIETH CHAPTER

FULL DAY UPON THE PLAIN

Beth awoke early Christmas morning, and leaned out of the window to look at the East. After a week of the year's darkest days, had come a lordly morn, bright garments fresh from ocean.... The night had shown her clearly the great thing which had befallen Andrew Bedient, a suggestion of which had come to her from the first Equatorian letter. And how wonderfully his life had prepared him for it!... Thirty-odd swift strange years—ships, Asia, queer voices, far travels, unspoken friendships, possibly a point or two of passion, glimpses into dim lands and dark lives, the adored memory of his Mother whispered only to one dear living heart, yet glowing over all his days—

"It was a man's love, then," Beth whispered.

She remembered his comings and goings, his sayings and silences. All were leveled and subdued by a serene and far-evolved spirit; and upon all was the flower of truth. His love had been an inner reverent thing which did not vaunt itself. All but once the passions he had felt were his own deep property.... The Shadowy Sister, who would live on when the worn-out earth of her being sank into its seventh year of restoring,—yes, the Shadowy Sister had been chastened and strengthened by his passing.

...Beth saw the little boy, faring forth alone without the Mother's hand—out into the great world of sea—under his star. Not a single preconception had his mind contained. Everything in the world had been for him to take, and when he would have taken something ill, the Mother had come and prevailed.... Only once he was denied—she, Beth, had done that. Did the Mother prevail against her?... But how mightily had he desired her!

Beth saw she had betrayed herself. She had been too much an artist of the world, too little a visionary. She had not seen deeply enough his inner beauty and integrity; too accustomed had she become to the myriad-flaring commonness of daily life.... But would the greater dimension have come to him, if she had given him the happiness he thought he wanted? Had he turned to Vina Nettleton the man-love she, Beth, had felt, and been answered with swift adoration, would he have met in this life the Great Light on his hills?

...Too much artist—how Beth understood what that meant now! There is a way to God through the arts, but it is a way of quicksands and miasmas, of deep forests and abysses. Only giants emerge unhurt in spirit. The artist is taught to worship line and surface; his early paths are the paths of sensuousness. He may be held true at first by the rigors of denial—but what a turning is the first success—his every capacity of sense is suddenly tested, as only an artist's can be! Then, the hatred of the unsuccessful; he must forge ahead in the teeth of a great wind of contemporary hostility, *which rouses the Ego and not the Spirit*. And finally the artist must choose between his visions, for alike come purity and evil. The road of genius runs ever close to the black abyss of madness. The human mind ignited with genius is like an old time-weakened building, in which is installed new machinery of startling power. What a racking upon old fabric!

The simple religious nature with its ventures into a milder spiritual country, puts on glory with far less danger and pain than the artist, and what a perfect surface is prepared within him for the arts to be painted upon!

Beth knew she had lived her art-life bravely, loved her work with valor, and served it with the best of her eye and hand. The life of *just-woman*, she had wanted more, and idealized as only an artist can—to be a man's maiden, a man's mate and the mother of his babes, but this was not for her. The man had come, and she had turned him away. *Just-woman* would have held him fast. Yes, it was the artist that had faltered at the right moment—the resolute creative force within her, weathered in suffering, not to be intimidated, slow, tragically slow to bow down.... A little Salvation band passed below:

> Joy to the world,
> The Lord is Come

Eight notes of the descending scale sounded mightily from drum and cornet....

* * * * *

Bedient was coming this morning. He had asked to, the night before; asked if he might come early.... What a morning for bleak December! She went to the window. Islands of rose and lily were softly blooming in the lakes of Eastern light. Heaven was building in the East—its spires to rise unto high noon....

His step was on the stair. Beth hurried to the door. She saw his strange smile, and the bundle in his arms.

"I thought you would like to play with him for a while," he said. "He's a wonderfully blessed little boy.... You really had to see him—"

Beth had taken the babe to a far corner—and rushed to shut the window. Now, she bent over the coverings.

"I have always wanted to see you, just like that," Bedient added. "...I know the little boy's story.... He is amazingly rich—they both gave him the blue flower. He is love-essence.... May I leave him a little while, until I get some other things?"

Out of the fervent heat—he had come. Beth looked up. Bedient had drawn back to the door. Light from the hidden sun was in the room.... He was gone.

Beth did not yet know the babe's story. Some dying woman's love-child, she thought.... She would give him her years—to make him brave and beautiful. It would be her gift to the world—her greatest painting—and the little child would name it *Mother*.

"He means me to have it!" she murmured. "I think this has been struggling to get into my heart for years—the child of some woman who has kissed and died for it! ... I think—I think this is the end of the fiery waiting.... Little boy, you shall heal the broken dreams, and I shall read in your eyes— the world-secret which aches so heavily in the breasts of women."

* * * * *

Long afterward she heard his step upon the stair again.... As she turned to the door from the far corner—there was a tiny cry—just as she had heard it before—in that high noon.

She went back to the child.

And Bedient with further bundles, waited smiling outside the door.

Choose from Thousands of 1stWorldLibrary Classics By

A. M. Barnard	Booth Tarkington	Edward Everett Hale
Ada Leverson	Boyd Cable	Edward J. O'Biren
Adolphus William Ward	Bram Stoker	Edward S. Ellis
Aesop	C. Collodi	Edwin L. Arnold
Agatha Christie	C. E. Orr	Eleanor Atkins
Alexander Aaronsohn	C. M. Ingleby	Eleanor Hallowell Abbott
Alexander Kielland	Carolyn Wells	Eliot Gregory
Alexandre Dumas	Catherine Parr Traill	Elizabeth Gaskell
Alfred Gatty	Charles A. Eastman	Elizabeth McCracken
Alfred Ollivant	Charles Amory Beach	Elizabeth Von Arnim
Alice Duer Miller	Charles Dickens	Ellem Key
Alice Turner Curtis	Charles Dudley Warner	Emerson Hough
Alice Dunbar	Charles Farrar Browne	Emilie F. Carlen
Allen Chapman	Charles Ives	Emily Bronte
Alleyne Ireland	Charles Kingsley	Emily Dickinson
Ambrose Bierce	Charles Klein	Enid Bagnold
Amelia E. Barr	Charles Hanson Towne	Enilor Macartney Lane
Amory H. Bradford	Charles Lathrop Pack	Erasmus W. Jones
Andrew Lang	Charles Romyn Dake	Ernie Howard Pie
Andrew McFarland Davis	Charles Whibley	Ethel May Dell
Andy Adams	Charles Willing Beale	Ethel Turner
Angela Brazil	Charlotte M. Braeme	Ethel Watts Mumford
Anna Alice Chapin	Charlotte M. Yonge	Eugene Sue
Anna Sewell	Charlotte Perkins Stetson	Eugenie Foa
Annie Besant	Clair W. Hayes	Eugene Wood
Annie Hamilton Donnell	Clarence Day Jr.	Eustace Hale Ball
Annie Payson Call	Clarence E. Mulford	Evelyn Everett-green
Annie Roe Carr	Clemence Housman	Everard Cotes
Annonaymous	Confucius	F. H. Cheley
Anton Chekhov	Coningsby Dawson	F. J. Cross
Archibald Lee Fletcher	Cornelis DeWitt Wilcox	F. Marion Crawford
Arnold Bennett	Cyril Burleigh	Fannie E. Newberry
Arthur C. Benson	D. H. Lawrence	Federick Austin Ogg
Arthur Conan Doyle	Daniel Defoe	Ferdinand Ossendowski
Arthur M. Winfield	David Garnett	Fergus Hume
Arthur Ransome	Dinah Craik	Florence A. Kilpatrick
Arthur Schnitzler	Don Carlos Janes	Fremont B. Deering
Arthur Train	Donald Keyhoe	Francis Bacon
Atticus	Dorothy Kilner	Francis Darwin
B.H. Baden-Powell	Dougan Clark	Frances Hodgson Burnett
B. M. Bower	Douglas Fairbanks	Frances Parkinson Keyes
B. C. Chatterjee	E. Nesbit	Frank Gee Patchin
Baroness Emmuska Orczy	E. P. Roe	Frank Harris
Baroness Orczy	E. Phillips Oppenheim	Frank Jewett Mather
Basil King	E. S. Brooks	Frank L. Packard
Bayard Taylor	Earl Barnes	Frank V. Webster
Ben Macomber	Edgar Rice Burroughs	Frederic Stewart Isham
Bertha Muzzy Bower	Edith Van Dyne	Frederick Trevor Hill
Bjornstjerne Bjornson	Edith Wharton	Frederick Winslow Taylor

Friedrich Kerst
Friedrich Nietzsche
Fyodor Dostoyevsky
G.A. Henty
G.K. Chesterton
Gabrielle E. Jackson
Garrett P. Serviss
Gaston Leroux
George A. Warren
George Ade
Geroge Bernard Shaw
George Cary Eggleston
George Durston
George Ebers
George Eliot
George Gissing
George MacDonald
George Meredith
George Orwell
George Sylvester Viereck
George Tucker
George W. Cable
George Wharton James
Gertrude Atherton
Gordon Casserly
Grace E. King
Grace Gallatin
Grace Greenwood
Grant Allen
Guillermo A. Sherwell
Gulielma Zollinger
Gustav Flaubert
H. A. Cody
H. B. Irving
H.C. Bailey
H. G. Wells
H. H. Munro
H. Irving Hancock
H. R. Naylor
H. Rider Haggard
H. W. C. Davis
Haldeman Julius
Hall Caine
Hamilton Wright Mabie
Hans Christian Andersen
Harold Avery
Harold McGrath
Harriet Beecher Stowe
Harry Castlemon
Harry Coghill
Harry Houidini

Hayden Carruth
Helent Hunt Jackson
Helen Nicolay
Hendrik Conscience
Hendy David Thoreau
Henri Barbusse
Henrik Ibsen
Henry Adams
Henry Ford
Henry Frost
Henry James
Henry Jones Ford
Henry Seton Merriman
Henry W Longfellow
Herbert A. Giles
Herbert Carter
Herbert N. Casson
Herman Hesse
Hildegard G. Frey
Homer
Honore De Balzac
Horace B. Day
Horace Walpole
Horatio Alger Jr.
Howard Pyle
Howard R. Garis
Hugh Lofting
Hugh Walpole
Humphry Ward
Ian Maclaren
Inez Haynes Gillmore
Irving Bacheller
Isabel Cecilia Williams
Isabel Hornibrook
Israel Abrahams
Ivan Turgenev
J.G.Austin
J. Henri Fabre
J. M. Barrie
J. M. Walsh
J. Macdonald Oxley
J. R. Miller
J. S. Fletcher
J. S. Knowles
J. Storer Clouston
J. W. Duffield
Jack London
Jacob Abbott
James Allen
James Andrews
James Baldwin

James Branch Cabell
James DeMille
James Joyce
James Lane Allen
James Lane Allen
James Oliver Curwood
James Oppenheim
James Otis
James R. Driscoll
Jane Abbott
Jane Austen
Jane L. Stewart
Janet Aldridge
Jens Peter Jacobsen
Jerome K. Jerome
Jessie Graham Flower
John Buchan
John Burroughs
John Cournos
John F. Kennedy
John Gay
John Glasworthy
John Habberton
John Joy Bell
John Kendrick Bangs
John Milton
John Philip Sousa
John Taintor Foote
Jonas Lauritz Idemil Lie
Jonathan Swift
Joseph A. Altsheler
Joseph Carey
Joseph Conrad
Joseph E. Badger Jr
Joseph Hergesheimer
Joseph Jacobs
Jules Vernes
Julian Hawthrone
Julie A Lippmann
Justin Huntly McCarthy
Kakuzo Okakura
Karle Wilson Baker
Kate Chopin
Kenneth Grahame
Kenneth McGaffey
Kate Langley Bosher
Kate Langley Bosher
Katherine Cecil Thurston
Katherine Stokes
L. A. Abbot
L. T. Meade

L. Frank Baum	Owen Johnson	Stephen Crane
Latta Griswold	P.G. Wodehouse	Stewart Edward White
Laura Dent Crane	Paul and Mabel Thorne	Stijn Streuvels
Laura Lee Hope	Paul G. Tomlinson	Swami Abhedananda
Laurence Housman	Paul Severing	Swami Parmananda
Lawrence Beasley	Percy Brebner	T. S. Ackland
Leo Tolstoy	Percy Keese Fitzhugh	T. S. Arthur
Leonid Andreyev	Peter B. Kyne	The Princess Der Ling
Lewis Carroll	Plato	Thomas A. Janvier
Lewis Sperry Chafer	Quincy Allen	Thomas A Kempis
Lilian Bell	R. Derby Holmes	Thomas Anderton
Lloyd Osbourne	R. L. Stevenson	Thomas Bailey Aldrich
Louis Hughes	R. S. Ball	Thomas Bulfinch
Louis Joseph Vance	Rabindranath Tagore	Thomas De Quincey
Louis Tracy	Rahul Alvares	Thomas Dixon
Louisa May Alcott	Ralph Bonehill	Thomas H. Huxley
Lucy Fitch Perkins	Ralph Henry Barbour	Thomas Hardy
Lucy Maud Montgomery	Ralph Victor	Thomas More
Luther Benson	Ralph Waldo Emmerson	Thornton W. Burgess
Lydia Miller Middleton	Rene Descartes	U. S. Grant
Lyndon Orr	Ray Cummings	Upton Sinclair
M. Corvus	Rex Beach	Valentine Williams
M. H. Adams	Rex E. Beach	Various Authors
Margaret E. Sangster	Richard Harding Davis	Vaughan Kester
Margret Howth	Richard Jefferies	Victor Appleton
Margaret Vandercook	Richard Le Gallienne	Victor G. Durham
Margaret W. Hungerford	Robert Barr	Victoria Cross
Margret Penrose	Robert Frost	Virginia Woolf
Maria Edgeworth	Robert Gordon Anderson	Wadsworth Camp
Maria Thompson Daviess	Robert L. Drake	Walter Camp
Mariano Azuela	Robert Lansing	Walter Scott
Marion Polk Angellotti	Robert Lynd	Washington Irving
Mark Overton	Robert Michael Ballantyne	Wilbur Lawton
Mark Twain	Robert W. Chambers	Wilkie Collins
Mary Austin	Rosa Nouchette Carey	Willa Cather
Mary Catherine Crowley	Rudyard Kipling	Willard F. Baker
Mary Cole	Saint Augustine	William Dean Howells
Mary Hastings Bradley	Samuel B. Allison	William le Queux
Mary Roberts Rinehart	Samuel Hopkins Adams	W. Makepeace Thackeray
Mary Rowlandson	Sarah Bernhardt	William W. Walter
M. Wollstonecraft Shelley	Sarah C. Hallowell	William Shakespeare
Maud Lindsay	Selma Lagerlof	Winston Churchill
Max Beerbohm	Sherwood Anderson	Yei Theodora Ozaki
Myra Kelly	Sigmund Freud	Yogi Ramacharaka
Nathaniel Hawthrone	Standish O'Grady	Young E. Allison
Nicolo Machiavelli	Stanley Weyman	Zane Grey
O. F. Walton	Stella Benson	
Oscar Wilde	Stella M. Francis	

www.ingramcontent.com/pod-product-compliance
Lightning Source LLC
Chambersburg PA
CBHW031926280626
47169CB00017BA/121